POLITICAL
PURGATORY

Veteran journalist **Brian Rowan** spent twenty-plus years of his career at the BBC in Belfast, including as a correspondent and security editor. In the Northern Ireland Press and Broadcast awards he was twice named 'Specialist Journalist of the Year' – as well as twice winning the online award. His 2005 book *Paisley and the Provos* was shortlisted for the Christopher Ewart-Biggs Memorial Prize, awarded to writers whose work promotes peace and reconciliation in Ireland. The late David Ervine – a former UVF prisoner and Stormont MLA – once described Rowan as having 'unrivalled access to all the protagonist groups'.

POLITICAL PURGATORY

THE BATTLE TO SAVE STORMONT
AND THE PLAY FOR A NEW IRELAND

BRIAN ROWAN

MERRION
PRESS

First published in 2021 by
Merrion Press
10 George's Street
Newbridge
Co. Kildare
Ireland
www.merrionpress.ie

9781785373817 (Paper)
9781785373824 (Kindle)
9781785373831 (Epub)

A CIP catalogue record for this book is
available from the British Library.

Typeset in Palatino 11/15 pt

Front cover: Winter theatre on the Stormont hill, January 2020.
Tánaiste Simon Coveney and Secretary of State Julian Smith
publish their New Decade, New Approach agreement in a
move to restore the Executive. Image courtesy of
Kelvin Boyes, Press Eye.

Back cover: Julian Smith with Sir Jonathan Stephens watching
Sinn Féin's response to the New Decade, New Approach
agreement. Image courtesy of Ross Easton.

Merrion Press is a member of Publishing Ireland.

Contents

Foreword   vii

Acknowledgements   x

Preface   xi

Prologue: A cake with 100 candles – but how many more?   xvii

1. Resignation – the nuclear option   1

2. 'Shadowy figures' in the Stormont corridors   24

3. See you later, alligator   45

4. McGuinness – 'part of the rage of his time'   68

5. A stage in the London lights – balance of power   98

6. Adams – the person least forgiven   103

7. Nearly fixed, but still broken – 'keep your ears open'   127

8. Stormont breakfast – 'tell me more'   138

9. No more road – election then agreement   161

10. 'Project Dignity' – politics and pandemic   183

11. Centenary and uncertainty – Union versus unity   194

Afterword: Hume – 'his long war for peace'   206

Chronology: From ceasefires to peace   210

Appendices   234

Index   242

For Aoife Violet Rowan

Foreword

Political Purgatory details many of the recent chapters in Northern Ireland politics. It is a fascinating account of the period following the historic Good Friday Agreement including new theories as to why the two main parties fell out, bringing down the executive in 2017. For voters and ordinary citizens, the reality of that decision had real-life consequences for over three long years. Thankfully, Northern Ireland's citizens were no longer faced with a daily diet of murder and terror – the peace dividend was, by and large, maintained. But still political stasis saw over 300,000 women and men in Northern Ireland on health waiting lists and forced ordinary workers to look on as their representatives continued to be paid without representing them, despite the desperate need for political decisions.

In the context of a toxic mix of events, notably the murder of Lyra McKee, the Renewable Heat Incentive Scheme (RHI) scandal and the protracted Brexit process at Westminster, trust appeared totally lost between politicians. Moreover, a corrosive relationship had developed between those who were supposed to be governing and the ordinary voter. And by the end of 2019, politics was holding its citizens to ransom, not this time by fear or terror but by the reality of mandatory coalition and the continued ability of both main parties to veto Stormont returning. From mental health to children's hospice provision, drain upgrades to broadband roll out, civil service reform to medical school places – voters from either side of the constitutional debate were losing out compared to almost every other part of the UK. In particular, the value of the large additional per capita spend provided to Northern Ireland each year was lost in this depressing state of affairs.

This book outlines just how far trust had disappeared between each of the political parties during this period. It also makes clear that it was only after the passage of time, brutal elections for the main parties, a clear path on Brexit and an aggressive approach to resuscitating Stormont by the UK and Irish governments that the executive and assembly got re-formed. The lack of meaningful dialogue between the two main parties for much of the period and particularly in the run up to restoration in 2020 are a painful reminder of how fragile the system is and was to deteriorating relationships and the impact this has on citizens.

But this book also recognises how fortunate it was that the assembly and executive were restored and able to deal with the biggest challenge and crisis to hit the world in decades. Whilst there have been some major breaches of trust during 2020, by and large, the work this five-party executive has done to protect Northern Ireland over the Covid crisis has been well received. Having lain awake at night in anticipation of the potential impact of no deal combined with no executive in the run up to the then EU exit date of 31 October 2019, the impact of Covid without functioning government could have been catastrophic.

As Northern Ireland moves out of the first phase of the Covid crisis, there are big positives – a more mature peace settlement, effective leadership to deal with the Covid crisis, progress on social issues like abortion and same-sex marriage and the victims' pensions on their way. But there are many issues that were agreed in the New Decade, New Approach deal which still need to be delivered and these are vital for the long-term future of Stormont – reforms of health, infrastructure and of the workings of the assembly. It is these genuine reforms that will build trust in the system. Above all, the UK and Irish governments and Northern Ireland parties agreed to work intensively to find a way of moving forward on the issue of the legacy of the past focused on families and victims. Dealing with the legacy of the past, of course, means different things to different people but there is now a real opportunity to find common ground, focused on bringing some form of resolution to the many families scarred by Northern Ireland's decades of violence.

Whilst the turbulence of Brexit continues to leave major issues to be resolved, and Northern Ireland enters its centenary year, there are huge opportunities to renew and reinvigorate the Good Friday Agreement North/South and East/West bodies, to rebuild the economy post-Covid and to tackle the biggest global challenge – climate change. With the UK taking the lead with Italy at the 2021 UN Climate Change conference in Glasgow, the EU investing billions in clean technologies and President Biden committed to bringing United States heft to the Climate Change challenge, there is a huge opportunity to create jobs and to deliver on the number one priority for the next generation. This is a reminder that while the constitutional debate will inevitably continue, there are many other things to get to work on meanwhile.

Julian Smith MP,
February 2021

Acknowledgements

We live in the smallest of worlds. Before July 2020, I had never spoken with publisher Conor Graham. Yet, in those first words of our first conversation, I discovered a connection that dates back to the early 1970s, when we all lived in a very different place. It was a period when we as a family had to leave our home in east Belfast – one of many families in the wrong place at that wrong time of conflict. Our escape was to Holywood, County Down – and to a house that a very young Conor and his family had lived in up to then. When he mentioned his father Tony's name to me, I immediately made the connection. Conor has since spoken with his sisters, who remembered being asked by their mother on the day they were moving out of their house to leave some toys for the Rowan children. My wife Val was also a young friend of Conor's eldest sister, Geralyn – these just some of the dots that connect us in our small world.

Today, we live in a better place, but not yet at peace with itself. 2021 will be another of those challenging years. I have called upon some of the biggest names in politics, policing and peace-building to help tell the story so far and to help us turn the next corner into another of those big conversations – that of UNION versus UNITY. I thank them all, including former Northern Ireland Secretary of State Julian Smith and Irish Foreign Minister Simon Coveney. I also want to thank Conor, Patrick and Maeve at Merrion Press, and my daughter Elle, Kelvin Boyes, Mal McCann and MT Hurson for their photography.

The book is dedicated to the youngest in our clan – our first grandchild Aoife Violet Rowan – in the hope that when she comes to read and understand it that some of the questions will have been answered and that our peoples will have found that peace of mind.

Preface

'It was a bounce and we had to surprise and move hard ... As the parties couldn't agree things up front – we had decided to lay it out and dare them to reject it.'

Julian Smith, Former Northern Ireland Secretary of State
(writing in this book on the January 2020 British–Irish
initiative that saved Stormont)

'We thought delay could be fatal to the credibility of the process and the participants. So, we made the call and we published.'

Simon Coveney, Irish Foreign Minister
(writing in this book)

The dictionary definition of purgatory describes a place or state of temporary suffering or misery. In those few words, we have the story of our politics from that moment when Martin McGuinness resigned as deputy First Minister in January 2017 through a three-year period when Stormont languished in a kind of limbo. On its hill overlooking Belfast, it became a wilderness – a political wasteland; directionless and dysfunctional – lost in some no man's land between devolution and direct rule from London. At times, we witnessed pantomime politics. It was a pretend parliament, until it was hoisted out of that misery and embarrassment in a rescue mission that, in the end, had the full weight of the two governments behind it. Stormont was saved from itself. Up to this point, there was no certainty about a functioning assembly and executive in time for the Northern Ireland Centenary of 2021.

The deal of January 2020 was forced by Secretary of State Julian Smith and Tánaiste Simon Coveney, both of whom write in this book. It was at the door of another deadline, and delivered with health as a headline priority, transforming the service with a long-term funding strategy. Little did they know what was waiting around the next corner: 'the tsunami of the Covid-19 pandemic', to borrow from Coveney's words. It was a new and different war that would demand a new and different politics. As it swept across the world, the coronavirus carried with it some dark reminders of past fears, of those still-haunting days of the seventies, eighties and nineties. Streets and workplaces emptied; people, once again, were afraid to come out of their homes. There was a lockdown, and we locked up.

Not a long walk from my home, an emergency mortuary was prepared on the old military site at Kinnegar in Holywood, County Down. New Justice Minister Naomi Long writes in this book about visiting it: 'Stepping into the storage rooms was a chilling experience.' It was worst-case planning; and, as I write, not yet needed, but there just in case. The senior police officer, Tim Mairs, also stood inside that 'sobering' space.

At two metres tall, he stands out in a crowd. So, also, do his words. He has that gift and ability to make and leave an impression. He entered policing beyond the era of the Royal Ulster Constabulary (RUC) and was one of the earliest recruits to the Police Service of Northern Ireland (PSNI). Forty-one years old, he is already an assistant chief constable on a journey, at pace, to the highest rank. He is now serving with Police Scotland.

Before Mairs left for Scotland in June 2020, we met and chatted, as we have done at times over the course of a number of years. I wanted to speak with him about something he had said in a telephone conversation. He had described a new house that is never quite right which, over time, you discover is built on a 'mass grave'.

What an image. What a choice of words. What a way of describing that struggle to get from our past to the present. The Covid-19 pandemic took him, and took us, back in time. Perhaps this time we were more afraid – afraid of what we could not see. In my conversation with Mairs, this is how his thinking developed: that the owners of that imaginary house come to realise that 'things will never be right until the mass grave is carefully and painstakingly opened and each soul lovingly identified, returned to their family and mourned for'. Being inside the morgue had played inside his head.

'There was courage and innovativeness', Mairs explains, 'investing in the construction of a resting place in a matter of weeks, and there was maturity and wisdom in managing the sensitivities of placing it on a Ministry of Defence site. So, maybe in all of that, there are lessons to be learnt about how we show dignity and respect to those who fell during "the Troubles".' There is nothing simple about trying to build politics on top of war. Not in a place so small, where the past is never far enough behind us – those broken stones of a different path and in a different time, still there as the reference points and the fall points of today. We have never allowed a pen free of emotional ink to write that story.

Una Jennings, another of the new generation of police leaders, now serving with South Yorkshire Police, writes in this book, 'We have collectively hurt and been hurt. Understanding and acknowledging that the space between truth and fact in Northern Ireland is and remains a contested one, is the perennial holy grail.' Jennings and Mairs will be needed back here; needed for their understanding of the pulse of the communities; needed for their use of words that, so often, can help people find the way.

In this place, there are layers to everything. So, the fall of Stormont in January 2017 is much more complex than is often reported. Sinn Féin did not walk at the first chance. There had been other opportunities. They could have collapsed those institutions long before they did. Remember also that Gerry Adams and Martin McGuinness had moved an armed organisation into a peace process. Having worked for that, you think before you throw away its political element. Everything had been invested in that strategy.

So, the Martin McGuinness resignation was about much more than an ill-thought-out Renewable Heat Incentive (RHI) scheme developed when Arlene Foster was minister in the relevant department. There was a deeper problem – that past still with us, and politics not working. 'An absence of violence but a conflict still whose root causes have been largely unaddressed and unresolved', to quote the west Belfast republican and one-time senior Irish Republican Army (IRA) figure Jake Mac Siacais, who writes in this book. He does so with considerable inside knowledge. In 1981, he gave the 'H' Block oration for the hunger striker Bobby Sands; he is an Irish language activist and the son-in-law of the late IRA leader Brian Keenan.

Our learning tells us that the journey out of war is long. It is not always clean. Writing in this book, the former Police Service of Northern Ireland (PSNI) Chief Constable Sir Hugh Orde puts it differently: 'Endgames in terrorism are messy. The experience across the world is that they don't just stop.' He is reminding us that this is a process; that there is nothing exact, precise or pure when it comes to the making of peace and politics.

Years before RHI, Stormont fell in an argument about IRA guns – the how and when they would be destroyed. It fell again when episodes of alleged republican intelligence-gathering and IRA training were exposed. It could have fallen in numerous other political battles. These include the dragging out of the devolution of policing and justice powers from London to Belfast, the Democratic Unionist Party (DUP) reneging on a programme for government commitment to build a peace centre on the old Maze/Long Kesh prison site, and the issue of welfare reform, where there were dire warnings accompanied by a commentary of a precarious and grave situation and of running out of road. All of this was there before RHI, corrosive and eating away at confidence and credibility.

That welfare battle almost derailed the Stormont government in 2015 – one of two crisis moments that overlapped in the space of a few months. The other was when members of the IRA were linked to the murder of a republican, Kevin McGuigan, in Belfast. That killing, the continued existence of the IRA and the arrests that followed 'pushed devolution to the brink'. Peter Robinson and the DUP could have walked then. Robinson writes in this book: 'In my seven and a half years as First Minister, the issue that held the greatest likelihood of bringing the Executive down was the McGuigan murder by those clearly identified as members of PIRA [the Provisional IRA].'

Politics was tested again in 2020, in the fallout from the funeral of Bobby Storey – one of the biggest figures in the IRA's war, who helped to make its peace. The news focus was on the crowd, on how the day and proceedings were organised, on the presence of the Sinn Féin Stormont leadership, and on the restrictions and guidelines of the time. One set of rules for this day and another set for the many other days of this pandemic.

These are just some of the complex layers that have made power-sharing government difficult, and at times, impossible. When I listen to some of today's commentary and read the analysis, I think we have forgotten what the peace process was about, how it started, what it entails and how long these things take. Moving 'shadowy figures' from their trenches in war into the open places of politics is part of what this process was meant to deliver. Some of the guest contributors to this book will take us back in time – to the mapping of the way. Because of their involvement in key moments of the peace and political processes, I contacted them to ask would they provide me with their thoughts in writing.

My writing here is not about the fine detail of RHI. *News Letter* political editor Sam McBride has written the brilliant and brave *Burned*, described by veteran journalist Ken Reid as 'an intriguing forensic examination of the scandal which brought down Stormont'. Here, I place RHI in a much wider frame. Yes, the final straw, but only one in a bigger bundle.

The pages turn from Martin McGuinness's resignation as deputy First Minister in January 2017 to the cold winter theatre on Stormont's political hill three years later, when Secretary of State Julian Smith and Tánaiste Simon Coveney somehow brought this place back to life. It was, in my opinion, the most significant British–Irish initiative since the Blair–Ahern years of the 1990s – so significant, because this was Stormont's last chance. Smith took it back to the learning and the basics of that period many years earlier. In the words of the loyalist Winston Irvine, it included and involved 'all actors' – meaning everyone had a voice in this conversation.

You will read later of a breakfast fry on the Shankill Road in Belfast and of Smith's direct engagement with Irvine and others in his community, 'rolling the pitch' as he moved with Coveney to bring this negotiation to the point of decision. By January 2020, he believed there was 'sufficient heat under this round of talks' to get a deal. Stormont was reborn on that coldest of winter nights.

Prologue

A cake with 100 candles – but how many more?

'We are being guided to and along different paths, moving towards very different destinations, the outworking of which means we are locked onto a collision course. Sooner or later, these two entirely legitimate political aspirations are certain to clash.'

Winston Irvine (writing in this book)

8 January 2017: That Sunday morning, Gerry Adams was travelling towards Limerick when he took time to call Jeanette Ervine at her home on the Braniel estate in Belfast. It was a few minutes of conversation to remember her late husband David on this the tenth anniversary of his sudden death. Ervine – a former prisoner who became a Stormont politician – was from the loyalist part of the Northern Ireland community, and ten years previously, the then Sinn Féin President had crossed the Belfast lines from west to east to be at his funeral. There was hope in those steps; hope that was now draining out of our politics like water running from a punctured pipe. We were on the eve of that resignation that would turn Stormont into a place of purgatory and at the beginning of what would become a remarkable period of change. For almost a decade, we had watched on occasions as Stormont was walked to the very edge only to be saved in some last-minute political surgery.

This time was different. Martin McGuinness, who, for decades, was a headline name on those pages of war and peace, was about to resign as deputy First Minister. Hours before then, we listened to an interview in which Democratic Unionist Party (DUP) leader Arlene

Foster thought out loud about a 'game of chicken', making it clear that she was not about to blink. In a fast-moving drama, unionists would lose their overall majority in the Northern Ireland Assembly – the start of an electoral trend that would make louder and more credible a conversation about a 'New Ireland'.

Brexit and its Irish Sea border have given impetus and energy to that debate. This and the electoral shifts were the winds of change in a place where politics moves slowly before it moves quickly. In this, its centenary year of 2021, Northern Ireland will have a cake with 100 candles – but how many more? How safe is the Union – that ground on which the loyalist ceasefire of 1994 was built? What is meant by a 'New Ireland'? These are the questions that become Ulster's next crossroads and nightmare. In this centenary, there will be celebration but also uncertainty – perhaps even danger – that 'collision course' and clash of aspirations described by Winston Irvine.

In the early weeks of 2021, the reality of that Irish Sea border – creating difference and further distance between Northern Ireland and Britain – caused a tremor across the unionist/loyalist community. There was a mood of anger and, once again, there was a crisis of confidence in the ability of politics to deliver solutions.

CHAPTER 1

Resignation – the nuclear option

'There was a complete acceptance within the leadership of the DUP [Democratic Unionist Party] that reaching an agreement with Sinn Féin would cause serious pain and problems for us both inside and outside the party.'

Peter Robinson,
Former First Minister of Northern Ireland

This opening thought from Peter Robinson helps us understand not just the political collapse of 2017 but also the context of the previous decade. The starting point in the DUP–Sinn Féin power-sharing arrangement in 2007 is an enemy relationship, with Ian Paisley and Martin McGuinness having to build on that ground, then Robinson and McGuinness, and then Arlene Foster and McGuinness. There were many times when the house could have fallen – yet it survived, until it could stand no more.

Over a period of a few days, 6–9 January 2017, we watched as our crisis politics was moved to intensive care – into one of those places of constant observation and attention, but of little hope. In the many different waiting rooms, there was a growing sense of inevitability about the news. The prognosis was not good. What was Gerry Adams thinking as he travelled towards Limerick on that Sunday morning in January 2017? Had the decision already been made? The course was set and McGuinness's planned resignation as deputy First Minister would be unanimously endorsed at party leadership level in Dublin that Sunday. Adams travelled there from Limerick, and McGuinness joined the meeting by telephone, reflecting a position already held by Sinn Féin's National Officer Board, which had met two days earlier. By Sunday, the discussion was about how the decision would be enacted, with McGuinness insisting that he would travel to Stormont the next day.

Almost twenty years previously, in that historic moment of the Good Friday Agreement of 1998, the then Social Democratic and Labour Party (SDLP) leader John Hume (who died in 2020) had persuaded Adams and McGuinness of the need for Stormont as a place to engage unionists. In a strategic sense, it was needed then, as it is needed now – needed as part of the long making of an 'agreed' or 'new' or 'shared' Ireland, whatever that might be. It could not easily be given up.

By now, however, there was a mood and a condition that determined it could not be saved. Not even by McGuinness, who, at times, had 'held it together', as former First Minister Peter Robinson had also, in crisis moments, held things together – particularly in 2015 after the murder of Kevin McGuigan in Belfast, to which members of the Irish Republican Army (IRA) had been linked. After the killing, there was an intelligence assessment that pointed to the continued existence of an IRA structure, including an army council. The chief constable at that time, Sir George Hamilton, explains, 'Within a short period of time, the investigation team were pursuing a strong line of enquiry that McGuigan had been murdered by members of the IRA. As the investigation developed, it became clear that there were reasonable grounds to suspect that this was with the knowledge and concurrence of senior figures within the republican movement.' His words here take the policing assessment further than was publicly disclosed at the time. In this same period, the fight over welfare reform could easily have broken Stormont.

Crisis was commonplace, not unusual. So, what was Arlene Foster thinking over that weekend in January 2017? Did Robinson's successor as DUP leader and First Minister still believe that somehow some way would be found out of this latest corner in which politics was stuck? That weekend, Foster gave an interview to the journalist Rodney Edwards, who, at that time, was working on the *Impartial Reporter*, a stone's throw from Foster's then office in

Enniskillen, County Fermanagh. The journalist asked if she thought McGuinness would resign. 'He may well do,' Foster replied.

We knew that Adams would speak at a republican commemoration that Sunday, 8 January. We did not know then that the Sinn Féin leadership – its Ard Chomhairle – was also meeting that day; and that its officer board had already met that Friday. There was also a speech on Saturday inside the Felons Club in west Belfast, used by Adams to place a message and to open out the republican mood for others to see. The media had been invited for this part of the proceedings, and that lunchtime, I watched the audience in that packed room hang on his every word. It was one of those days when you sense immediately that something is afoot. You know because of those who are present – the people who matter. You read it in their faces. In the words and in the reactions. I interpreted the Adams speech as an ultimatum. That afternoon, he described a worsening crisis – and said this was a 'defining point' in relation to the future of the political institutions. I believed the prospect of Martin McGuinness resigning as deputy First Minister, and thus collapsing those institutions at Stormont, was now centre stage in this political play. In these developing events, it would be three years before Stormont would breathe again – a long coma on life support.

In the final weeks of 2016, we had watched as the knot tightened – politics tied up in a mess that would require some remarkable escape. By now, the fiasco of the RHI scheme had made it into the headlines as 'cash for ash' – a phrase first used by the Press Association Editor in Ireland, David Young, as he untangled the complex jargon of RHI.

DAVID YOUNG:

Credit for the phrase should really be shared with a source who patiently walked me through how a little-known scheme called RHI actually worked. I was aware of the Renewable Heat Incentive, and had filed a brief story on its closure in early 2016, but that was long before allegations of misuse and huge overspends became public knowledge. Those were the claims I was trying to stand up some months later when a helpful industry insider explained the fatal errors that created the burn to earn incentive. After lots of puzzling talk of capped tariffs and varying kilowatt outputs, I needed to distil the information down into a concept that was easy to convey in a story for the wider public. 'So, basically the more ash pellets you burn the more cash you get?' I asked, somewhat incredulously. The source replied in the affirmative and a few days later, when PA Media published the first story on the critical flaw that had left Stormont with a multi-million-pound bill, 'burning ash to make cash' was how I described it.

By mid-December, Stormont's survival had become a battle of wills – Sinn Féin pushing for Arlene Foster to step aside and the First Minister stubbornly resisting. In this very public argument, loosening the knot became an impossible task. It was too tight. On Monday, 19 December, Foster made a statement on RHI without the approval or authority of the deputy First Minister, and as we watched a pantomime of politics at Stormont, I wondered whether we were witnessing another of those 'cry wolf' moments. We had been here before – with policing and justice, Maze/Long Kesh and welfare reform – when Sinn Féin showed its teeth, then put them away.

There was a build-up that had created an expectation of something decisive. In mid-December, Martin McGuinness had a phone conversation with Arlene Foster – telling her that the credibility of the political institutions was being undermined 'by the serious and ongoing allegations surrounding the design, operation, abuse and ending of the Renewable Heating Incentive scheme'. He said she should 'stand aside from the role as First Minister' while there was an investigation – advice immediately dismissed by the DUP: 'The First Minister does not take her instructions from Sinn Féin but from the electorate.'

Given the talk of 'grave consequences', that 'crisis' Monday at Stormont closed with a feeling of false alarm; still no indication that Foster was willing to step aside, and Sinn Féin not yet ready to push the nuclear button of a McGuinness resignation. On that stage of

December 2016, politics was disorientated, becoming dysfunctional – perhaps even desperate.

We had witnessed this before in the battles between these parties over the how and when to transfer policing and justice powers from London to Stormont and watched another falling out – this time in 2013 – over plans to build a peace centre on the old Maze/Long Kesh Prison site.

Peter Robinson, Ian Paisley's successor as First Minister, buckled under the weight of opposition from within the loyalist-unionist community. He had no choice and no cover. The Maze/Long Kesh row took place in a period when events on the streets unnerved the unionist political leadership.

Within the unionist community, there was talk of republicans engaging in 'cultural war' – battles that threatened the Union Flag and loyal order marches. Talk, also, of Sinn Féin glorifying terrorism and causing further hurt and pain to the 'innocent victims' – including in a commemoration in Castlederg, County Tyrone. And there was an ever-louder argument that the Maze/Long Kesh peace centre would inevitably become a shrine to the ten hunger strikers who died there in 1981. In the heads of some, all of this was adding up to yet more evidence of republicans rewriting history, and in the noise of these times and in the angry street protests linked to a decision to reduce the number of days that the Union Flag would fly on Belfast City Hall, the Maze project was lost. Peter Robinson stepped away from that plan.

I thought Martin McGuinness might resign as deputy First Minister and that the power-sharing executive could collapse. With my colleague Eamonn Mallie, I had spoken with McGuinness in Derry on Tuesday, 27 August 2013 – a meeting at 11 a.m. in the City Hotel. We were not allowed to report that we had met him. The conversation was for background. It could not be sourced to him. This was one of two meetings we had with McGuinness that day. The second was in the grounds of Saint Eugene's Cathedral. Both Mallie and I wanted to be sure that we had read his lines and his mind correctly; that we had properly understood the meaning and seriousness of what he had said and shared with us earlier.

You read between lines in these conversations and try to assess the mood and message. McGuinness and Sinn Féin considered the Robinson decision as an act of bad faith. We believed that there was the potential for this to escalate into a bigger crisis – that McGuinness was reassessing the worth of that partnership at the top of the executive. These conversations in Derry took place twelve days after Robinson – on 15 August 2013 – had sent a letter to DUP Members of Parliament (MPs) and Members of the Legislative Assembly (MLAs) putting the peace centre project on hold.

McGuinness, in a power-sharing arrangement and in a joint office at the top of government, had no pre-warning. Robinson was on holiday. The correspondence he sent to party colleagues came to be described as his 'letter from America'.* McGuinness was due to see him in New York on 9 September. When Mallie and I spoke with him, his anger was obvious. This was not just about the Maze project. It was about power-sharing and partnership – how joined-up decision-making was meant to work and how it was not working.

McGuinness believed a red line had been crossed. If the peace centre was on hold, then so too was everything else in that planned development. 'Not a brick', the deputy First Minister told us. The row was becoming the backdrop to new negotiations on the vexed questions of flags, parades and the past, which US diplomat Richard Haass would lead with Professor Meghan O'Sullivan – a negotiation in another storm of angry words and in that mindset of 'cultural war'. Within a couple of days, Mallie and I wrote a joint article. Its headline, 'Has Robinson's US missile demolished Peace Centre and Executive', spoke to the seriousness of the situation. It was our reading between the lines of those McGuinness conversations – the working out and the writing out of what we had been told. Every brick in that planned Maze development was now in jeopardy; and so also, we believed, was the highest office at Stormont.

When you walk the path of how this story developed, these are the stepping stones. On the evening of 15 August 2013, as news

---

* In August 2013, Peter Robinson, who was on holiday, wrote to party colleagues detailing his plan to put the Maze/Long Kesh peace centre on hold.

of the Robinson letter began to emerge, Dominic Doherty, one of Sinn Féin's press team in Derry, contacted party MLA Raymond McCartney. In media interviews the next morning, McCartney would be Sinn Féin's first responder into the political row and rubble of this collapsing Maze project – and into another of those moments when the cracks could not be concealed. They were there for all to see. 'Further evidence of weak political leadership', McCartney said of the Robinson letter. McCartney was part of the 1980 IRA hunger strike at the jail, and in the developing peace process beyond his release, he represented the Foyle constituency in the Assembly in the period 2004–2020. Here, he explains the consequences of that letter from America in August 2013.

RAYMOND McCARTNEY:

Dominic Doherty phoned me at about 10 p.m., and in the familiar manner told me that: '[Radio] Foyle is looking for you in the morning', and went on to say that it was about the Long Kesh issue. Funding had been secured from the EU for a Peace Centre on the site, and in recent days some unionists were beating the drum in opposition to it. Dominic went on to say that there was an embargoed statement from Peter Robinson, so I asked him to try and suss what it was about. He came back and told me that the speculation was that Robinson was pulling the plug on the Peace Centre. We agreed that Dominic would phone Martin and that I would then phone Martin to get the agreed approach. Dominic came back again and told me that Martin was unaware of the statement, never mind its content. When I spoke to Martin, he was as measured as ever. I said despite the politics of bad faith, the obvious question would be about the future of the site. Martin's view was that I should not be explicit, but take the approach, that if such a strategic development was not proceeding that it would be difficult to see how any future developments would ever be approved. After the interview with Foyle, and other interviews in the following days, it was obvious that the DUP buckling to pressure ensured that the future of the site was in obvious jeopardy.

Over a period of weeks, the row got louder. In public, McGuinness was measured, calling the Robinson decision 'a mistake'. Privately, other republicans were less restrained. There was talk of an 'untenable' situation and a description of 'a letter bomb from Florida'. In a speech in Warrington, McGuinness accused the DUP of reneging on a programme for government commitment: 'For many, given the journey we've all trodden and the changes that have come about, and our work abroad as advocates of peace-building, it beggars belief that we cannot agree, on the building of a peace centre.'

In the Irish parliament, Adams described 'a crisis within political loyalism and unionism' and spoke of the 'infamous letter from the USA'. There was 'clearly a big problem'. By 25 September, the senior republican Gerry Kelly was describing a 'crisis' in power-sharing; this was dismissed by Robinson, who urged everyone to 'cool their jets'. Then, there was another development. On 1 October, Sinn Féin's former publicity director Danny Morrison wrote an article on the eamonnmallie.com political website: 'I hope I am wrong but I suspect that the Assembly could collapse. If unionists are thinking this cannot happen, they should think again.' It felt like the build-up – the choreography – to some big moment, some big decision, but then it was reined in. Three days after Morrison wrote that article, McGuinness said he would not 'be part of any agenda that sees the institutions collapse'. Someone had changed the record – changed their mind – decided, for some reason, to give Stormont some more time.

Richard Haass and Meghan O'Sullivan were by now chairing those negotiations on flags, parades and the past. Was there a decision by the Sinn Féin leadership to allow this to be a breathing space – or that cooling-off space – in which something might change? Perhaps. There may also have been a view that this was the wrong issue on which to collapse those institutions? I don't know.

What I do know is this: that those republicans who described 'a letter bomb from Florida', an 'untenable' situation, a 'crisis' in power-sharing and the possibility of the Assembly collapsing have been around a long time – too long to misread the tea leaves. Mallie and I had also understood what McGuinness had intimated to us when we met in Derry several weeks earlier; we understood the seriousness of the situation and wrote and spoke about that over a period of weeks. There was no contact from McGuinness to say we had the wrong end of the stick or had got things wrong. To be clear, he did not tell us that he was going to resign, but since our conversations with him, we had listened as other significant republicans took this suggestion, or this sense of crisis at the top of the executive, to a higher pitch; then, suddenly, the volume was turned down. On 4 October 2013, I chatted with the deputy First Minister on the phone. Again, he spoke to me of 'severe difficulties', with the emphasis, he said, on *severe*. His relationship with Robinson had not improved: 'It's not going to improve until Peter repairs the damage that has been done.' He also told me that the DUP believed Sinn Féin were talking to me and Mallie.

In terms of the overall mood and tone, it felt like I was in the same conversation I had with McGuinness in Derry those weeks earlier – the argument and the issues were the same – but Stormont was being given more time and another chance. A veteran and senior republican, with whom I spoke in June 2020, believes that was a mistake: 'In any relationship, if you let someone away with it, they will go further, and by not drawing a line, they [the DUP] go further and further and further.' Another republican holds the view that from that point onwards, Stormont 'was holed below the waterline'. It was waiting for the opportunity that RHI presented. Here, in our politics, there are many sides to every story. Peter Robinson has had time to reflect on that historic political agreement between the DUP and Sinn Féin in 2007 and the challenges of government, including when he succeeded Ian Paisley as First Minister. There were times of anger in his community, when the much easier option for him would have been to collapse the political institutions, but like McGuinness, Robinson was trying to make this work. When you stand in his shoes and in his community, you better understand the dilemma of working politics alongside security and intelligence assessments that report on the continued existence of an IRA army council.

PETER ROBINSON:

By the turn of the century any carefully tuned political antenna could sense that the time for a deal had arrived and most keenly observant practitioners could sense the broad scope and shape of a potential agreement between Northern Ireland's two largest parties. Yet, the downdraft of history was always capable of blowing the process off-course. These were two parties who were enemies with a capital 'E'. Two parties so fundamentally at odds in every area that touches upon day-to-day political priorities and economic outlook, never mind matters relating to culture and identity. The optimist could conceive they might just be able to agree to sit and talk together and perhaps with fortuitous mutual goodwill they might even agree terms, but could they, even if they succeeded in accomplishing that monumental task and used their best endeavours, work positively thereafter in partnership. Agreements are less about negotiating skills than leadership qualities. They are about calculating what can be achieved; is it a worthwhile advance; how sustainable would it be, and can it be delivered by both your adversary's team and your own.

There was a complete acceptance within the leadership of the DUP that reaching an agreement with Sinn Féin would cause serious pain and problems for us both inside and outside the party. We were certain that there would be a price to pay. While the bulk of the party and its support base were practical and level-headed there were those in the party who were born to be in opposition rather than government and they and a few others were genetically incapable of reaching and accepting any deal with Sinn Féin. The terror toll, community division, distrust and loathing for the IRA and all those associated with its murder campaign was, understandably, palpable within the unionist constituency. Unquestionably many in our support base would be confused, distrustful of whether republicans would end their terrorist campaign, and some would consequently, and at least temporarily, withdraw their support from the party. We had witnessed the failure of the Ulster Unionist Party to sell an admittedly poorer deal to the unionist electorate and indeed a large section of its own party. We had in parallel observed the failure of Sinn Féin to deliver on key elements of that previous deal. This deal had to be different in both content and outcome. We sought to close the key gaps in Trimble's deal which had collapsed three times and was by now lifeless. Permanently ending the IRA campaign, decommissioning paramilitary weapons, government accountability, support for the police and recognition of the Courts all had to be resolved satisfactorily.

Back as far as 2004, when the exploration of a possible deal with Sinn Féin had first begun inside his party, Robinson was probably ahead of the posse in his willingness to examine the potential of a once unimaginable or inconceivable agreement. There was so much bad history. He had his benchmarks, of course: a better deal than the one that David Trimble had made; more certainty on a definitive end to the IRA campaign; the destruction of weapons; and publicly declared support from Sinn Féin for policing and the courts. As the DUP moved into the lead unionist role, he would find that it was all much easier said than done, that the IRA moves at its own pace – not at unionist pace. That demands don't work. That governments will tell you what you want to hear. From outside the tent, it was easy to criticise Trimble. Inside it, there was a very different reality. This process has been about phases, and what is achievable within each of them. Think of the ground that Trimble had to cover; back in 1994, Jim Molyneaux, Trimble's predecessor as Ulster Unionist leader, had spoken of the ceasefire as 'destabilising' and as a potential threat to the Union. Just a few years later, Trimble was part of an agreement that would see Sinn Féin in government, decommissioning set in aspirational terms and paths opened up to police reform and prisoner releases. In correspondence with the author, the former Presbyterian Moderator Dr John Dunlop recalled how republicans dragging their feet 'almost ruined David Trimble and the Ulster Unionist Party'.

PETER ROBINSON:

One by one the issues were dealt with, but it still left a difficult conundrum. It was Sinn Féin's view that if the IRA army council was to shut up shop significant numbers of its so-called volunteers would be without the control, influence and leadership to support the process and could follow new leaders who would continue what they described as 'the armed struggle'. Our view was that those who were in leadership and with influence did not need the contradictory structure of an army council to persuade republicans to embrace peaceful and democratic institutions and the most belligerent republicans would find a new vehicle for violence anyway and would have to be dealt with firmly. For a very good reason the devolution of policing and justice had been set aside in every previous set of negotiations. It had to be resolved though the thinking had been that the Executive needed to establish itself and take root before the matter was tackled. Sinn Féin had moved considerably to bring their support base to accept policing and recognise the authority of the Courts and had, for some time, been *chomping at the bit* to move forward with the devolution of policing and justice powers. Against a backcloth of scare stories about terrorists becoming Ministers in charge of the police service whose members they had murdered and in charge of courts they had blown up and whose judges they had attacked, the atmosphere was toxic and within the unionist community people were both very wary and very worried.

My approach was to put every step I intended to take into the public arena before I took it. I needed to ensure that there were vetoes on who could hold Ministerial responsibility and the extent of any Executive role in decision taking. While my own feedback from the public showed we were on the right lines and people were content with the shape of the deal we were constructing there was massive and undisguised hostility from a significant number of our Assembly team, party officers and the DUP Executive. When we entered government with Sinn Féin the cost had been considerable. This was not so much about the loss of the small number of members who resigned, it manifested itself in the loss of electoral support. About 40 per cent of our support evaporated and there was, understandably, concern that taking another hit could destroy the party. In the event it never became an electoral liability and by 2011 the DUP had not only regained the votes it had lost when entering the mandatory coalition but returned more Assembly Members than ever before. Every day of Executive life involved the First Minister and deputy First Minister in negotiations on some matter of Executive policy or potential future changes.

When reading this contribution from Peter Robinson, I remembered sitting with him and the now DUP Chief Executive Tim Johnston in a restaurant in Holywood in December 2004. It was lunchtime, about a week before Christmas; it was just days after it had become clear that the first arms-length negotiation conducted through the British and Irish governments, and designed to achieve a DUP–Sinn Féin agreement, had failed. It did so on the question of IRA weapons, or more specifically, on the DUP demand for photographic evidence of decommissioning. That executive was not achieved until 2007, and years later, I watched at Stormont as Robinson tried to hold it together. He was battling against the headline assessment of IRA involvement in a murder in Belfast. It was 2015, with devolution hanging by the thinnest of threads. The IRA still a question and a factor in our political frame. Had the policing assessment – as outlined by then Chief Constable Sir George Hamilton earlier – been as clear at the time, Stormont may well have fallen.

PETER ROBINSON:

Only a few of the more intractable issues became public knowledge. Welfare Reform, the Maze and the Kevin McGuigan murder aftermath were the most difficult. Martin and I accepted we were repeatedly asking our colleagues to stretch to accept uncomfortable compromises. On a few occasions our best endeavours were not enough. The Sinn Féin senior executive rejected the first Welfare Reform package that we had jointly reached while there was wide disapproval within the DUP for the Maze development proposals we had worked up over a protracted period.

However, in my seven and a half years as First Minister the issue that held the greatest likelihood of bringing the Executive down was the McGuigan murder by those clearly identified as members of PIRA. At the time we were informed there was no evidence to show that the murder was sanctioned by the republican leadership but the proximity of those involved to those we were partnering in government meant that the issue had to be addressed and resolved. The demand from some within the unionist community was for the DUP to walk out of the Executive – a move that would bring devolution to an end at least for some years. At the other end of the spectrum there were those who thought we should do no more than register our strong condemnation. While the former would have brought the institutions down the latter would have been a signal that no matter what line the IRA crossed in the future, we would merely have to *suck it up*. The only feasible route for the DUP to take that assuaged justified unionist anger and sent a message that the party would not tolerate this behaviour was to have the Intelligence Services provide a detailed report on paramilitary activities and intentions that we could use to make an assessment while, in parallel, the Executive was frozen by the resignation of our Ministers and the periodic rotation of successors to hold the posts. It halted Executive meetings and while it was indelicate, inelegant and tedious it provided space for the intelligence report to be prepared and acted as a censure on the conduct of republicans.

All forms of power-sharing are difficult even when it is a voluntary coalition of willing and like-minded parties. Our process is slow and ungainly, its surfaces are rough, and, at times, it gets tied up in its own inherent contradictions and inconsistencies. But it was custom made for a society that is deeply divided and often pulling in different directions. There should be no surprise that it falters from time to time. Given our history and divisions, the fact that the Executive is operating to this day is a tribute to the determination and eagerness of all who are contributing to making politics work and who, bit by bit, edge us towards a more prosperous, shared and peaceful future.

Recently, as a columnist with the *News Letter*, Robinson has re-entered the debate and discussion. Here he has given us an insight into, and detailed critique of, his experience inside that highest office of government here. It helps us better understand the background and the challenges as Stormont moved into its next period of crisis.

The executive is operating today, but after a three-year absence between January 2017 and January 2020. It had survived those many battles up to this point, but it did so at a cost. All of this becomes debilitating, damages the foundations, weakens the structure. In late 2016 into the turn of the year, with Arlene Foster now DUP leader and First Minister, patience snapped. McGuinness and Sinn Féin brought it down.

Someone watching from inside that party described a momentum in the language 'that could take us over the edge'. If there was some way out of the political corners and crisis of this moment, it was not obvious. Arlene Foster had repeatedly rejected the soft exit option. Each time and every time, she dismissed the suggestion that she should step aside for several weeks pending some preliminary report into RHI. This made a hard exit more likely – forced by McGuinness resigning.

At the top of the executive – in that joint office – if one goes, both go. The words and language were taking us ever closer to that point, but I was conscious that in our politics, you remain in that last minute until all sixty seconds have gone. For now, the clock was still ticking. I also remembered those days in 2013 and that battle for the peace centre. All seemed lost until some more time was found. So, the challenge was not to race beyond the argument but to keep pace with it. On 2 January 2017, I wrote of growing concern. This was linked to a sequence of statements from the top tier of Sinn Féin: Michelle O'Neill, Gerry Adams, Martin McGuinness, Matt Carthy and Declan Kearney.

Writing in his blog in the republican newspaper *An Phoblacht*, Kearney – the Sinn Féin chair – described an 'unprecedented tipping point', and Carthy, one of the party's MEPs at that time, and later elected as a TD for the Cavan–Monaghan constituency, spoke of 'the greatest threat to the political institutions in over a decade'. There was no easy way back from those words; this was the momentum that would take things over that edge. In that same piece, I also made this point: that those who thought that this latest political crisis was about a single issue were missing the point.

The RHI fallout was a jigsaw piece, a big piece, but not the whole picture or anything like it. The partnership politics envisaged in the political negotiations and agreements of 1998 had been undermined. The Irish language, legacy, reconciliation and other issues were back in the conversation. Another negotiation would be needed, but was there the mood for such?

The pace was about to change, to quicken. We were now in the endgame. On Wednesday, 4 January 2017, Arlene Foster restated her position. She told Sky News, 'I'm not going to roll over to Sinn Féin. I'm not going to roll over to my political opponents.' DUP and Sinn Féin leadership teams met that day: Foster with the MP Nigel Dodds; Martin McGuinness with Michelle O'Neill, now in a more prominent leadership role and taking on some of the responsibilities of McGuinness, who was ill – more seriously ill than was known at that time. Nothing changed in that meeting. A source spoke of a knot that could not be untied.

Days later, 7 January, we arrive at the place and the defining moment in this drama: the Adams ultimatum to Foster, which I referenced earlier. This was the point of no return. Inside the Felons Club, in west Belfast, there was standing room only for that speech by Adams, which was his last word before the political breakdown. 'If the First Minister does not take the actions that society desires and deserves and which a sustainable process of change requires, then Sinn Féin will bring this ongoing and totally unacceptable state of affairs to an end.'

When Adams finished his speech, there was a pause as the media were asked to leave and ushered down the stairs and out a side door; the meeting was then resumed in private session. I went for a coffee nearby to think over what Adams had said, and afterwards, by chance, I met Eibhlin Glenholmes walking on the Falls Road. During the conflict years, in a headline case, Britain sought her extradition from the Irish Republic in relation to IRA attacks. The request failed and she went on-the-run, only returning to Belfast in the period of the peace process. That Saturday, in January 2017, she had been to that meeting in the Felons Club. The Belfast republican, whose life has been the war and peace of this place, spoke of 'gridlock'. As the day developed, that picture became clearer.

Through Saturday into Sunday, I spoke with several others, all of whom had been at that private briefing. In different words, they all described an endgame. There was a need for a 'new agreement', or more accurately, the implementation of old agreements. Everything I was hearing was confirmation that the political fallout was about more than RHI. It was about the power-sharing project and whether a 'workable relationship' was possible alongside the DUP, and there was an even bigger question: Was the North ungovernable?

I was told the loudest cheer came in response to a shout from the audience to 'bring the institutions down now'. Even if Arlene Foster stepped aside, it 'wouldn't be enough'. Another source described 'growing unease'. 'It could all happen very quickly', he said. I shared my observation with him – a belief that minds were set. He replied, 'That's my view of that meeting today.' A third source spoke of 'uncharted waters': 'I don't think we've long to wait,' he said. Given his rank and influence, he is someone who would have known.

When you work these threads of information together, you see the picture. Stormont in its last days. The crash about to happen. I wrote that weekend about politics in the trenches. Adams' speech was not a hint. It was the final word on this matter. We were watching the Stormont project disintegrate before our eyes. The question now, what happens on the other side of such a falling out? I was told that in that private briefing in the Felons Club, Adams had said it could take years to fix. He was right.

It was important to be there that Saturday in order to keep pace with developments. Not only to hear the Adams speech but also to see that packed room – and to try to read its mind. Adams was joined on stage by the party's Stormont Executive team minus Martin McGuinness. Michelle O'Neill was there; also, Mairtin Ó Muilleoir, Chris Hazzard and Megan Fearon. In my experience, these set pieces always have a wider purpose. I can remember two other similar occasions, in different times. Both were inside Conway Mill in the lower Falls area – the first in 2001, the second in 2005; and both times, there was an Adams speech. They were signposts to other developments. One on the eve of an IRA statement on the first act of decommissioning. The other, the beginning of something that, months later, would bring the announcement formally ending the IRA armed campaign.

There were two other significant happenings out of our vision that weekend in January 2017 – a meeting of the Sinn Féin officer board, and then a meeting of its Ard Chomhairle; all of this paving the way for the McGuinness resignation that Monday. That weekend, in Enniskillen, Arlene Foster gave an interview to the journalist Rodney Edwards of *The Impartial Reporter*. It was recorded on Friday and published on Monday, 9 January.

RODNEY EDWARDS:

For years a portrait of Rev. Ian Paisley, the founder of the Democratic Unionist Party, hung on the wall above Arlene Foster's desk in her now former office on Enniskillen's East Bridge Street. That image of her late party leader was later replaced by one of her shaking hands with Prince Charles, her favourite Royal, and always caught my eye when I sat in her cramped office in between piles of documents, correspondence and thank you cards from constituents. The *Impartial Reporter* office was a few yards down the street. So, I could nip over when I wanted to grab a quick word with Foster much to the annoyance of the DUP press office. Friday was always a good time to get her as she'd be in town dealing with constituency issues. She'd have her team around her and sometimes her children would be there. So, the interview could be interrupted by her son Ben discussing his chickens or her colleagues engaging in some local gossip which she loved to hear. I always maintain Fermanagh sees a different side to Foster; she's more personable, more approachable and chattier and open to people like me calling over and catching her on the hop. 6 January 2017 was no different, except of course Foster would make a comment that would anger deputy First Minister Martin McGuinness and the rest of the Sinn Féin hierarchy that weekend.

Politics was in one of those phases when every word was read and heard – especially those spoken by Foster in this crisis period – but it was Sinn Féin who had control of the board in terms of the next move. With hindsight, we know it was already too late for Foster to rescue the situation. That Friday, as Edwards stepped into the First Minister's constituency office, neither would have known just how close politics was to collapse. It was that same day that the Sinn Féin Officer Board was meeting, shaping its thinking ahead of a critical Ard Chomhairle meeting that Sunday.

RODNEY EDWARDS:

I called her to see if she was free for a chat and she asked me to nip over later that afternoon, which I did. Her close protection officers were waiting outside in a bullet proof jeep with the engine running. Inside, there was Foster, sitting under that photograph of a grinning Prince Charles, tapping away at her iPad. She put it to one side and lifted the lid of her laptop and the Backstreet Boys started to play before closing it again, nervously laughing at her choice of music. With the office phone almost constantly ringing Foster was clearly preoccupied and wanted to get out of there. It was Friday after all.

She stood up, perhaps to hurry things along, and I asked her if she would step aside, as McGuinness was asking, to which she replied: 'What I say to [Mr McGuinness] is this: if he is playing a game of chicken, if Sinn Féin is playing a game of chicken and they think we are going to blink in relation to me stepping aside they are wrong. I won't be stepping aside.' I asked if she was damaged goods as suggested the previous week by DUP biographer John Tonge and she threw it back at me, saying: 'Well, you should ask him what he means by that because I am not damaged goods.' Asked to respond to the charge that she possessed 'overarching arrogance', Foster said: 'These are the sort of things that are fired at you when you are a strong leader, particularly when you are a strong female leader. If you have strong male leaders, they are strong, they are hard, they are tough. If you have a strong female leader, they are arrogant.' While she was answering my questions, she put her coat on, one of her close protection officers appeared at the door, and she lifted her iPad and placed it in her handbag. I asked her if she thought McGuinness was going to resign. 'He may well do,' she replied, as she walked out the door with her children in tow and got into the jeep. 'He may well do.' Days later he did.

That Edwards interview with Foster captured the building drama. It was recorded before Adams spoke in the Felons Club but did not run until afterwards. There was no announcement yet from McGuinness, but there was a growing inevitability. The quickening pace became a race away from the Stormont institutions and along a road that was far from certain.

After treatment in hospital that Monday, a visibly frail Martin McGuinness travelled to Stormont to tell Arlene Foster directly of his decision. It would take effect from 5 p.m. and there would be 'no return to the status quo'. The First Minister's response was in a scripted, scolding, pre-recorded statement.

Within days, on 12 January 2017, I quoted a senior DUP source (one of the party's MPs) as he outlined this assessment: 'We believe the republican movement is hunkering down for a period outside government to manage the transition to their new leadership. If you can't crack something in the next three days, it's not happening. The election will happen. It solves nothing. It will be bruising. It will be over [this phase of devolution].' Then what, I asked. 'A lengthy period of direct rule,' he responded. 'We might not be talking months. We could be talking years.'

The time frame of years was correct, but the working out of the reason was wrong. This had nothing to do with the transition to the new Sinn Féin leadership. It was about the brokenness of politics and a relationship that was not working. Just read back into that Adams speech in the Felons Club: 'The deliberate flouting of any notion of partnership government by the DUP, and recent remarks in particular by the First Minister about the Executive Office, have caused huge difficulties … Arlene Foster is not a Prime Minister.'

The DUP was still looking at and blaming Sinn Féin for this breakdown when it should have been looking into the mirror. What was its contribution – its part – in the making of this mess? 'It's nothing to do with a transition', a senior republican responded at the time. 'The mood is: enough is enough.'

In the procedure of these things, there is a short breathing space – a chance to mend and to reconsider, and for Sinn Féin to re-nominate for that office at the top of the executive. It was too late for that. By now, there was an election mood and mode. By 16 January – a week after the McGuinness resignation – Secretary of State James Brokenshire had set the date of 2 March. Martin McGuinness would not run in that assembly election. On Monday, 23 January at a news event at Stormont, Michelle O'Neill became the party's leader in the North. That day, I wrote an article for the *Irish Times* entitled 'Sinn Féin meeting that brought political crisis to a head' – thinking back to that speech and briefing in the Felons Club those two-plus weeks earlier and to the mood in that moment. So much had happened and changed since then. In that run and that race away from Stormont, there was an irreversible momentum; but where was its finishing line?

'SINN FÉIN MEETING THAT BROUGHT POLITICAL CRISIS TO A HEAD':

Almost 20 years after Good Friday 1998, the threads of that historic agreement – one that was held up internationally as the way to confirm and consolidate peace – have loosened and are coming undone. Republicans are now questioning the worth of the Stormont institutions and a decade-long relationship with the DUP at the head of the Northern Ireland Executive. This was the mood inside the Felons Club that Saturday in January ... 'People have reached the end of their tether,' a senior republican said that evening. 'The anger in our community is palpable.' The question being asked he said, is: 'Why are you up there [in Stormont]?'

For over two decades, a key consideration for the republican leadership has been the cohesion of its movement and party and community. During that period, Adams and McGuinness have relied on a small group of senior republicans to be their eyes and ears, to take the pulse and know the mood. Among that small group are a number of Belfast republicans, who were significant figures in the IRA leadership and who have been part of the transition into peace and into politics. Bobby Storey, Sean Murray and Martin Lynch were all inside the Felons Club. 'They are not just reflecting it, they are the mood,' another republican told me. He means that key group, working closely with Adams and McGuinness and other senior republican figures such as Ted Howell, have come to that point of questioning the credibility and viability of the Stormont political project. When such figures speak, they cannot be ignored ... So, there is a mood, seen and heard in the Felons Club, that has to be managed; managed at a time of transition in the republican leadership, which is having to be accelerated because of McGuinness's illness. Health Minister Michelle O'Neill, who has taken on a more prominent role in recent times and who was on stage with Adams in the Felons Club, now steps into that position of leading the Sinn Féin Assembly group.

For many in the Northern Ireland communities, McGuinness will only ever be seen in an IRA frame, his name linked to the bombs and bullets and death and destruction of a decades-long conflict, but his story reads from war to peace. There have also been remarkable moments of reconciliation. His meetings with Queen Elizabeth and his participation in a debate with PSNI [Police Service of Northern Ireland] Chief Constable George Hamilton in west Belfast in 2015. Within the republican community, there was recent anger and criticism of McGuinness's presence in London at the unveiling of Irish artist Colin Davidson's portrait of Queen Elizabeth. 'They [republicans] saw it again as him reaching out, stretching, and nothing coming back,' said a source with knowledge of events, meaning nothing coming back from the unionist political leadership. This criticism is part of that wider mood and questioning. Now, after almost a decade in government, there has been a very public breakdown in the relationship between the DUP and Sinn Féin. Leaving another Sinn Féin event at the Felons Club last week, the influential Belfast republican Bobby Storey shouted across the road towards journalists: 'Let's go.' It was a reference to the election – scheduled for 2 March. But, let's go where? This is the unanswered question.

A new agreement to achieve the certainty of partnership in government and to settle impossible issues such as legacy will take time. If there is no Northern Ireland Executive, what fills the gap?

Some unionists are predicting a long period of direct rule; the pressing of a rewind button until some way forward can be found. That new agreement to achieve the implementation of old agreements could mean a very long negotiation before the Northern Ireland Executive is rebuilt. Beyond the election, politics will enter what a senior republican called 'uncharted waters'. There is also concern that dissident republicans will attempt to step into the space, fears underscored when a police officer was wounded in a gun attack in north Belfast on Sunday evening.

Some of those I mentioned in that article, and who held some of the most-senior IRA positions, have become a big part of today's politics. Not elected, but hugely influential. In the words of one republican, they have 'authority' and are 'trusted' – respected because of their 'nous' and 'savvy'. Inside that transition and debate that moved the IRA from its war into peace, they, along with others – including the late Brian Keenan – 'became an intellectual force'. In another description, they are 'shadowy figures'.

CHAPTER 2

'Shadowy figures' in the Stormont corridors

Sometimes in peace-building, we have to go back to the basics – remind ourselves from where we have come. How do conflicts end? How do we judge the success of a transition towards peace? Who needs to be involved? The starting point is dialogue and persuasion – the work of trying to convince armed groups that there is an alternative. This is where John Hume began in the 1980s. Firstly, persuading those at leadership level such as Adams and McGuinness, who then have to prove to others that another way is worth the journey. Bobby Storey, Martin Lynch and Sean Murray, as well as many others, including Brian Keenan, Sean Hughes and the former IRA chiefs of staff, Kevin McKenna and Thomas Murphy, had to believe in this if others were to follow. If they didn't, then there was no point.

Their involvement in a peace process or initiative was not something that could be considered as optional or desirable. It was absolutely essential. We know now, although we forget at times or become impatient, that all of this is a long negotiation. There is a beginning but no clearly defined end. Peace and its politics are always a work in progress.

As I stepped out of that Stormont news event on Monday, 23 January 2017 at which Michelle O'Neill was confirmed as the Sinn Féin leader in the North, I bumped into a conversation in the corridor – Storey and Lynch sitting, Gerry Kelly and Sam Baker standing. I used my phone to take a quick photograph, and there was some quip about where it might turn up. I think I used it on Twitter that afternoon alongside a link to that *Irish Times* article. It is a picture that illustrates and explains the story of the republican transition out of war and towards peace and the related politics.

In the conflict period, Storey and Lynch were senior IRA leaders. Storey was that organisation's director of intelligence – always, it seemed, one step ahead of the Special Branch and Security Service (MI5). Lynch was a member of the IRA army council; he was also the target of a bugging operation many years after the ceasefires and in the course of critical political negotiations on the implementation of the Good Friday Agreement. Viewed from inside hurt and hurting communities, their involvement with the IRA is the beginning and the end. Pages of terrorism, destruction and death – and then a full stop.

Yet, that Stormont picture says something else and something more. It represents the chapters of the peace process – a new, distinctive, phase. The what next after conflict. By the time I took that photograph, Storey and Lynch had become part of the political furniture. But beyond that date in 2017, they would, at times, still be characterised – along with others – as those 'shadowy figures' in the republican backroom. Sean Murray and Ted Howell, whom I mentioned in that *Irish Times* article, are also written into that script. So, too, Padraic Wilson – the IRA jail leader at the time of the Good Friday Agreement.

I wrote earlier that they are unelected. This becomes part of the story. But if, at any time, Sinn Féin had run any of them in an election, they would have won comfortably, even if running in their heaviest boots. For decades, they have been main stage and centre stage in the republican community and story – part of every discussion and debate, including those that were about turning corners away from the armed campaign and, eventually, into political and policing structures. Ted Howell has been through every dotted 'i' and crossed 't' in that forest of papers that shaped the negotiations and agreements both before and after Good Friday 1998.

You have to go back more than three decades to find the beginnings of those conversations as part of that long and, at times, contradictory peace initiative. Many have forgotten the detail and the challenge in all of this – how to move an armed organisation into politics. That is the purpose of a transition. What had to happen. How success is judged. I asked the Belfast republican Jake Mac Siacais to write here – to remind us how that peace initiative evolved and contextualise its place in the bigger jigsaw of our politics then and now. He writes with deep inside knowledge of those key developments in the 1980s and 1990s – the first bricks on which the past thirty-plus years have been built – and the task facing Adams and McGuinness and those around them at that time: How to move the IRA.

JAKE Mac SIACAIS:

The current imperfect peace, which, for twenty years, has tottered from crisis to crisis can best be described as an absence of violence but a conflict still whose root causes have been largely unaddressed and unresolved. A pathway to our current position, began as a republican 'peace initiative', whose origins were a leadership strategy begun in the 1980s. Republicans by the end of the '80s were in effect aiming for a long-term position where it would be possible to remove the gun from Irish politics. The challenges were daunting and there were no certainties or guaranteed outcomes.

Nothing was certain or guaranteed. Peace is not some worked out plan. It happens and doesn't happen – punctuated by challenges and contradictions. Those involved do not all move at the same pace. Some are quicker than others. Some are slower. Some also believe sooner than others. Today, in our politics and communities, there are those who remain to be convinced.

JAKE Mac SIACAIS:

Armed conflict had been a constant and recurring feature of Irish politics throughout the twentieth century ever since unionism introduced guns to the equation in 1912 by arming itself and setting its face against any form of Home Rule in Ireland. For the republican leadership to move the IRA and its active support base towards a wholly political struggle would require, extremely careful and skilful management, infinite patience and a good degree of constructive ambiguity. It would also call for strategy capable of convincing those who held armed struggle against British Rule as something akin to a Sacred Cow, that another route was possible. This task was all the more difficult given that the IRA had, by the 1990s, been waging a thirty-year-long ferocious armed insurgency ever since the Northern Unionist State had imploded under its own inherent contradictions in the late sixties.

The notion that the IRA and the republican movement was a coherent monolith is a mistaken notion. The IRA leadership which emerged in the late 1970s was one of the most consistent and capable which had existed at any time in the organisation's history. It nonetheless oversaw a disparate number of constituencies and centres of local power, including the General Headquarters Staff, The Northern and Southern Commands, The England and Overseas Department, The Quartermaster General's Department and various powerful brigade structures including Belfast, Tyrone, South Armagh, Derry, South Derry and others. Articulating the position reached by the early 1990s the IRA stated publicly on April 24th 1993, in the aftermath of the Bishopsgate bombing: 'The British establishment should seize the current opportunity and take the steps needed for ending its futile and costly war in Ireland. We reiterate that they should pursue the path of peace or resign themselves to the path of war.'

Mac Siacais was inside the republican debate through to 1997, when he left the movement. He sings from his own hymn sheet; lives in west Belfast; knows the pulse and mind of his community and is not programmed to repeat the leadership line. His involvement in those years before 1997 gives him the stripes to speak his mind. He believes the IRA statement of 1994 did not go far enough, that the armed campaign should have ended then with an order to dump arms. Instead he believes the IRA became a bargaining chip in negotiations.

JAKE Mac SIACAIS:

In effect, alongside its developing 'peace initiative', the IRA leadership was escalating conflict so that it could enter any endgame from a position of relative strength. The unfolding republican 'peace initiative', which sought a comprehensive process addressing the root causes of conflict, rested on an agreed nationalist position shared by republicans and nationalists and supported by the Dublin Government and a powerful constituency in Irish America. The IRA leadership had agreed that this initiative, which had become known as the Hume/Adams agreement, could form the basis for a ceasefire. It was, however, fatally undermined by the Dublin Government's signing of the Downing Street Declaration on 15 December 1993. The Declaration underwrote the unionist veto and set the framework for an internal settlement, something which the IRA had said they would not countenance. There was, however, no other game in town. The republican leadership would have no inclusive and comprehensive talks process addressing the root causes of the conflict and would instead have to play out their hand as best they could. The strategy which would govern this would be known as TUAS, an acronym which in constructively ambiguous terms could be sold as a Totally UnArmed Strategy or a Tactical Use of Armed Struggle.

These are the complications and the contortions that occur in a peace initiative – that as armed groups move in that direction, violence remains an option or a part of the negotiation. Leaderships have to consider both the internal management of organisations as well as the task of building trust with enemies and political opponents. There are many contradictions along the way. The road is rarely straight.

JAKE Mac SIACAIS:

It must be borne in mind that the republican 'peace initiative' was a leadership-led strategy, which came as a huge revelation to the bulk of the IRA and its active support base at the same time as it came to public attention. In the circumstances the IRA leadership played a sterling hand and could by 2005 effectively signal the end of the armed campaign without the spectre of republicans turning in on themselves as had so often happened in history. It was an imperfect peace in that it left a largely unreconstructed unionism on one extreme as well as a tiny republican rump still wedded to the use of 'armed struggle'. That it was an imperfect peace was recognised by the IRA in their July 2005 statement which noted: 'There is also widespread concern about the failure of the two governments and the unionists to fully engage in the peace process. This has created real difficulties.'

Keeping the process on the road at all costs and avoiding the recurring bouts of crisis at the heart of the process was the inevitable outcome of the very flaws inherent in a process which saw both governments and all the parties failing to comprehensively address the root causes of conflict. What we have been bequeathed is a balkanised society. Its underlying dynamic is self-reinforcing and ensures that both the unionist and republican leaderships must constantly reassure their respective bases that they will remain vigilant in ensuring that the other will not be allowed to prevail. We live in a present haunted by an unresolved past.

You read in those words a real sense of being underwhelmed. There have been three major legacy consultations and negotiations – Eames/ Bradley, Haass/O'Sullivan and the Stormont House Agreement. A decade-plus of reports and proposals but still no process on the past – no serious attempt or demonstration of intent to address those questions of causation in relation to the conflict years. This is part of the deep background of discontent that surfaces as part of the fallout in 2016–17, part of the disconnect from Stormont. The weariness that comes with all of this. No Irish Language Act. Those draining battles over the devolution of policing and justice powers, the peace centre and matters of welfare reform. That list becomes part of the questioning and the question: Why are you up there in Stormont? And, on the other side of the coin, there is suspicion – dating back to 2015 – as reports and assessments are read that point to parts of an IRA structure, including an army council, still in place, albeit with an entirely different purpose. It is in this that the story of 'shadowy figures' opens out into the question of who is in control. Who is in charge? Is it Sinn Féin, or is it still the IRA?

Sir Hugh Orde served as PSNI Chief Constable in the years 2002–2009 and, before then, was part of the Stevens Investigation that examined the loyalist murder of Belfast solicitor Pat Finucane and the wider allegation of state collusion with loyalists. He has seen the 'dark side' and understands the 'dirty war'. He understands, also, the nature of a transition: that for peace to work, policing has to work; that the two are always a negotiation – a negotiation that did not end with the political agreement of 1998 or the Patten report on police reforms the following year.

SIR HUGH ORDE:

End games in terrorism are messy. The experience across the world is that they don't just stop. As most endgames, the Northern Ireland settlement was a negotiated one, but the negotiations had to continue post-event if we were ever to underpin the Good Friday Agreement with a sustainable and lasting peace. Will you talk to ex-terrorists, was one of the first, and I suppose most predictable, questions I had on taking office. I can't remember who asked it, but it was, in my judgement, an effort to create some unhelpful and sensational headline. If I remember correctly, my response was that I would talk to anyone who wanted to make a difference to policing. No headline appeared. This was my benchmark for seven years and allowed me to meet all sorts of individuals, many of whom had difficult histories. I never forgot what these people had done in their past, but my determination was to deliver a new style of policing against the new environment, and to prevent another set of pages of material for Lost Lives [the highly acclaimed book that logs the deaths of the conflict period]. To try and achieve this without talking to those who represented every community would have been stupid.

Orde arrived to change things. He was from outside of us, had a mind and a way of his own and was part of the next steps – how to take the pages and the plans of Patten and to begin to make things better. In the same way that the IRA would move at its pace, so, also, would policing. These transitions don't happen in a rush. They take time. They are tedious; tiresome. They are still happening: part of that work-in-progress.

SIR HUGH ORDE:

The more one understood the challenges the better the chance of success. In the early years, when Sinn Féin were not supporting policing, I met privately with many players who didn't want any public knowledge of the conversations, but wanted me to know the inevitable would happen. These were not by any measure all ex-combatants (from both sides) but people who had clear connections with such operators. Many just wanted me to know what it was like for them during 'the Troubles', with much of the conversation, depending on the community, being about 'the police' or 'our police'.

In positions of leadership, you have to think beyond yourself and, as Chief Constable, Orde knew there would be difficult challenges and conversations. Who to talk with? Who to avoid? How would his decisions be interpreted both inside and outside the police service? Part of this was trying to understand the hurt on all sides. As with everything, you learn as these processes develop.

SIR HUGH ORDE:

I was always concerned about how my officers would feel about such conversations, but, as ever, I underestimated them. No one, including colleagues, wanted to go backwards, and compromise was an inevitable part of the process, however difficult it was going to be. Some of the most challenging experiences were when, with proper facilitation, different players (including police) came together to discuss both the past and the future. Often highly charged and emotional, the benefit definitely outweighed the considerable risk ... If 'shadowy figures' hadn't engaged in this process it would have been worthless.

I remember one meeting with combatants from both sides, clergy, police, ex-military and others when there was a heated debate over state killings. It was asserted that all murders of republicans during 'the Troubles' were a result of collusion. It ended with a stark observation from a loyalist to a republican that 'We didn't need them [albeit in more colourful language, pointing at me and another colleague] to kill you, we were good at it.' The point here being that challenging different versions of the past had to be worked through if the peace process was ever going to work.

Some of the conversations between my officers and shadowy figures were equally challenging, but, also, in my view, critical to the future. It has to be remembered that many players were now in positions as a result of a democratic process. So, engagement was not an option but an obligation. The more one could create conversations, the more chance we had of delivering policing across the divide, and the more inevitable Sinn Féin joining policing would become. My sense was bottom up pressure from communities wanting effective policing would be an essential part of the Sinn Féin decision to join.

From a policing perspective, I was convinced that in parallel with talking, local empowerment of District Commanders to work without too much central direction was essential. There was no point building relationships if everything came from the top. Giving those who knew the territory best the authority to move forward, at different speeds and in different ways, was the key to success.

Orde is absolutely right. A peace process would not have worked without the so-called 'shadowy figures' – without their influence and that ability to turn the handles that take discussions and debates into different places. Into the rooms of give-and-take, compromise and agreements that, then, have to be sold because they fall short of expectations. The republican political leadership could not have delivered this without the weight of those who fought the war. So, the 'shadowy figures' script either misunderstands or ignores the processes of peace-building or results from skipping through those pages, not wanting to know.

In the *Irish Times* article of January 2017, I wrote that Murray, Lynch and Storey represented a mood. For decades, their thinking – alongside that of others – was the test of what was possible. At crucial moments, had they not moved, then Adams and McGuinness could not have moved either. This was their influence. As the peace process developed, they became regulars in the Stormont canteen. I have seen them with their boiled eggs and breakfast and with their lunches, feeding off the same menu as everyone else, drinking the same tea and coffee – often 'on-the-run' for milk or something else – and walking in the same corridors. There to see – and be seen so many times that they became part of the political routine and picture. They melted into it, and they fitted into it. If you say hello to them, they will say hello back. They too had to find their way in these different places where there are different responsibilities and decisions to be made.

When convenient or beneficial to do so, all of this is disregarded – at times, by those in politics and government on the other side of the border. There is a screaming double-standard, most evident after the Irish general election of 2020, 'That unionists have to go into government [with Sinn Féin], but they [Fianna Fáil and Fine Gael] don't want to soil their hands.' These are the words of a veteran of the Northern Ireland peace and political processes.

Much has happened since I took that photograph in the Stormont corridor back in January 2017. Bobby Storey died in June 2020. The youngest man in that photograph, Sam Baker, became Sinn Féin chair in the North; he is one of today's republican leaders and influencers. Beyond 2017, Murray, Lynch, Wilson and Howell continued to be part of the talks that were about the re-making of Stormont. The latter two are co-authors with Adams of *The Negotiator's Cook Book*. Inside its pages, there are photographs of them inside Stormont – out in the open and outside that description of being 'shadowy figures'. And it was inside those long negotiations that the recipes for peace and politics were eventually found – something that had been impossible to imagine in the hell of previous decades.

When I talk with republicans, there is a routine description of Howell: private, senior, very close to Adams, well read, talented. One source, in a conversation with the author in June 2020, said, 'He's been around the leadership all his life – highly trusted ... He's a highly-skilled, self-taught negotiator.' In a later conversation, there was a reference to his 'searing intellect ... capable of analysing and making quick decisions'. In July 2020, in the course of my research for this book, I spoke with another republican who has been inside those rooms and discussions and debates with Howell. I asked for a sentence or two – for the words that would give us a sense of his role and significance. 'Probably the single most important strategist within that leadership ... he coordinated and chaired all of the critical negotiations.' This source spoke of someone who made assessments and identified hurdles, likening all of this to the thinking moves of a chess game.

I know Ted Howell only to say hello, and by way of what others have told me. I have never heard him discuss his role or involvement in the past fifty years of this place. I did hear him speak briefly, because I called on him to do so at a private event that I chaired for the Healing Through Remembering project in Belfast in the summer of 2011. Recalling that moment, Dawn Purvis, a former Stormont MLA and board member of the project, said, 'I thought it was Gerry Adams speaking.'

Only a photograph of the panel was ever made public (Mitchel McLaughlin of Sinn Féin; Kate Turner, director of Healing Through Remembering; loyalist Jackie McDonald; Sir Hugh Orde; and the then PSNI Chief Constable Matt Baggott). Nothing was said of the fascinating audience that packed the room that evening other than a reference to victims' groups, security forces, ex-combatants, religious organisations and other non-governmental organisations (NGOs). As well as calling on Howell to speak, I also invited Raymond White, the former head of Royal Ulster Constabulary (RUC) Special Branch, to do so. Lord Robin Eames and Denis Bradley were also present.

Years later, I read the minutes of that meeting taken by a stenographer. Howell spoke of the need for a range of processes to address the past – supplementary, supportive processes to assist the truth recovery and the causes of the conflict process. This, he said, was the 'broad umbrella within which to deal with it'. The British and Irish governments should fund the process, but, according to Howell, 'beyond that, it should be independent … they shouldn't design it'. All combatants should be involved. This meeting and its minutes are from a decade ago. The legacy debate has moved and not moved since then. Republicans wanted an independent truth process, but through the Haass/O'Sullivan and Stormont House negotiations, different proposals emerged. These were for a new Historical Investigations Unit (HIU) and Independent Commission on Information Retrieval (ICIR). Included in the proposals was an Implementation and Reconciliation Group (IRG) and an Oral History Archive. As I write, these things have not been implemented. The proposals and agreements have become disagreements.

Part of the mystery of Ted Howell is that he holds no formal position within the republican leadership yet he can hold everyone's attention, both inside and outside of that structure. You learn a little about him when you read back to 2004, the year his wife Eileen died. She was a prominent and well-known community activist and leader in west Belfast. At the time, the Belfast republican Jim Gibney wrote in *An Phoblacht*, 'It is difficult to write about Eileen without reference to Ted, because to me it was always Ted and Eileen. They had an old-fashioned relationship, which took root in the midst of war in the early '70s. The pattern of times to come was set early on. On their wedding night Ted was arrested and narrowly escaped internment when he was released the following morning on false identification papers.'

Gerry Adams said, 'During the early 'seventies Eileen was a frequent visitor to the Maidstone prison ship and Long Kesh where her husband Ted was interned.' From the hunger strikes in the 1980s through the political negotiations and agreements that stretch far beyond the ceasefires of the 1990s all the way to January 2020, you find Ted Howell in the republican kitchen cabinet. So, in all of those moments when there were big decisions to make and take, Howell was there, and you are not in that circle unless you have reason to be there, which comes with significant influence.

He might, within a different political frame and circumstance, be described as a minister without portfolio – someone whose responsibility stretched across a range of kitchen cabinet matters.

Padraic Wilson spent long years in jail and has spent longer years of involvement in the republican peace and political projects. He was on the inside of all of those big developments that extend and stretch across the ending of the armed campaign, the process of putting arms beyond use, and the exploration and explanation of the steps into the 'new policing' structures. He has also been inside the Stormont negotiations that have failed and worked. When you piece all of this together, you read the one evolving story. All of the elements – of war and politics – are there to be scrutinised as one piece.

Sean Murray – a former IRA prisoner who, during the conflict period, was one of that organisation's most senior leaders – is now the key figure in the Sinn Féin negotiation team on matters of legacy, policing and parades. I am told that he was one of the last to be persuaded of the alternative to 'armed struggle'. He then persuaded others. His story reads onto the pages of the peace process. He has been photographed and filmed alongside other Sinn Féin negotiators at Stormont, and in 2018, he was part of a panel discussion hosted by Féile an Phobail in west Belfast. That panel also included Chief Constable Sir George Hamilton, Victims' Commissioner Judith Thompson, loyalist Winston Irvine and Queen's University Professor Louise Mallinder. The event, which I chaired, was titled 'Stuck in the Past'. Long ago, Murray stepped out of the shadows; now he is out in the open. As Kate Turner, Director of the Healing Through Remembering project, now explains, some once-unimaginable friendships have become part of this developing process and story – friendships that some still struggle to understand or accept.

KATE TURNER:

In 2016, a few days after the funeral of my father (a senior Church of Ireland cleric) a friend and former parishioner of his confronted me angrily: 'How could you have that republican carry the Canon's coffin?' she spluttered, waving a newspaper showing Dad's coffin leaving the church. Over the years, my father Edgar met many of my colleagues and people from my wider work circles.

Healing Through Remembering is one of those quiet projects that every peace process needs. It has been a safe space for difficult conversations and has brought together people from the different sides of the conflict – all with different perspectives on what happened and why. Think back to that 2011 event I referenced earlier. That type of gathering, with such wide participation, was only possible because the project is trusted.

KATE TURNER:

For more than twenty years, I have coordinated the work of Healing Through Remembering (HTR). At HTR, we consider the challenging question of how to deal with the legacy of the conflict in such a way as to support and meet the needs of society, both in remembering and in healing and collectively moving towards a better future. HTR aims to work with a wide range of groups and individuals to ensure this debate takes into account the deep difficulties and subtle nuances of that legacy for all those affected by and involved in the conflict. In these conversations over decades we have come to understand that it is just as important to engage meaningfully with the staff in government departments as with their ministers, who change from year to year. It is just as necessary to establish relationships with party advisors and office staff as it is to develop a rapport with the high-profile politicians. And it is just as important to forge relationships with the people who spend long hours in the offices – drafting the words, considering the options, weighing the impact – as it is with those who deliver the speeches in public. Building common purpose with the people who know what is possible and what the practicalities of legacy work mean for their constituents – be they victims/survivors, ex-prisoners, former RUC, British Army; whether they are seeking answers, traumatised by the past, or those who wish to just move on – is a vital part of the process. The slow work of nurturing trust in the present moment matters for dealing with the past.

This work goes into every corner of the conflict period. In its conversations, it hears of the many hurts – the different truths of that dark past – and its reports are like a kind of torch showing a way into the future that respects the past while understanding the need to find the present. We cannot live in 'the war' forever.

KATE TURNER:

Amongst these diverse individuals, I have worked with both Ted Howell and Sean Murray. More than work with them, I have come to know them well enough to hug when we meet – but then, it's true that I hug everyone. Ted is one of those quiet people who listens intently, but tells you little. While it seemed immediately apparent to me that he's one of those important 'behind the scenes' characters in our society's story, I was surprised to find that many people don't know him or know about him. He's reported to be a very good cook – but, unfortunately, I don't know him well enough to be able to confirm that. Sean is a more well-known and outgoing character. At a residential meeting focused on reconciliation, Sean and Dad met and immediately struck up a rapport. They formed what many onlookers seemed to view as an unlikely bond. People challenged my father – a city centre rector throughout the sixties, seventies and eighties who had seen and experienced the horrors of the conflict – about his friendship with Sean (who he refused to call 'Spike'). Dad would carefully explain that he was not naïve to Sean's past, and that it was Sean's present and his work for the future that mattered now.

I looked at the newspaper image in the indignant parishioner's hand. 'This man?' I asked her, pointing to one of those carrying Dad's coffin. 'Yes,' she said, 'how could you have Gerry Kelly carry your father's coffin?' 'No,' I replied, 'he's just a friend of Dad's that looks a bit like Gerry Kelly. The man in front of him – that's the republican. He's Dad's friend, Sean.'

Another Belfast republican, Martin Lynch, is now Sinn Féin's political director in the North. Jailed in the 1980s, he was the target of a bugging operation discovered in 1999 during a phase of political negotiations in which Senator George Mitchell was reviewing progress on the implementation of the Good Friday Agreement; this was long after the ceasefires of 1994 and 1997, but before the IRA had formally ended its armed campaign. The intelligence war was not over. Twenty years later, you see him on political platforms with today's Sinn Féin leaders, Mary Lou McDonald and Michelle O'Neill – part of the one leadership, part of that transition and peace-building process. This is not some re-writing of Lynch's history, or Murray's history, or Storey's history, or Wilson's history. It is their story developing into another phase and into different places and positions. It is a story in and of different times.

It does not remove or erase the IRA pages, whether specific to these individuals or to the wider organisation. Nor should the many other pages be erased or rubbed out – political, intelligence, security, loyalist and other. These are all the parts of the past – the different, disputed, divisive, competing, complicated and contested narratives that can never be, and will never be, reconciled. Some pages are more deeply hidden than others, more difficult to find. The point here is that the conflict period is not just about the IRA, and this is both a reality and also the highest obstruction preventing some truth or legacy process. When, or if, it occurs, there will be questions not just for republicans and loyalists but also for many others, who will run a mile from such scrutiny and examination.

In the writing of the shadowy figures script, there is another point that is missed or purposely ignored. McGuinness and Adams survived an attempted coup in the late 1990s, out of which the dissident IRA threat emerged. Back then, had Murray, Lynch, Storey and Wilson rejected the republican peace strategy, there would not have been a Good Friday Agreement and that dissident threat would have moved to a very different level. The so-called 'shadowy figures' helped make the peace and have since helped make the politics. Today, they are part of it; part of where this process had to get to if it was to have any chance of succeeding. If we cannot understand or accept this, then peace will always be an argument and a fight – the heavy weight or burden that we then ask the next generations to carry.

John, Lord Alderdice was part of the Independent Monitoring Commission (IMC) that watched and reported on the IRA transition from conflict into a peace process. The commission gave their assessments to the British and Irish governments. In 2008, this was one of their findings:

> PIRA's commitment to following the political path has been further reinforced in the period under review with a number of people making the transition to positions in Sinn Féin and thereby engagement in democratic politics. Since the time of its announcement nearly three years ago [ending the armed campaign], PIRA's strategy has included the movement of members into political life and we view these changes as important further evidence of the move to a peaceful and democratic role.

Alderdice is an experienced politician. A former leader of the Alliance Party, he was the first speaker of the Northern Ireland Assembly after the Good Friday Agreement, and he now sits in the House of Lords. He has watched that slow process into peace, and as part of that monitoring commission, he read the intelligence assessments and reported the progress of this transition. Going back decades, to the earliest days of an exploration of possibilities – while Alderdice was leader of the Alliance Party – it was the then SDLP leader John Hume who convinced him of the need to engage with republican leaders; he convinced him that there would be no process and no peace – no point – without them.

LORD ALDERDICE:

It seems only common sense now that in the context of a violent political conflict you can have a political process without involving the violent organisations, but you cannot have a peace process without someone engaging them. However, it did not seem like that at the time. The shared view across the spectrum was that we should try to reach agreement with the so-called constitutional parties and that this would give the momentum to marginalise the extremists on both sides and bring peace. The only problem was that it didn't work. The talks amongst the four constitutional parties – Ulster Unionists, SDLP, DUP and Alliance kept running into brick walls and, from time to time, breaking down.

Getting through those walls would demand a new approach, including widening the dialogue. The Hume argument made sense. It was the only way forward, no matter how difficult that would be for some. The hard learning in this place is that peace is hard work, but nowhere near as hard as burying the dead of conflict.

LORD ALDERDICE:

My first clear recognition of the necessity of including Sinn Féin and the IRA in talks came out of a private meeting with Ian Paisley [DUP leader], Jim Molyneaux [UUP leader] and John Hume [SDLP leader] at Stormont during that earlier stage of the process. When things seemed to be stuck, the four leaders would get together without the British and Irish Governments. Jim would persuade Ian to come and I would talk to John and explain why I thought it worthwhile to meet at that point and we would get together on our own. In one of these meetings John explained how he felt that he had to talk to republicans because otherwise we could never solve the problems. I will never forget it. Jim's face just went white. 'Well, that is an end of it then,' he said. It was not said angrily, but with a sense of anxiety and despair. I knew that John was frustrated that we were getting nowhere with real change on the unionist side, but without John there could be no power-sharing. I strongly disagreed with him, but I resolved to follow his line and test it to destruction because frankly there was no alternative. Eventually that completely changed the analysis and ultimately, the outcome.

You do not make peace if people and sides hold rigidly to fixed positions. There has to be room that allows for a change of mind and direction. The learning in dialogue here is that peace is not some fine-detailed or worked-out plan, immediately available as a full stop on conflict. It is a hope that can only be achieved if people and processes are flexible. Think about what Lord Alderdice has just written – how Hume was persuaded of the need to engage with republicans, and then, how he persuaded others. Alderdice allows himself to be convinced. Many years later, Paisley enters government with McGuinness. Different leaders moving at a different pace.

LORD ALDERDICE:

Some people believed that it was unethical to engage with terrorists, and I acknowledged that there was a moral problem, but it was a much bigger problem than the critics recognised, for either we would engage and the accusation would be made that we were betraying the past and those who had been injured or had died *or* we would refuse to engage, there would be no resolution and we would be betraying our children and grandchildren. In such a moral dilemma, I chose the generations to come rather than those that were past. It was not about persuading republicans to abandon their vision of a United Ireland, that would never have got anywhere. What was needed was to persuade them that there was another, more legitimate and possibly ultimately more successful way to achieve their ambitions and that was through democratic politics. If that door was *not* open to them there was no prospect of agreement or even of a workable process. It is the non-violent alternative that is the road to peace, not force or confrontation and not persuading people to abandon their vision when they do not believe that they have even been defeated. It was about a new analysis – the understanding that simply talking about the border in Ireland and British withdrawal would get nowhere. We had to address all the disturbed historic relationships between Britain and Ireland, north and south, east and west, and that involved not only new analyses, but new language, imaginative choreography and creative and symbolic steps on a 'long and winding road'.

The Independent Monitoring Commission did not exist at the time of the ceasefires or the Good Friday Agreement; it emerged much later in the process as a 'new way', and at a time when the DUP first began to explore the possibility of an agreement with republicans. It would produce reports and assessments on many aspects of peace-building, including on how the IRA began to dismantle its war structure and move people into politics. Those reports helped politicians and others to assess progress and to understand where work was still needed. The reports could also cause difficulties and, at times, the commission was criticised both by loyalists and republicans.

LORD ALDERDICE:

The IMC work was essential because without it the Belfast/Good Friday Agreement would have collapsed. There was no way that unionists would go into government with Sinn Féin on the basis of assurances from them, nor indeed by that time, from the Blair Government who they did not trust any more. Sinn Féin were angry, including with me personally, but I knew it had to be done and sometimes you just have to accept that people will not understand you, and do what is right anyway. In the end I did get cooperation from republicans, albeit never openly or acknowledged, but the leadership came to recognise, not least when it was made clear to them by the Irish Government, without that covert cooperation we could not have completed our work and the whole peace process, so painfully and painstakingly put together, would have collapsed, with terrible consequences all round.

It all seems so logical when we look back from the relative peace and calm of now. The benefits of talking, so obvious. But it was different then. Choices had to be made in the noise of the battle – in the news of what had just happened in those days of the 1980s and 1990s. And we are reminded of just how difficult it was in the words that Alderdice uses to articulate the dilemma of having to choose between the generations to come or those that were past. It was not easy – not just for those who engaged with republicans but also for those republicans who stepped into the unknown of dialogues with others. The success of the story is this: that the 'shadowy figures', so-called, are in the corridors of Stormont and no longer in the trenches of war. And the missing lines in the script are about other sets of 'shadowy figures' on other sides who rarely if ever get mentioned.

There are outstanding challenges. The final dismantling of the 'war' structures of the IRA, the loyalist groups and, here in Northern Ireland or the North, the MI5 presence as well. Loyalists still issue statements under their organisational titles; their presence, some two-plus decades beyond the first of their ceasefires, is still far too obvious. Then, there is the matter of MI5 and the question I have asked many times: What is it they do that the police cannot? There are many shadows – only some get noticed, but all of them are the reason why the past remains so large and so loud in the present.

CHAPTER 3

See you later, alligator

Twenty years after that attempted coup to oust Adams and McGuinness inside an IRA convention in the late 1990s, those leaders faced another challenge – different in its nature, but a significant point on the road, because the political project at Stormont was now being openly questioned within the republican community. Two decades previously, the Adams and McGuinness fight was with others in the secret meeting places of the IRA. It was about strategy – conflict versus peace. When this happens inside an armed organisation, there are obvious dangers. Just months before the Good Friday Agreement, the peace of the ceasefires of 1994 and 1997 was again being questioned and tested. What had it achieved in terms of advancing republican objectives? Back then, Adams and McGuinness won because of those they had on their side. In late 1997, the big republican leaders and influencers stayed with them; indeed, more than that, they then helped make the path to Stormont – to that place of ghosts, to which republicans said there would be no return.

To achieve this, another IRA convention was needed. It happened in the republic on the first weekend in May 1998, and it cleared the way for members of the organisation to take seats in the proposed new assembly. It meant a change to part of the IRA constitution, which had read that 'participation in Stormont or Westminster and in any other subservient Parliament, if any, is strictly forbidden.'

After the Good Friday Agreement, there was, of course, a different political construct. A place of power-sharing as part of a new beginning in politics. The Northern Ireland Assembly and

Executive was but one part of a wider relationship that extended north-south and east-west. But, by 2016 – indeed, probably long before then – that sense of something new had gone. The excitement and euphoria of the achievement had long since faded. 'There was something fundamentally wrong at Stormont,' was how one republican put it. This time, the discontent was not locked inside some secret convention or convulsion. Things had moved away from those days. It was out in the open and being talked about within the republican community. The question was how to manage it.

There had always been doubts about that relationship with the DUP, particularly after Ian Paisley's retirement. Could it work? Would it work? I found an example of this in a note I came across while researching and reading for this book. It detailed a conversation I had with a republican in December 2009, when the Sinn Féin battle with the DUP was over the devolution of policing and justice powers. As far back as then, there were concerns that Stormont could fall. This is what that republican source said to me then: 'I was just talking to Ted [Howell] about it and we were shaking our heads about this being groundhog day – having the same conversations about Peter [Robinson] that we had about [David] Trimble … There is nothing that is not retrievable, but at some point people have to stop digging the hole.' My source told me that he thought the institutions could collapse. When I asked when that might happen, his response was, 'I don't know.'

There was a reason for this conversation and this examination of the condition of the Stormont project at that time – a sequence of speeches, writings and statements that meant that cancer of crisis was once more visible within our politics. Declan Kearney, who had nothing like the public profile he has today, addressed a republican commemoration and spoke of DUP 'intransigence' on this issue of policing and justice powers: 'It's a train-wreck political strategy and political consequences will be inevitable.' His words, in late November 2009, were shaped and sharpened to deliver both a message and a warning.

Then, days later, on 4 December 2009, a blog by Adams was published, including these pointed lines: 'the institutions are not there for the optics. They are there to deliver. If they aren't doing that, then what's the point? Common sense stuff you might have thought. But not for the DUP.' Under the St Andrews Agreement, that transfer of policing and justice powers was set for May 2008. 'We are long past that agreed date,' Adams wrote. It took until February 2010 to get the agreement, with a date set in April that year for powers to be transferred. Stormont was saved at the eleventh hour.

By 2016, there was not the energy or the mood for some rescue mission. It was the cumulative effect of those many visits to the treatment room – too many times in those political places of last rites. 'The integrity of the struggle kicked in at that point,' a republican commented. What he is articulating is the constant running after and chasing agreements that had already been done. Dates were being stretched, which meant that credibility was being undermined. A line came into the conversation and commentary that the DUP was running rings round Sinn Féin. When you look back, the pieces in the jigsaw become more obvious – a disappointing election, a different looking executive, Brexit now part of the mix, and a sense that the legacy and reconciliation efforts were not delivering.

Dawn Purvis was on the inside of those negotiations out of which the Good Friday Agreement and the Stormont political institutions emerged; she was part of the loyalist delegation that helped the then Ulster Unionist leader, David Trimble, carry the weights of compromise. There would not have been an agreement then but for that loyalist presence and cover. Trimble, on his own, could not have delivered. The DUP was outside those talks, shouting in and accusing other unionists of a sell-out.

After the sudden death of David Ervine in 2007, Purvis became the Progressive Unionist Party leader and, later that year, held the East Belfast seat with an increased vote. She was an MLA at Stormont until 2011 and, years later, watched the plays that became the fall of 2017.

DAWN PURVIS:

In January 2017, as the Northern Ireland Executive was on the brink of collapse, I tweeted that Unionism needs to end their war. The reference was to the DUP and their constant needling of Sinn Féin. It was not RHI on its own that lead to a crisis in the Executive. It was a series of events that culminated with the RHI crisis as the proverbial straw that broke the camel's back. These events included the failure to introduce an Irish Language Act, and the then DUP Minister for Communities Paul Givan removing funding for an Irish language project. Later, during the Assembly election campaign, there was Arlene Foster's description of Sinn Féin as a crocodile. As individual acts, one could say they are trivial, but, as a series of events, the nationalist community was not only feeling disrespected, but that the devolution experiment was proving pointless. Unionism was never going to treat nationalists as equals. Unionism, in other words the DUP, needed to stop this 'war' and this getting at Sinn Féin and the wider nationalist community. The DUP needed to show maturity, leadership and magnanimity for the sake of the peace process and the future of devolution.

Purvis, like Ervine, was not afraid to engage with republicans, to be seen with them, and to argue and debate with them. All of this is a necessary part of any peace process, and loyalists understand this better than some unionists. There are those in the DUP who still struggle with this. They want government but would prefer it without partnership with republicans. Unionists paid a price for the fallout of 2016–17, and some appear blind to the damage they are doing to their own cause. The more Stormont is undermined, the more Northern Ireland is undermined, and the more others will think about this thing that is now called a 'New Ireland' – what it might look like and how it might work. Purvis can see the foolishness – the unionist self-harm – in the actions and words leading to the Stormont collapse in January 2017.

DAWN PURVIS:

When Martin McGuinness announced he would not run in the Assembly elections, I tweeted that 'his contribution to peace was immense'. I meant it. I was not ignoring his contribution to the war. I was not ignoring the fact that Special Branch once described him as a dedicated and ruthless terrorist or his own admission to being in the IRA. I do not doubt that. I have heard Martin McGuinness talk about how he was motivated by what he experienced and what he saw happen to his community in Derry. My friend David Ervine spoke in similar terms about what motivated him to join the UVF. He often asked the rhetorical question: What came first, dirty stinking politics or a dirty stinking war? Martin McGuinness helped lead the IRA towards peace. He became deputy First Minister in the Northern Ireland Executive. He developed a good relationship with First Minister Ian Paisley and, later, with Peter Robinson. He tried to make the Northern Ireland Executive work. In the lead up to January 2017, his efforts were not reciprocated.

Arlene Foster had been First Minister for just a year as Stormont fell in those rows of 2016–17; she was First Minister in a very different looking executive. The Ulster Unionists and the SDLP were in opposition. Alliance was also outside the executive. It was a DUP–Sinn Féin coalition, with the independent unionist Claire Sugden as Justice Minister. Dawn Purvis correctly identifies a number of the factors that undermined the devolution experiment, but there was a wider problem, seen in a build-up throughout 2016.

The assembly election that year was both a disappointment and a warning for Sinn Féin. The twenty-eight seats it won fell below party expectations. Martin McGuinness had switched from Mid Ulster to run in his home constituency of Foyle. The hope was that his presence on this patch would give Sinn Féin an additional seat – three out of the six. It did not work out. McGuinness was elected along with Raymond McCartney; Maeve McLaughlin did not make it back to Stormont. Eamon McCann of People Before Profit won a seat at the expense of the SDLP – the seat Sinn Féin was after. And, elsewhere, Gerry Carroll of People Before Profit was elected on a big vote in West Belfast. These numbers meant some 'soul searching' for Sinn Féin. In the words of a veteran republican, the party had been 'out manoeuvred on the left' both in Derry and in West Belfast; this was the beginning of some bigger worry. Across the eighteen constituencies, Sinn Féin was down a seat.

Quietly, some republicans will admit that Stormont had become too cosy or too comfortable a place – that, over a period, Sinn Féin had begun to lose contact with part of its base, part of what it is about, and that those who raised their voices on this issue were not being heard. This became part of the build-up – a mood and pressure that could no longer be ignored. Add to this the Brexit referendum in June 2016, producing a UK-wide result to leave but a Northern Ireland vote to remain. Here again, the DUP and Sinn Féin are on completely different pages. Of course, this is part and parcel of our politics – something Peter Robinson highlighted earlier – but when the pages are so different and so difficult, then things become unworkable – relationships become more strained.

The past was still – is still – part of the picture and part of the problem; and it is still one of the loudest arguments. In October 2016, Martin McGuinness wrote to Prime Minister Theresa May, 'Unfortunately, we are rapidly coming to the conclusion that the British Government isn't serious – and never was serious – about resolving the outstanding legacy issues.' This is another example of the fight and the fatigue of the effort to get agreements over the line – the draining battles that created a tiredness and, then, a turning away from the Stormont project. Politics not working – not delivering. And to go back to the Adams thought of 2009, the question then becomes: What's the point? This is where we were in 2016 – still no indication of when the proposals of the Stormont House Agreement of 2014 would be implemented.

When politics becomes a problem, so, the past is always a part of it: that going back to get the bricks to throw – searching in the worst of times to find something to try to win. The dead are called from their graves. Names and dates from the seventies, eighties and nineties used as reminders of where we were rather than where we are trying to go. The pain of war becomes the point-scoring of politics. Rarely does anyone step outside the rigid arguments or positions. Yet the republican Leo Green – part of the IRA hunger strike of 1980 – was able to walk into a more difficult space to make the case for no more conflict-related sentences. I first heard him speak on this at an event in the Ulster University in November 2016, and I later asked him to be part of a panel discussion for an analysis piece on television. Beyond prison, he became part of the Sinn Féin negotiating team, often working alongside Ted Howell and then with Martin McGuinness at Parliament Buildings. So, he knows the complicated nature of those long years of negotiation and that long road away from the armed campaign. He is no longer a member of Sinn Féin and has been carrying out PhD research on power-sharing. On the question of the past, I asked him to share his thoughts – why it is still so large in the present.

LEO GREEN:

The seemingly interminable delay to the implementation of the Stormont House Agreement (SHA) proposals for 'dealing with the past' can scarcely have come as a surprise. Although the proposals were cast by the Irish Government as a comprehensive framework for dealing with the legacy issue, they represented no more than a consensus on a 'Heads of Agreement' that was sure to unravel once attempts began to match the modalities required for credible implementation with their likely outworking. In terms of substance they simply rehearsed the core recommendations of the Consultative Group on the Past [better known as the Eames/Bradley report], which had concluded its deliberations five years previously. The absence of explanation as to how or why proposals, which had sat on the shelf from 2009, suddenly found favour in 2014 leads inevitably to the conclusion that their trimmed-down regurgitation in the Stormont House Agreement was more of a box-ticking exercise than a manifestation of a new found collective political will to endorse and advance the Consultative

Group on the Past recommendations. Although a lack of political will in some quarters has certainly been a contributory factor in maintaining the ongoing stalemate on legacy, something more fundamental and glaringly obvious lies at the root of the impasse. Local political parties, with or without the two governments, are simply unable to move the legacy issue forward.

It seems a statement of the obvious, yet it is rarely acknowledged, certainly not by the two governments or from within the main political parties. How many times does a political negotiation have to fail, or a consultation with proposals have to be rejected or dismissed, for us to understand and accept that leaving this to politicians is to abandon the past in some hopeless place, and to leave it there to look over our shoulders forever.

LEO GREEN:

Whilst 12 years of failure offers a persuasive testimony to this, a more meaningful explication for why it is so is found in the routine characterisation of Northern Ireland (NI) by political scientists as a 'deeply divided society'. As a classification of a society, 'deeply divided' represents much more than a clichéd description of the obvious. It highlights the role of the principal segmental fault line in a society as a critical determinant in both the orientation of political policy and the positioning of political parties with respect to its implementation and outworking thereafter.

The North of Ireland is archetypal 'deeply divided'. Both its past and its present represent contested space, bound up in competing claims, counter-claims and unresolved disputes about the legitimacy of the state, the causes and consequences of three decades of conflict along with the role and legitimacy of the actions of state forces and armed groups in all of this, and including the more than 3,500 deaths, the excess of 45,000 injured, and the innumerable human rights abuses.

Whilst this both argues a clear and compelling case for an urgent addressing of legacy issues and presents a persuasive argument for the commissioning of external assistance to realise it, it also defines the prism through which the acceptability of measures to do so will be filtered. In effect, what this means is that political pragmatism, rather than the victim-centred approach promised in the Stormont House Agreement (SHA), will, for the foreseeable future, continue to govern the viability of all proposals for addressing the past. Moving forward on legacy requires a renewed, frank, and open discussion as to the implications of this for the 'doability' of the SHA proposals.

In March 2020, the UK government, in a unilateral move, all but binned the Stormont House Agreement. It outlined its latest thinking. There would be a swift and final examination of cases. Only those where there is new, compelling evidence would go forward to investigation. The vast bulk of cases would be closed and the focus would switch to information reports for families and an emphasis on reconciliation. At the same time, the UK government made clear its intention to build in further protections for military veterans. It looked like, and read like, a race away from the past. Leo Green believes these developments might provide the opportunity for that new and frank discussion on legacy matters.

LEO GREEN:

The 2020 announcement by the British Government that British Army veterans who served in NI will be afforded the same immunities as their counterparts who have served elsewhere might serve as a useful starting point for such a discussion. Their announcement effectively nullifies the prospect that any British soldier will be prosecuted or imprisoned as a result of investigations into conflict-related offences. Whilst they have been heavily criticised for this clarification, they might also, perhaps more usefully, be commended for their candour. The imprisonment of anyone – republican, loyalist, British Army/ UDR or RUC personnel – for conflict-related offences is directly at odds with the prisoner release provisions of the Good Friday Agreement and can only impede rather than facilitate truth recovery. Taking the prospect of imprisonment off the table might not totally unlock the legacy impasse, but it will surely remove an obstacle in the way of its progress. The British Government assertion that they will legislate to ensure their soldiers are provided with immunities has opened the door for a renewed discussion on an all-round amnesty and its potential positive impact on advancing the search for truth.

Leo Green is now free of the chains that held him to party lines, and he makes a cogent argument for amnesty to assist some truth-recovery or information-retrieval process. It is not the Sinn Féin party position, which still insists on implementation of the Stormont House Agreement, including an Historical Investigation Unit (HIU) and an Independent Commission for Information Retrieval (ICIR). Weeks after the McGuinness letter to Prime Minister May back in 2016, British Secretary of State James Brokenshire spoke on the issue of legacy, how there would be 'one chance to get this right', and of the importance of 'broad political consensus'. On the past, of course, there is no such thing – not in those divided and broken communities that Green referenced earlier. Brokenshire's comments in a BBC interview on 12 December 2016 will have been heard as yet more delay and as a confirmation of the McGuinness assessment those few weeks earlier.

What Sinn Féin misses in all of this – indeed, what some ignore or avoid – is the hurt the IRA caused across the unionist/loyalist community. There is a gaping wound that will never heal. Also, the hurt inflicted across the broad military and policing families. At times, these things get mentioned almost, it seems, as some afterthought. On 1 August 2005, I first met and interviewed Colonel Mark Campbell, the most senior officer in the Royal Irish Regiment at that time. It was for an interview detailing the military response to the IRA statement ending the armed campaign. That response would include a phased end to the longest-running operation in British Army history, including disbanding the home service battalions of the Royal Irish Regiment. Now, many years later, I asked him to share his thoughts on a legacy process, which he fears will be used by some only to refight the past.

COLONEL MARK CAMPBELL:

As we, as a society, seek to address the legacy of the Troubles there are two almost irreconcilable positions that will wrestle uncomfortably throughout the process. The first holds to the primacy of the law, imperfect as that may be, and the belief that the only legitimate way to seek change is through peaceful, democratic processes. The counter position is that by its very nature, state oppression vindicates the use of violence to rectify injustice. The innocent will be exposed to both, and in any circumstances when force was used questions of necessity, reasonableness and proportionality must always arise. Sectarian brutality, self-evidently, can have no vindication. The bald statistics of the Troubles set the context; 60 per cent of deaths are attributed to republican paramilitaries, 30 per cent to loyalists and 10 per cent to the security forces. Yet almost one third of all those killed were members of the security forces; a high proportion when off duty and particularly vulnerable. As the security forces were the most numerous, overt and heavily armed participants, those figures do indicate very high levels of security force discipline and control.

I would also hold that members of the security forces must be held to a higher standard than paramilitaries. Security forces are upholders of the law, and for the primacy of the law to prevail, they must be held to account if the law is broken, to maintain legitimacy. The primacy of the law cannot be upheld by those breaking it, even in the face of extreme provocation. On the other hand, the paramilitary has, by definition, set themselves outside the law and can only try to justify their actions in the context of state oppression or thinly disguised sectarianism. One really has to question the level of state oppression necessary to justify the murders, atrocities, destruction and suffering caused by paramilitaries over the years. Is it even remotely arguable that the levels of paramilitary violence NI witnessed were necessary, reasonable and proportionate? The vast majority of those who served in the security forces did so honestly and credibly and will maintain there is no moral equivalence between soldier and paramilitary. They will also rightly condemn any ex-colleagues who lost their moral compass.

> The greatest problem thereafter is that a legacy process will be seen by some, not as a source of healing and reconciliation, but as a continuation of the struggle by alternative means. Seeking to undermine the moral authority of the State by highlighting those occasions when members of the security forces may or did breach the law, whilst airbrushing their own highly significant brutality. If any process were ultimately to conclude that such political violence was justified, then we set a very difficult precedent for future generations. At its core, any legacy process must seek to move society forward whilst promoting the wellbeing of traumatised citizens, not principally be a vehicle to highlight selective grievances and further political agendas. Unless all parties can approach a legacy process in that mindset, with humility, objectivity and openness – whilst recognising the tremendous waste and loss of opportunity caused by the Troubles – then we have little to offer future generations for which they would be thankful.

Campbell highlights the irreconcilable narratives in that battle for the past – how far apart they are, and how they will never – can never – be brought together in one agreed 'truth'. It is why, I argue, that the writing of any legacy report has to be from outside of us – some independent and international analysis of the many 'truths', and presented as such.

Like Tim Mairs, Una Jennings arrived in policing when it had stepped out of its RUC title and uniform. She was part of the class of 2001 – among the very first recruits to the PSNI – and graduated the following year. A Catholic from Derry, she had a tough decision to make. She was from a community that had been hurt by policing, and from a community that had hurt the police. History here is never history. She made a difficult choice, and her career has taken her to senior rank in South Yorkshire Police. Jennings is of a generation that will be needed back in Northern Ireland: to lead policing, to treat the past with respect and dignity and, with others, to try to win the future – win it for everyone. I asked her about understanding hurts – the many hurts of past and present.

UNA JENNINGS:

Time heals all wounds ... does it? I think we know, where we are from, it definitely does not. I am from Derry. Londonderry. A place on the edge. Economically and geographically. In the words of others, between the light and the half-light of west coast sunsets. It's a place that gets in your very bones and catches your heart off guard. I love where I am from. It is who I am and it is why I do what I do. That sense of being in between is one that resonates deeply with me. I am from a community that has, in the past, hurt policing. A community, deeply hurt, by policing itself. So, I know, at least as well as most, if not a bit better than others, how sacred that contract is, how holy the relationship between people, ordinary people, and the police service, who should in all cases protect them. Because good policing, the policing that we deserve and should expect, changes lives. Good policing is about inclusion. It is about feeling connected, valued, listened to. It is about belonging. Good policing is about so much more than responding to crime. It is about hope, education, equality, social mobility and good policing is about peace. Science will explain to us the impact of trauma on communities, on individuals, on children. We have lived and shared experience of that in Northern Ireland. Be it the inter-generational impact of violence or the absence of opportunity. It crushes our spirit. It puts out hope. Whether you live in the Shankill or Shantallow, adversity does not discriminate.

Una Jennings understands that the past is a battlefield; that the different truths are dug into the deepest trenches; and that there is no one story, but many stories, and that there is a need to be careful, both in how we store them and how we tell them – to ourselves and to others.

UNA JENNINGS:

We have collectively hurt and been hurt. Understanding and acknowledging that the space between truth and fact in Northern

Ireland is and remains a contested one, is the perennial holy grail. What science is less able to articulate is the impact of courage and resilience. The root of the word courage is *cor* – the Latin word for heart. In one of its earliest forms the word courage meant 'to speak one's mind by telling one's heart'. For us in policing, for the communities we serve, a part of the 'telling of our hearts' has to be to acknowledge each other's truth, accept responsibility for what we have done, connect with others about it and using that experience to transform. To become truly inclusive. Despite our, at times, very evident mistakes in the police service, I can tell you this, the people I have worked with are some of the most extraordinary I have ever met. They are heroes and heroines, they have humour and humility, and a profound sense of duty and responsibility.

Resilience means you face the things that scare you, that make you feel uncomfortable, not avoid them. Sometimes that might just be each other. That you make mistakes but you learn from them. I can attest to that. Resilient people get that really tough things happen, they know that suffering is part of life, this doesn't mean they welcome it. It's just that when the tough times come, they seem to know that suffering is part of the human condition and knowing this stops you feeling discriminated against when those times, as they always do, come. Resilient people do not ignore the negative but they have also found a way of tuning into the good. It's called benefit finding. In my brave new world, it is called trying to find things to be grateful for. That's why I'm so careful about language. So careful about my story. Our Story.

Too many others are not careful about language. In the absence of a legacy process, the past, at times, becomes a poisonous tit-for-tat of exchanges on Twitter. One hurt is remembered and many others ignored. Would we have got to ceasefires and political agreements if the processes and engagements of those times had been exposed to the vitriol and abuse that is so often presented as debate and free speech on social media?

UNA JENNINGS:

This concept of story is very important to me. My Granda was just the best at them. As a 40-year-old woman now I can still remember him lying beside me, every single night, reading me a story, telling me a story. There were so many life lessons tied up in that connection between him and I. I remember one time, him telling me, 'be careful the stories you tell yourself Una, you will have to listen to them for a long time ...', wisdom, in truth it took me many years to understand and put into practice. Because the fact is, we don't tell stories, stories tell us, and the stories that I listened to, I hope the stories I tell now were wide enough and broad enough to allow me to be open to the possibility of imagination. Stories that shaped my ability to move beyond the limitations, my people and my place would have imagined for me. A story that shapes how I chose to live.

It has been said, 'your wound is where your light enters you'. So, I challenge you. I know you've been wounded, I know you've been hurt. Find it – use it; use it to make sure we never end up where we began. Use it for you. Use it for us. Use it to lift your sights and hearts and dream for our place, and shape and guard our story carefully. Believe in our promise, the duty to ensure that we leave a legacy for our children that is better than anything they can imagine. Understand how the stories we tell ourselves, and of ourselves, have to be wide enough and broad enough to allow us to imagine all that we could be, not simply what we should be.

Outreach and reconciliation are key to peace-building. They are parts of the challenge – better understood by some than others. In November 2016, McGuinness was criticised by republicans for his presence, alongside other political leaders, at a London event where Irish artist Colin Davidson's portrait of the Queen was unveiled. 'He'd so bought into peace and reconciliation that he stretched people beyond their limits,' a senior republican said in conversation with the author. 'Your pride kicks in. He [McGuinness] kept turning the other cheek.' Another republican, with whom I spoke for this book, said the event had added 'to this whole history of anger and disappointment'.

By now, republicans – including at a senior level – had had enough. They were not seeing the 'quid pro quo' of the Sinn Féin outreach or reconciliation effort – certainly nothing coming back from the DUP. But perhaps this was to misunderstand the initiative. McGuinness was reaching out to the unionist people more than he was reaching out to the unionist parties – trying to build trust and reconciliation as part of putting the 'New Ireland' house together. One source summarised the initiative as being 'firm with the unionist parties and flexible with the unionist people'. In moments of anger and impatience, such arguments are not heard.

Arlene Foster was also present at that event in London. She is part of a community in which many still see the republican reconciliation initiative as bogus and self-serving. They remember how Sinn Féin snubbed/ignored the Queen's visit to the Irish Republic in 2011. Like the rest of us, the DUP leader has watched the various legacy processes and proposals come and go. Over a period of a decade or so, she had also watched those occasions when the power-sharing government was in danger, only for Sinn Féin to step back. The Maze/Long Kesh peace centre argument and the battle to get those policing and justice powers devolved are but two examples.

Perhaps, in that Christmas–New Year period of 2016–17, she thought that Martin McGuinness would step back again, but this time he was not in control of that decision. Others were determining the steps – the mood and anger of the republican community had been heard. That storing and stacking of grievances, over a period of long unhappy years, had become too heavy a weight to manage. This was the 'tipping point'; RHI was the opportunity, not the reason – certainly not the only reason – for the collapse of Stormont. The only question now was whether this would end in divorce or in a long-term separation.

That resignation moment in January 2017 represented the failure of the Stormont project. 'Republicans turned their backs on the administration, and turned to the national project – unification,' one source commented. So, why had it taken so long to arrive at this moment, when there had been previous opportunities? This is how it was explained to me by one veteran republican: 'The army [the IRA] changed its strategy from armed struggle to a peace strategy – had invested enormous energy [in this]. The pressure of what they had invested, meant trying to sort this out from within [the political institutions].' This is one explanation of how Stormont survived those earlier battles over policing and justice powers, and the Maze/ Long Kesh peace centre. The change in strategy – the emphasis on politics – meant any collapse of Stormont could only be as a last resort; this is an analysis that goes deeper than the charge of Martin McGuinness turning the other cheek.

The war of words continued into the election campaign – and one news conference, on 6 February 2017, stands out above all the rest. It was that moment referenced earlier by Dawn Purvis when Arlene Foster likened Sinn Féin to a crocodile – saying that if you feed it, it will keep coming back for more. It was a reference to another of the unresolved political battles – the question of a stand-alone Irish Language Act.

Delivering that crocodile comment, Foster's tone was terse. 'It's not the way the Democratic Unionist Party does business,' she said. Adams' four-word response was jokingly dismissive: 'See you later, alligator.' It was humorous, flippant, but we were watching a deepening political crisis. The question was: How much later? How long would it take to fix what was broken? Could it be fixed? The war of words was making all of that more difficult. Unless Foster and Adams could make a post-election agreement, there would be no return to government, no First Minister and deputy First Minister, and no executive. Politics in 'suspended animation' was how one insider described it.

For unionists, the elections were an earthquake moment encapsulated in this opening paragraph of a page-one lead story by the *News Letter* political editor, Sam McBride, on Saturday, 4 March 2017: 'Northern Ireland is today waking up to a fundamentally altered political reality: unionism is no longer a majority in the Stormont chamber for the first time since the creation of the Province a century ago.' The *News Letter* headline read, 'Unionism loses its

Stormont majority'; the *Irish Times* headlined 'big gains' for Sinn
Féin in Northern elections. As part of my election commentary for
the BBC, RTÉ and Ulster Television, I had watched this remarkable
story develop through the hours of Friday.

In the 2016 election, the DUP had a ten-seat advantage over
Sinn Féin. A year later – with the assembly now reduced from
108 to 90 seats – that gap was down to one. In the final count,
just over a thousand votes separated the two parties. Sinn Féin's
decision to pull the institutions down had been hugely popular
within the republican community. It had reconnected with parts of
a disillusioned and disengaged base and re-energised the vote. At
a news conference on the Falls Road in Belfast on Saturday, Adams
said, 'Clearly the unionist majority in the Assembly has been ended,
and the notion of a permanent or a perpetual unionist majority has
been demolished.' The combined unionist total was forty seats.
Nationalists had thirty-nine, and Alliance (eight seats), Green Party
(two seats) and People Before Profit (one seat) meant there were
eleven MLAs in the category of other. I tweeted about a day of
shocks that would take time to manage. The Ulster Unionist Party
was so bruised that its leader, Mike Nesbitt, resigned. In the fallout
from the Kevin McGuigan murder in 2015, he had taken his party
out of the executive and, after the 2016 assembly election, had opted
for opposition. Here he explains his thinking.

MIKE NESBITT:

A day or two after the McGuigan murder, I crossed the corridor from
my office on the second floor of Parliament Buildings to visit the Gents.
Standing at a urinal, I was joined by someone I knew well. He was wearing
a Sinn Féin staff member's security pass. He was also by reputation a
member of the army council of the Provisional IRA, an organisation the
Chief Constable had just told me still existed in a structured manner,
and members of which had participated in the McGuigan murder. Yet
here was this man enjoying the same right of access to Stormont's
facilities as the 108 elected politicians. My question was whether this
would be tolerated at Westminster, in Edinburgh, Cardiff, or Dublin. The

answer, of course, was 'no', especially in Leinster House. So, I began the process of recommending my party withdraw from the Northern Ireland Executive, aware that if successful, I would be responsible for the Ulster Unionist Party having no role in government for the first time since Northern Ireland's creation when there was a devolved administration at Stormont. The party backed me unanimously.

I have known Mike Nesbitt a long time. In the 1970s, we were both involved in athletics. He ran for Irish schools, and on a couple of occasions, I represented Northern Ireland at junior level. My first running club was Willowfield Harriers. On Tuesday and Thursday nights, they met in a hall on Hynford Street in east Belfast, the same street on which Van Morrison once lived. Years later, I learned that the IRA hunger striker Bobby Sands had run at the same club, and that Nesbitt was also a member. The former Sinn Féin MLA and Belfast Lord Mayor Máirtín Ó Muilleoir picked up a story that all three of us had been there at the same time. On Twitter, he offered a king's ransom for a photograph. We were there at different times. No such photograph exists, but the story captures how small a place we live in. In a different decade, I was interviewed by Nesbitt on BBC radio about the early exploration of a peace process, and more recently, I watched his steps into politics – his climb to leadership – and his decision after the 2016 assembly elections to stay out of the executive.

MIKE NESBITT:

We formed the first Official Opposition since 1998 alongside the SDLP. Alliance also stayed out of Stormont Castle. Did Opposition work? In my view, too well, because when we left the DUP and Sinn Féin alone around that large circular Executive table, they had no one to give them cover for their inability to get along. Take out summer recess and that Executive lasted only a matter of weeks before Martin McGuinness pulled the plug, affirming my analysis that the two parties simply cannot share. When the votes are counted, parties to a coalition government are supposed to stop being rivals and start becoming partners. That is not how the DUP and Sinn Féin do business. The 2017 Assembly Election result was a disaster for unionism and I identified two reasons, not mutually exclusive, but both down to the actions and words of the DUP. Firstly, there was Peter Robinson's decision to support reducing the number of MLAs from six to five per constituency. The 2017 results show that shrinking the Assembly from 108 to 90 seats saw unionism lose 16 of the 18 seats that were taken away. The second factor was Arlene Foster's infamous 'crocodile' remarks. In that one sentence, she energised nationalism/republicanism in a manner Gerry Adams could only ever have dreamed of, resulting in astronomical turn outs in many nationalist polling areas.

While Nesbitt believes that his party's time in opposition exposed the cracks in the DUP–Sinn Féin coalition, he also accepts that when it came to the 2017 assembly election, there was no benefit in terms of votes.

MIKE NESBITT:

I had spent our time in Opposition promoting the idea of a post-sectarian election, based on policy. We produced policy paper after paper – Mental Health, Cancer Treatment, Animal Welfare, the Knowledge Economy, the Arts, you name it, plus an election manifesto of course. I don't think they secured us a single additional vote. Assembly elections are different and the results on my watch prove it. During my time, we had significant success in every other type of poll. In local government in 2014, we returned 88 councillors when my advisers thought 78 would have been a good day. We easily retained our seat in the European Parliament and then in 2015, we not only got ourselves back into the House of Commons, we got there with two MPs, unseating a Sinn Féin member in Fermanagh South Tyrone, surely the most remarkable electoral victory for unionism over republicanism in recent times. But when it came to the 2016 Assembly Elections, we stalled, with 16 seats, the same as 2011. Why? In my view, because of the change agreed at St Andrews to the way the First Minister is elected. It allowed the DUP to tell voters that if they voted for Nesbitt's team, they would split the unionist vote and Martin McGuinness would sail through the middle to the top post. It was a shrill emotional tug; the very thought too much for too many unionist voters and one that can only be deployed for the Assembly elections.

Nesbitt had a life and a career outside of politics. He spent many years as a presenter at the BBC in Belfast and at Ulster Television. He was now asking himself the questions he would have asked other political leaders in his previous roles. He knew that the 2017 assembly election had been a disaster for unionism. He also knew that Arlene Foster's 'crocodile' remark had been a big part of that and that, in the results, the Ulster Unionist Party had suffered. He did not need time to sleep on his decision.

MIKE NESBITT:

By 2017, I had spent months attacking the DUP in general and Arlene Foster in particular over RHI. I could not in all conscience go on to give a preference vote to the DUP. Plus, I wanted voters to think differently and more deeply about their Single Transferable Vote. Why should unionists only offer a view on which unionist party they wanted to run the Executive out of Stormont Castle, when they could go on to say whether they would prefer to see the SDLP or Sinn Féin as their partners. And vice versa for nationalists. So, I made public my intention to offer a personal preference to the SDLP. Many colleagues disagreed, although voting analysis indicates cross-community voting elected three of the 90 MLAs, Pat Catney and the late John Dallat of the SDLP and Rosemary Barton of the Ulster Unionists. Our first preference vote also increased slightly on 2016, but all this was drowned out by the tsunami of nationalist energy that swept away the unionist majority at Stormont.

As the results came in, and our losses mounted, I reflected on Einstein's famous warning that doing the same thing over and over, expecting a different result, was a definition of insanity. I judged there was insufficient electoral support for my call for a post sectarian election and rather than try to hang on to the leadership and risk undoing five years of effort to unite my Party, I resigned before the counts were even complete, so members could focus on the future. Since then, many people have told me I was too early, ahead of my time. Watching the so-called Alliance surge of 2019, I wonder if all I got wrong was the timing.

That 2017 election analysis from Nesbitt, alongside the writing of Sam McBride and the words of Gerry Adams in actual time, gives us a better understanding of the historical significance of these results and the utter shock to the unionist system. It was too big a blow for anyone to seriously contemplate any early possibility of a resolution at Stormont. After interviews with the BBC, Ulster Television and Sky News correspondent David Blevins, I made my way to the Falls Road for the Adams news conference. The story now was much bigger than a broken parliament. The more significant element was the directional change that was the story of the vote and the new numbers – and what this would add to the conversation about a 'New Ireland'.

With the cameras in place in west Belfast, this was one of those walk-in moments. Adams at the front, a file and a water bottle in his left hand. Michelle O'Neill and Mary Lou McDonald alongside him, as well as Declan Kearney, Martina Anderson, Conor Murphy, Matt Carthy, Pearse Doherty and Gerry Kelly. A picture that spoke of an all-island party on a one-island political mission. They stayed in that frame as Adams took selfies on that Falls Road street where the mural to Bobby Sands is painted large.

The strategic decision in January – if not before then – to bring Stormont down had produced this reaction and this result. In the ructions of this time, there were whispers about Arlene Foster's leadership, but not then, or since, has anyone stepped out of those quiet conversations and corners and into some public challenge. That said, the whispers are always there, some times louder, including in the early weeks of 2021 as I completed my writing of this book. Something did happen after that vote in 2017. It shook the unionist electorate out of its slumber and out of its certainty – out of its carelessness, even smugness, in relation to the future of the Union. Within months, there would be a fight back – and a place for the DUP in the London lights. Before then, we witnessed a remarkable day in Derry – a day of choreographed steps and careful words at the funeral of Martin McGuinness, who, for decades, was one of the biggest figures in our divided place and politics.

CHAPTER 4

McGuinness – 'part of the rage of his time'

I^f Martin McGuinness was just a terrorist, why would former US President Bill Clinton speak at his funeral? Why would the Irish President, Michael D. Higgins, and political leaders north and south attend, as well as the most senior police officer in Northern Ireland at that time? Why would Queen Elizabeth send a private message to the McGuinness family? And why would clergy – who in the speak of this place, 'kick with the other foot' – be part of the service? Why did so many people want to be there – both inside and outside the church? There is no one-word description of the late Martin McGuinness. In changing circumstances, he moved and then moved others. It was not some simplistic conversion from 'bad' to 'good'.

That day in Derry – Thursday, 23 March 2017 – outside St Columba's church, I scribbled a few words on a now-faded taxi receipt – words from one of those times when you are made to stop and think. They were spoken by Clinton. It was a little more than ten weeks since McGuinness had resigned as deputy First Minister. The news of his death came two days earlier, in an email from Sinn Féin at 6.22 a.m. on Tuesday 21 March. He had died during the night.

That evening, at a candlelit vigil in west Belfast, I noticed a face in the crowd – the woman who, in August 1994, had read the IRA ceasefire statement to both myself and my journalist colleague Eamonn Mallie – the statement that announced 'a complete cessation of military operations'. New words marking the beginning of another new chapter.

These many years later, as Clinton spoke at the McGuinness funeral, it was about acknowledging his contribution to peace – one part of his story that stretched and spanned from that period of the first ceasefire right through to that moment and decision at Stormont in January 2017. I noted two thoughts from Clinton. His urging those present, including the leaders of the DUP and Sinn Féin, to 'finish the work of peace', and the words he chose to place McGuinness in the madness and the upheaval of the conflict years. Clinton spoke of him being 'part of the rage of his time'.

Read some of the headlines on the news of his death. In a few words, they try to mark out a journey on a long road. 'McGuinness – IRA leader who forged path to peace' (*Irish News*); 'Both saint and sinner, Martin McGuinness leaves more than just one legacy' (*Belfast Telegraph*); 'From IRA terrorist to Stormont statesman' (*News Letter*); 'A Complex Legacy in Life and Death' (*Irish Times*). You cannot tell the McGuinness story in a sentence or two, or in a page or two. That complex legacy is a book. The same man, the one story – all of its different parts seen and read through many different eyes. The 'rage' of 'Bloody Sunday' and the 'rage' of many other 'Bloody Days', including in 1972. That same year, McGuinness, 22 years of age, with other republican leaders, met British Secretary of State William Whitelaw in London.

Think about his age – that time in life when most young people are still trying to work out the next steps, and the paths to take and follow. McGuinness – like so many others of the many different sides – was young and at war. In all of the scrutiny and agonising over the past, this is something that is often missed.

Denis Bradley is a former priest and journalist; he was a part of a secret back-channel used in contacts between the British government and the republican leadership right through to the 1990s, and he was co-author, with Lord Robin Eames, of the first proposals to try to address and answer the questions of the past. In Derry he had watched the McGuinness story develop through its many parts. He wrote about this in the *Irish Times*, remembering back to those younger years. These were his opening thoughts:

> It was the very early days of the Troubles. A group of IRA men was gathered in a hall in the Bogside in Derry. Someone came running in to say that there was a camera crew outside wanting an interview. Those were the days before press officers and, since none of the IRA men had ever appeared on the media, the young Martin McGuinness was chosen because, as one of his comrades said, he looked innocent and angelic. Years later, that same comrade, in typical Derry humour, said that was the day they had put McGuinness on the public stage and he hadn't come off it since.

That piece by Bradley was published on 22 March 2017. It was the following day that Clinton chose his words to try to contextualise that period – those days of 'rage' that eventually turned to days of hope.

Go back into those conflict years and you will find other descriptions of the Derry republican: 'McGuinness, for all his public posturing, is a ruthless, dedicated terrorist.' Those eleven words were spoken by a special branch officer in December 1991. 'Take the human proxy bombs,' he continued. 'Someone gave the go ahead and that was the leadership [of the IRA]. That was the Provisional Army Council.' The special branch officer was speaking with me at RUC Headquarters in Belfast. He placed McGuinness inside that leadership, both on the army council and as a 'vital component' of its Northern Command. He was its Officer Commanding. In the late 1980s, McGuinness was considered 'central' to a decision to escalate the IRA campaign, with Libyan-supplied arms, on three fronts – in the North, in Britain and on the continent.

'Gibraltar was a fiasco to them,' the special branch officer said. This is a reference to the SAS killings of three IRA members in March 1988. In a previous special branch briefing, I had been told, 'If Gibraltar had come off [the planned bombing], that would have been the trigger – would have been the lead into a major push.'

There were no ceasefires then, only battlefields – the bloodiness, the bitterness and the bile of war. McGuinness was in the middle of it. These briefings, in conflict time or 'wartime', came with the language and the lines you would expect as part of an enemy relationship. There is much, of course, that the special branch would want to hide – many questions still to be answered about the so-called 'dirty war' and the 'shadowy figures' in the corridors of that intelligence world. More pages of missing detail in the book of this place and its past.

In December 1991, I also interviewed Martin McGuinness. This was in my time at the BBC. He spoke of the IRA at war, of the need for talks between the British government and the republican movement. He was 'absolutely convinced' that the British wanted to engage and said that it was 'incumbent upon them' to find a way in which it could happen. The interview ran on 7 January 1992:

> The IRA have their own agenda. They fight a war against the British forces of occupation. It is a dirty war. All wars are dirty. All parties to the conflict are involved in deeds, which all of us, in normal times, would not think right. But we have an exceptional situation which exists in this part of Ireland. What I would be more concerned about, and what people like Gerry Adams is more concerned about, is addressing the reasons why these things are happening. We can talk about the politics of the last atrocity until we are blue in the face, but we are never going to resolve anything.

Those atrocities are the pages, referred to previously, that cannot be erased and should not be erased – pages that extend much wider than the IRA's involvement in the conflict, and which still mean that the past is with us. The detail of what happened then is chiselled into the here and now – forever present in the minds of those who witnessed and remember as if it were yesterday. Because of government broadcasting restrictions at the time, I had to illustrate the McGuinness interview both through graphics and by using an actor to voice his words. On that question of talks between the British government and the republican movement, he said:

> I must make this quite clear. We are not on our knees begging for talks with the British Government, but we think it is a sensible thing to do. We think that it could lead to a different situation. We think that there is an onus of responsibility on us but also on the British Government to engage in discussions recognising each other's positions and, at the end of the day, seeing if there can be a solution worked out to this problem.

McGuinness said that republicans would endeavour to make any such talks 'as easy as possible'.

What did he mean? Further up the road, we would learn of that secret back-channel (in which Denis Bradley was an intermediary) linking the British government and the republican leadership. Learn, also, that in the period of this interview, there had already been some reaching out. McGuinness knew that. I didn't. In my preparations for that BBC report, I also met representatives of the IRA leadership – a man and a woman, both of whom were masked. I was told that they were representatives of the IRA General Headquarters Staff and Northern Command. The meeting happened in a house in west Belfast to which I was taken. I made none of this detail public in that BBC report at the time. Again, the lines were those you would expect: that the IRA was confident in its ability to 'prosecute the war', and that sooner rather than later the will of the British government to remain locked into a conflict would 'weaken and break'. There was no give or take in those words. Yet weeks earlier, Sir John Wilsey, an army general, had spoken to me of 'people within the Provisional Movement who would like to see this thing come to an end, who would settle for an honourable draw'.

Were there straws in the wind? We know now, of course, that there were, but in that period, they were not obvious. When I think of 1991, I remember the mortar bombs launched at Downing Street in February of that year, and the attempt by the IRA in September to target a military checkpoint at Annaghmartin, County Fermanagh, with the largest bomb of the conflict years. Our learning is that these transitions are complex; they are not some simple adding up and assessment of what is visible but an understanding, now apparent, that there is always another stage and another play. The republican Jake Mac Siacais wrote on this earlier in the book when recalling that period of the early 1990s: 'In effect, alongside its developing "peace initiative", the IRA leadership was escalating conflict so that it could enter any endgame from a position of relative strength.'

Years before the ceasefire announcement, McGuinness would be part of the early exploration of some peace process. We know now that it took years to develop, and we also know that he – along with Gerry Adams – was at the heart of every initiative. There would have been no peace without them.

Beyond his 'war', we watched as McGuinness and others stepped into once-unthinkable conversations. I witnessed two of them from close-up, both events staged as part of Féile an Phobail – the west Belfast festival. The first was in 2010, when McGuinness was on stage with William 'Plum' Smith, who chaired the 1994 news conference at which the Combined Loyalist Military Command (CLMC) ceasefire was announced. The second was in 2015, this time with the Chief Constable of the PSNI, Sir George Hamilton. I chaired both events. In my introduction to the first, I read part of that special branch briefing from the early 1990s – that description of McGuinness as a 'ruthless and dedicated terrorist'. I read it not for comment there and then, but as a reminder, some twenty years later, of those conflict years – what we called 'the Troubles'. It was a line from the past to give some context in the present.

So much grows out from inside the McGuinness story – happenings viewed by some as ground-breaking but seen by others as controversial, even traitorous. Another loyalist, Jackie McDonald, was also present in the audience in 2010 and afterwards was photographed shaking hands with McGuinness at the Bobby Sands mural on the Falls Road. It became a front-page picture – one that caused McDonald some problems with some of his own people. It was not just the McGuinness handshake, but the fact that it happened beside that wall painting of an IRA hunger striker.

Reconciliation – the gestures and mechanics of such – is a process of challenges. When McDonald attended a funeral soon afterwards, another loyalist refused to shake his hand. The photograph with McGuinness had been too much. McDonald told me he turned the conversation round by asking, 'Have you thought about what it was like for him to shake my hand?' He added, in typically blunt style, 'We weren't fucking boy scouts.' Much of this happens out of our vision and out of our hearing.

McDonald and McGuinness had met previously – some years earlier, at the second term inauguration of President Mary McAleese in Dublin. Now, they would chat again – over coffee in the library after that festival event on the Falls Road. The loyalist leader remembers every detail of that day, both inside the event and over coffee afterwards. How he spoke of his concerns about the ceasefire period of 1994 – concerns because he believed that the IRA leadership 'had given notice to their operators that any loose ends/revenge attacks had to be carried out before their ceasefire deadline [31 August 1994]'. 'Martin McGuinness denied that that was true,' McDonald recalls. Back in the 1990s, he had argued for a delay in the loyalist response to the IRA ceasefire. Friends of his, including Ray Smallwoods, had been killed just weeks before the IRA announcement. The loyalist leader believed the Ulster Defence Association (UDA) 'might seek revenge'. He would have known that was the case; he had been around the 'wars' long enough to know the score.

'It wasn't that I didn't agree with the idea of a ceasefire. I just didn't want it to be broken once it had been declared,' he said. After the event and subsequent coffee, he recalls driving a veteran republican, Harry Thompson, to a hospital appointment across the city. Why is it that some of those once at war with each other have been more able to step onto this new ground? To try new conversations, look for different ways – go into places that some in politics have not, and will not, explore? As McDonald explains, none of this is cosy – not just what is said during these events, but what is said in the margins.

He told me one of the things that he spoke to McGuinness about was 'Bloody Sunday'. McDonald made clear what he thought about the killings that day and how they should be described – that those shot by soldiers were 'innocent victims'. But he also spoke to the republican leader about the allegation that he was in possession of a machine gun that day: 'And, if that was true, then the Paras should have shot him. He never blinked. Never made any comment. Just continued drinking his coffee.'

McDonald then recalls leaving the Falls Road that day, and the detail of that short journey that he and a friend shared with Thompson on his way to a hospital appointment. Think about it. A republican in a car driven by a loyalist. Unimaginable in those decades of fear from which this place is still trying to escape. McDonald and Thompson knew each other through their interest in junior soccer. Thompson, McDonald said, made some quip 'that not too many of his sort' – republicans – would get into the back of this car, and the loyalist had replied with one of those dark lines of Troubles humour. When Thompson died in 2012, McDonald attended his funeral.

How did Harry Thompson fit into the republican frame? We get some of the detail when we read a piece that Gerry Adams wrote at the time of his death – detail about Thompson being recruited into the IRA; how he was also active in Sinn Féin; that he was one of the last internees to be released in December 1975; how they 'were always close'; that he was 'a trusted friend'; and 'When John Hume and I started our talks in the 1980s we used to meet regularly in Harry's home.' When we read this, we better understand the wider significance to those stories of McDonald attending that event on the Falls Road – the handshake with McGuinness and driving Thompson to a hospital appointment, and then attending his funeral. It is the building of trust and the building of peace. How hard that is and how it takes guts. It becomes a fight of a different kind.

JACKIE McDONALD:

Conversations with the likes of Martin McGuinness, Harry Thompson and other republicans were made possible by members of all the main paramilitary groups working together for [the project] Prison to Peace in cooperation with the Community Foundation for Northern Ireland. Loyalist and republican ex-prisoners/ex-combatants met over a period of several years with members of each group joining together to visit schools, youth clubs and universities to de-glamorise paramilitary activity; to explain how the conflict wasn't all fame and glory. Members of Prison to Peace played a very important role in deterring many young men and women from becoming involved with republican or loyalist paramilitaries ... the dialogue between those rival factions has saved countless lives and has helped create a much safer environment for us all to raise our families in.

That day on the Falls Road a group photograph was also taken at the Sands mural, McDonald, Smith and the senior loyalist Winston Rea standing in a line with McGuinness and Thompson. The former senior police officer Peter Sheridan was in its frame. So, also, was the former Methodist President Harold Good, who was a church witness in 2005 when the IRA put its arms beyond use. The *Belfast Telegraph* published the photograph with pen portraits under the heading, 'A picture from another planet'. William Smith, who chaired that loyalist ceasefire news conference in 1994 and who shared the stage with the deputy First Minister those many years later, died in 2016. So, his is another story left for others to tell, although in this case his book *Inside Man*, which details his jail experience and his role in the peace process, helps with that task. Here his niece Mandy McDermott writes on what conflict and peace meant to him and his generation. Smith – involved in a loyalist gun attack – knew prison in his teens.

MANDY McDERMOTT:

I believe his time spent in prison was to be the beginning of his lifelong journey towards bringing peace, conflict resolution and reconciliation to Northern Ireland and beyond. William believed in embracing his past. He recognised, created and developed his own personal foundation of self-knowledge and inner growth. He 'understood himself'; his 'own' motives and character, eventually leading to a strong sense of inner peace, tranquillity and freedom from disturbance … Plum [William 'Plum' Smith] never denied his past. He came to understand the process if war cessation in Northern Ireland was to happen. This meant engaging and building key relationships with those who also shared similar experiences and who had a vision for a peaceful future. This became the norm. The long journey to ceasefire was the focus for many years to come.

Once the negotiations started, a sense of belief that 'change was possible' became real for all involved, and that peace in Northern Ireland would eventually become a reality – putting an end to the 'bloodied war'. 31 August 1994 [the date the IRA announced its complete cessation of violence] remains a hugely important date in Northern Ireland's history; the day that the possibility of peace, of change, of a new dispensation and a New Northern Ireland – one no longer defined by sectarian conflict and violence – became possible. On 13 October 1994, William 'Plum' Smith opened the news conference and set the rules as the loyalist ceasefire announcement was made, making history. Plum, along with colleagues, dedicated and contributed a huge part of their lives to building peace in Northern Ireland.

I interviewed Smith many times and we spoke regularly. He was part of a small group, with David Ervine, Gary McMichael, Gusty Spence, Davy Adams and Jim McDonald, who, with the leaders of the UVF, Red Hand Commando and UDA, shaped the loyalist response to the IRA ceasefire. Smith understood the steps and challenges beyond that response – the work that still had to be done on a range of issues: prisoner releases; the making of a political agreement; the task of managing day-to-day life on the 'peace lines' and interfaces that still divide communities across Belfast. And, on the question of a legacy process, he believed expectations were unrealistic. 'The more we dig at the truth, the more we bury it,' he told me in an interview for the *Irish Times* in January 2016. A few months after that interview, Smith asked could he see me. In May, I visited him at his home and, then, at the Mater Hospital – that second visit just days before his death in early June. At his funeral, his great nephew Glenn sang 'Where Have All the Flowers Gone', a song about the consequences of war. It had been requested by Smith, perhaps his way of underscoring the importance of a peace process that he had helped to build.

MANDY McDERMOTT:

For him, the meaning of peace did not end once the Good Friday Agreement was announced in 1998. Right up until his untimely death, he used various methods and platforms to continue his work. He helped international students and academics understand the importance of building relationships and conflict resolution. He used his own experience to influence and educate young people in using non-violent methods of managing and resolving conflict. He wanted people, especially young people, to learn about, and really understand, the impact of 'the Troubles'; the trauma, resilience, building relationships and the journey towards healing. In his later years, William became extremely disillusioned. He felt let down when the Historical Enquiries Team (HET) was set up to investigate unsolved murders during 'the Troubles'. Previous guarantees and negotiated arrangements leading to the Good Friday Agreement were not honoured.

Smith's niece also shared some words her uncle had written just two weeks before his death. He believed we had come a long way from the ceasefires and from the firefighting of conflict management, but he understood the work that still had to be done, that the 'entire community' had to be responsible for change, and that young people had to be part of that transformation: 'Therefore, I call on our community, in particular those from my era and influence, to encourage our youth and support their opinions and allow them the freedom to promote their new ideas.' What is the reading between those few lines that Smith wrote? That, at some point, the conflict generation has to step back and give those who will be the future the chance to shape their present. It means politics and politicians have to let go of that past, giving it to those who can write it with all its competing narratives and in a way that explains why it should never be repeated. This is what a legacy process should be.

Otherwise, we will bury the present and the future in those conflict years.

When you take any of the big figures from that conflict period and you study them, so much more and so many others become part of the telling of the story. In 2015, there was another of those moments. This time, McGuinness was in conversation with Chief Constable Sir George Hamilton – a conversation under the title, 'Facing the Questions of the Past'. The biggest hall in St Mary's University College was packed. Outside there was a protest – a reminder of the still uneasy, uncomfortable, tense relationship between the republican community and the police. Inside, officers from Hamilton's close protection unit stood nearby, and there is a photograph of Bobby Storey and Martin Lynch sitting on the steps of the stage. There is another photograph of Gerry Adams standing and listening, again, not far from the main table of the event.

As I introduced the discussion, I spoke of the first time I met Martin McGuinness in the 1980s. I was helping with research for a BBC *Panorama* documentary, 'The Long War', by the veteran journalist Peter Taylor. Speaking to that festival audience, I said the title of the film told us where we were then. There was no sign or sense of peace – no hint of the type of conversations that would become possible as this process evolved. Taylor's closing thought in that film was that a military victory was unwinnable: 'Both sides agree on one thing … that politics, not guns, will win the long war.' Introducing that festival event in August 2015, I said 1988 had been the beginning of the SDLP–Sinn Féin engagement (what was to become the Hume–Adams talks), and that while we did not see it or understand it at the time, it was the beginning of a move in another direction.

There is a segment in that Taylor film when he asks McGuinness about the IRA killing of an agent:

McGuinness: If republican activists, who know what the repercussions are for going over to the other side, in fact go over to the other side, then they, more than anyone else, are totally and absolutely aware of what the penalty for doing that is.

Taylor: Death?

McGuinness: Death, certainly.

Sir George Hamilton will, of course, have known the different chapters in the McGuinness story – his involvement with, and leadership of, the IRA before his steps into peace and politics. How does Hamilton remember that festival event, his participation in it, and the questioning and questions that sit alongside such decisions?

SIR GEORGE HAMILTON:

Having experienced policing in England and Scotland as well as Northern Ireland I knew that policing here was different. Many aspects were much the same at an operational level – protecting people, preventing harm, investigating, enforcing the law and bringing offenders to justice. However, the big difference, especially for a Chief Constable, was that policing in NI is an integral part of maintaining and building the peace. This place has a fragile, complex and dynamic political infrastructure in which policing ofttimes becomes either a stumbling block or a stepping stone in maintaining some momentum in our collective slow journey towards a normal society.

In accepting the role of Chief Constable, I knew that this 'bigger' responsibility would rest on my shoulders for five years. I was determined to play my part, as Orde and others had done before me. That would mean dealing with personal dilemmas, being criticised by 'both sides' at different times and even from within the police family – present and past. At times it would be lonely and challenging, but I was determined that I would stretch myself to fulfil the unique and broad responsibility I had been given as Chief Constable. One of those challenges came with the invite to participate in a public debate with Martin McGuinness in St Mary's University College in west Belfast as part of Feile an Phobail on 6 August 2015.

There was much more to this than simply agreeing to participate and then turning up. Many things had to be considered, including the security arrangements that would be required. This was not an unannounced visit. It was part of a festival and included in the programme. Dissident republican organisations still consider the police to be 'legitimate targets'. So, all of this becomes a part of the planning and preparations – how to protect the Chief Constable, as well as those officers tasked with keeping him safe.

SIR GEORGE HAMILTON:

This was a festival held in republican west Belfast and owned and developed over many years by the republican community. It was 'their' event; participation was on 'their' terms. I believed the invite was respectfully made with a view to being inclusive and constructive. There were many operational challenges in me attending. There would be the inevitable protest and attempt at disruption from dissident republicans who despised both McGuinness and I in equal measure. It would be a distraction of police resources away from 'normal' police work. It would require a major public order and close protection operation. It would be seen by parts of loyalism and unionism as me pandering to mainstream republicanism. I was aware that this could backfire on me. After all, I was sharing a very public platform with the man who in 2007 said he was leading his party into the devolved policing arrangements 'to put manners on the police'. Was I setting myself up for a public and professional humiliation? I agreed to participate.

I knew, of course, that this was a big occasion – something different, and the electric atmosphere as we entered the hall was a confirmation of all of that. There was applause. I could hear the cameras clicking. I was both nervous and excited. You don't want to mess up on an occasion like this. There wasn't a seat in the room – not even for Gerry Adams, who was standing. It is in moments such as this that you better appreciate the challenges of peace-building. Twenty-plus years after the ceasefires and this was still a big-deal conversation: two leaders on a public stage – one a republican, the other, the most senior police officer in Northern Ireland. I looked into the front row; Eibhlin Glenholmes was sitting beside Katherine Finucane, the daughter of the murdered Belfast solicitor Pat Finucane.

SIR GEORGE HAMILTON:

The venue was packed to capacity with upwards of 500 people in the hall and many more people outside including the anticipated dissident protests. Barney Rowan facilitated the debate with a wide range of questions from the audience providing the stimulus for a robust and frank debate between Martin and myself. I was treated with courtesy and respect by my hosts and the debate provided opportunity for me to answer questions and provide a form of informal accountability to a community still not entirely convinced of the bona fides of their police service. It was slightly surreal to sit at the desk at the front of the hall and address the challenging questions from the audience with Gerry Adams standing over my shoulder to the right and other senior republicans – Bobby Storey and Martin Lynch – sitting slightly behind me on my left-hand side.

The presence of such senior republicans was a confirmation of just how important a conversation this was. Their presence was a statement to their community and to the protesters outside that they endorsed the event. Had they not, Martin McGuinness would not have shared that stage.

SIR GEORGE HAMILTON:

Just six days later, Kevin McGuigan was murdered outside his home in east Belfast. McGuigan had been an active member of the IRA and fallen into dispute with other senior republicans. Within a short period of time, the investigation team were pursuing a strong line of enquiry that McGuigan had been murdered by members of the IRA. As the investigation developed, it became clear that there were reasonable grounds to suspect that this was with the knowledge and concurrence of senior figures within the republican movement. There was public and private commentary of 'told you so' regarding my decision to attend the West Belfast Festival and engage so publicly with republicanism.

For my part it was uncomfortable, but transition out of conflict right across the world is never straightforward. There is often a feeling of one step forward and two back. The murder of McGuigan was several steps back in the peace process and of course police actions and commentary were under considerable scrutiny with some suggestion, rather ironically, that it was the police rather than those who had murdered Kevin McGuigan who were putting the peace and political process in jeopardy. For my part, I was prepared to stretch myself to do uncomfortable things to nudge us along in the right direction. However, I was a police officer and legally obliged to go where the evidence took the investigation and to maintain the integrity of the police under the rule of law. Those sorts of dilemmas are not unique to policing in Northern Ireland, but they are much more prevalent and magnified.

On 23 March 2017, Hamilton then took another step, this time into that church in Derry on the day of Martin McGuinness's funeral. There is an unwritten code that comes with peace-making about the importance of quiet conversations and honouring confidentiality. In the words that follow, Hamilton does that, but he also shares enough to let us look inside and think inside the challenges in all of this. He reminds us that none of this is easy. Not when there has been an enemy relationship; and not when you are reminded of your dead. There are steps in reconciliation that some will never understand and will not forgive. And there are sides in peace, as there are sides in war. Hamilton's time as Chief Constable overlapped with a period when McGuinness was deputy First Minister. Both in leadership positions, they had to set an example – show that peace could be and would be different. In March 2009, McGuinness's description of dissident republicans – behind the killings of two soldiers and a police officer – as 'traitors to the island of Ireland' was one example of such leadership. So, also, was Hamilton's decision, eight years later, to step into that church in Derry/Londonderry; and to sit not far from some of those who had directed and participated in the IRA's campaign.

SIR GEORGE HAMILTON:

The decision to attend Martin McGuinness's funeral presented another dilemma. I had known 'about' Martin all my working life. I was well aware of his history including his involvement in the IRA campaign at its very worst. I had known him more personally since 2011 due to the positions we both held, including in my time as Chief Constable. The two positions we held necessitated constructive engagement. I knew that my attendance at his funeral and paying my respects to him was going to be controversial and potentially uncomfortable. There were two reasons to attend and many more to absent myself.

Firstly, at a professional level I felt it was appropriate that the Chief Constable would attend the funeral of the dFM. He had a history that made him different to most other senior politicians but he also had a mandate and had moved mainstream republicanism away from violence in pursuing their political aims through entirely peaceful means. Secondly, at a personal level, I had got to know McGuinness and will not breach the confidentiality of our private conversations. But, in general terms, we had spent time discussing the peace process; the challenges of maintaining support for it, the impact of policing and the need to nudge that process on to the next level of reconciliation. We had discussed concepts such as 'grace' and 'generosity' and the need for those ingredients to be obvious in the words and actions of leaders across all sectors.

On the other hand, I knew the hurt that had been caused in the past by Martin and his IRA comrades. In my opinion the violence was never justified and could never be justified. Under Martin's leadership the mainstream republican movement had moved away from violence as a means of achieving their political aims. However, I still struggled with the shallow and crass republican narrative that attempted to justify the violence of the past. The heavily caveated words of 'regret for the suffering caused' was too qualified for me and lacked authenticity. With these personal and professional dilemmas, I decided to attend the funeral after confirming with his colleagues and family that I would be welcome.

Inside the church, a multitude of thoughts raced through Hamilton's head – not just his, I am sure, but those of many others in attendance. This was a day to reflect on many other days – those bits we forget as the peace process becomes more certain and creates further distance between itself and the 'war'. There is a rewind button in all of us that takes us back and plays us back into that conflict period.

SIR GEORGE HAMILTON:

Sitting in the Long Tower Chapel in Derry's Bogside, looking at his tricolour draped coffin, I thought of the coffins of the many police officers that I had carried and walked behind. I knew I would be pilloried and criticised for attending the funeral of this 'unrepentant terrorist' and I knew that me being there would cause upset to victims of IRA violence. However, I was the Chief Constable and he was my deputy First Minister with a democratic mandate and despite my past and his being polar opposites we had both shared a journey and we were both committed to never returning to the past that we had lived through.

As the coffin was brought into the chapel to a lone piper playing 'Amazing Grace', I was reminded of those private conversations about the need for grace, generosity and healing that I'd shared with this leader of Irish republicanism. I also thought of the progress that had been made that meant that I would be made welcome in the church. I sat in the third row from the front with the President of Ireland, the Taoiseach, and local and international political leaders in front of me and beside me. The myriad of thoughts, emotions, memories, events and trauma that raced around my head as I sat on that church pew on 23 March 2017 was to make it a day never to be forgotten and yet another example of why civic leadership in Northern Ireland is just so unique.

Like Gerry Adams attending the funeral of David Ervine ten years earlier and being accepted into that place by the loyalist community, here was Hamilton being welcomed by the republican community. These gestures – these acts of reconciliation – go beyond individual experiences and hurts and think of others. They are examples of those ingredients of 'grace' and 'generosity' that Hamilton and McGuinness had discussed.

That day in March 2017, I travelled to the funeral with colleagues Eamonn Mallie and Deric Henderson. The latter is the one-time Ireland Editor of the Press Association and a co-author with Ivan Little of the book *Reporting the Troubles*. In that long career spanning forty-plus years, he had watched the McGuinness story evolve from the headlines about the IRA into the places of politics – from the Bogside in Derry onto the biggest of stages. Watched, also, peoples' fascination with McGuinness.

DERIC HENDERSON:

It was the first day of the G8 summit in 2013 and Peter Robinson and Martin McGuinness strolled close to the water's edge, swatting the midges and taking in the air on a beautiful June evening a few hours before sunset. Amid one of the biggest ever security operations staged in Northern Ireland, all was well with the world. Or so it seemed. The First and deputy First Ministers had just completed their interviews for the tea-time television news bulletins when I caught their attention under one of the trees on the sloping grounds of the Killyhelvin Hotel, the official media centre for the hundreds of print and broadcast journalists covering the conference. The mood was relaxed. They were talkative and keen to reflect on the opening stages of a momentous event, before sitting down to dinner with David Cameron, Barrack Obama, Vladimir Putin, Angela Merkel and the six other global leaders. Both were smartly dressed, wearing tiny circular lapel badges; maroon in colour with a gold rim, confirming their identity as one of the 12 VIPs on the heavily protected site. Unlike the rest of us who had to undergo rigorous checks at every entry and exit point, the international dignitaries were left with uninhibited access, and free to come and go as they pleased.

Pause for a moment and take in those names – Obama, Putin, Merkel and Cameron. Then think back to Denis Bradley's story of the young McGuinness being put on a stage by the IRA in those early days of conflict. When 'war' becomes 'peace' all things are possible. McGuinness, in this moment in County Fermanagh in 2013, was proof of that. We need reminders – such as this writing from Henderson – to properly appreciate just how remarkable this journey has been.

DERIC HENDERSON:

It's roughly 55 miles between Derry and Enniskillen, and here was Martin McGuinness, once a feared IRA commander, but now a fulltime advocate for the developing peace process, sharing the same space as the G8 leaders on the banks of Upper Lough Erne – another important road stop on his personal journey since his days fighting the police and military on the streets of the Bogside. Who would have believed it back then when he was involved in a vicious campaign that he would get this far? I'd monitored his public movements for more than 40 years, not all of them as relaxed and convivial as this one, especially in the run up to the August 1994 ceasefire. By that stage, IRA activity in his home city had more or less ceased – long before republican guns had fallen silent in other parts of the country – and when he declared his war with the British was over. Gerry Adams might have been the chief architect of Sinn Féin's vision for the future, but McGuinness was an astute political strategist never far from his side and who was also ahead of his time. He had history. Without disclosing the details of that terrorist offensive, he never denied his past, and it's difficult to imagine the bloodshed and grief he must have inflicted on so many victims and their families. I can understand the reasons for the loathing he frequently invited, but on the evening of our encounter in Co Fermanagh he was a changed man who had long re-invented himself to embrace a process with political bona fides which I, and many others in the media, readily accepted.

Circumstances had changed. The peace process was the way out of conflict for all sides. It changed everything. Go back to my interview with Martin McGuinness in 1991. He was urging the British government to engage in talks then. The Hume–Adams dialogue was happening privately. The British were using a backchannel to reach out to the republican leadership. Think also of Peter Taylor's line back in the late 1980s that politics and not guns would end the long war. The process that evolved through the ceasefires and the political agreements is what brought about change. McGuinness was ready for that political stage, and had been waiting for a long time.

DERIC HENDERSON:

I once got into trouble with the DUP after suggesting that Peter Robinson could be 10 times a better leader if he possessed only half the social skills of some body he once detested but grew to respect. It was difficult to dislike Martin McGuinness, the deputy First Minister, and it probably explains why he and the late Ian Paisley got on so well. I recall standing in the lobby of Fitzpatrick's Hotel in Lexington Ave., New York, in 2013 as McGuinness and Robinson – on a joint economic mission – prepared for the first engagement of the day and I watched as guests queued to secure a selfie and McGuinness's autograph. Robinson stood unnoticed by the reception desk with a couple of his staff and advisors. McGuinness could be charming and, frequently, a touch disarming. Just ask any of the civil servants, a majority of them from different religious persuasions who worked for him. Always on top of his brief; sharp on detail; a problem solver; and unfailingly courteous no matter who was in the room or at the opposite side of the table. Even the Queen had a good word for him, as he had for her; something that developed from that memorable handshake at the Lyric Theatre in 2012. That's the sort of peace time impression he made. Was this really the same man I observed in north Belfast [in 1987] as he supervised a tense republican stand-off with the RUC outside the home of Larry Marley, a former IRA man shot dead by the UVF in Ardoyne, and whose funeral was delayed for three days?

Thirty years later, as McGuinness's coffin was carried from the church, the crowd outside applauded and, standing beside me,

Henderson joined in. The hard-nosed, no nonsense news editor, with decades of experience in his pens and notebooks, was acknowledging a journey that began in war but, later, found another way. McGuinness helped make that possible. He noticed a turn on the road and took it. Conflict and peace are the two parts of his one story. Separate but joined. Not the stories of two different people, or some later-life crisis and conversion.

DERIC HENDERSON:

His death at 66 from amyloidosis in the weeks following his resignation from the Northern Ireland Executive was a huge setback for politics on all sides at Parliament Buildings and triggered a poisonous Stormont Assembly election campaign. His calming influence and steady hand were badly missed, even by those who didn't share his political viewpoint. On the day of his funeral I stood outside St Columba's Church, Long Tower with the journalists Eamonn Mallie and Brian Rowan, who knew him much better than I did, and waited for the cortege to pass. Just behind me was a man from Omagh who I hadn't seen since the morning of my wedding in June 1978. He was there with his son, both wearing Easter Lily emblems, and no doubt like myself curious to see who else was crowding the footpaths to pay their respects.

How would I describe my working relationship with Martin McGuinness? Apart from on one occasion, there was never a bad word exchanged. It was a civil, professional relationship conducted on first name terms, and he later presented me with his G8 security badge as a gesture of goodwill, and a memento of one of those never-to-be-forgotten moments. We were friends as well. I liked him. I was glad to be at his funeral and – I don't mind admitting – to be touched by the emotion of the occasion. I've been to scores of IRA funerals to witness the placing of the Tricolour; the beret and gloves; the traditional volley of shots; police in full riot gear, and then the usual chaos and mayhem which inevitably erupted at some stage. His was different. Solemnity and good order prevailed throughout, leaving the main part of the republican farewell restricted to the graveside out of respect for those

with differing allegiances, and who were openly welcomed to take
their places inside the church.

Since that day, Henderson has thought deeply about why he chose
to be in Derry, and he thought also about those who stepped inside
that church, including Sir George Hamilton, Peter Robinson and
Arlene Foster. Those would have been difficult steps. Could I ever
have imagined such a moment? Certainly not when I was talking to
McGuinness in the 1990s, and talking to him because I knew his role
and influence with the IRA. People across our divided communities
believed McGuinness's commitment to peace, and that was also
believed across the world. War is not forever, but McGuinness
clearly believed there was a time when it was necessary. I never
heard him change his mind on that. There are those who will never
forgive him, and there are those who know that forgiveness does
not have to be part of trying to understand his circumstances and
journey. His funeral and those present have challenged us to think.

DERIC HENDERSON:

The likes of Bill Clinton, the Irish President Michael D. Higgins, and
the Taoiseach Enda Kenny would hardly have noticed the careful
choreography in the arrangements, but the PSNI Chief Constable
George Hamilton, Peter Robinson and others in the reserved seats
up near the front might initially have found it slightly awkward. Their
presence at such a gathering would have been unthinkable a generation
ago, and what must Arlene Foster have thought as she slipped into her
place? I'm reliably informed that she texted Martin McGuinness in the
days before he died when her future was in serious doubt and the
entire political process hopelessly adrift. She has never forgotten the
day when aged just eight, an IRA man wounded her policeman father
at their isolated home. Years later, McGuinness delivered the oration at
the funeral of the gunman she believed was involved. So, if she was
conflicted about what to do beforehand, then the agonising over her
decision to ignore the abuse and leave home for the Requiem Mass
didn't last long. Her critics, and there were a good few back then

within the party, probably haven't forgiven her. She'd be dammed if she did, and dammed if she didn't. But like myself, she did the right thing.

From outside that packed church, I watched and listened with Henderson, and the following day, I chose these words, in an article on eamonnmallie.com, to mark one of those moments when you hold tight to the detail of what is happening around you.

'NO ORDINARY DAY IN DERRY':

It was a remarkable day in Derry – a day of measured words and steps. No ordinary day. A day that if listened to and built upon might even make a difference. Thousands of people wanted to be there; be there for the funeral and the mass for Martin McGuinness – see it, hear it, witness it so as to be able to remember and recall this day from the vantage point of presence. In the conflict years, McGuinness was a leader in the IRA but, on Thursday, there was none of the trappings that once accompanied such funerals. No beret, no gloves, no marching or stamping or shouted orders and instructions but, rather, those measured steps and words – every one of them careful and considered.

In the waiting for the mass to begin, those with whom I stood outside the church shared conversation and the chips that Eamonn Mallie had bought and brought in brown bags. They were passed among those around us, including some who had travelled on a bus from Cork in the earliest hours of Thursday morning. Travelled to be there, to see for themselves – to hear for themselves. There was nothing to embarrass or intimidate those who are not part of the republican community – and who stepped into St Columba's Church on Thursday afternoon, including the DUP leader Arlene Foster. Such steps are not easy, but were made easier by the conduct and the choreography of this occasion.

Martin McGuinness was part of an organisation that caused much hurt – the horrors that screamed out in the headlines of the conflict years, human bombs, the disappeared, the dirt and ugliness of wars.

He was also part of a community upon which much hurt was visited. Those who talk about hands that drip in blood, forget and ignore the poison that dripped from politics and discrimination, what can drip from security and insecurity, the fear and anger – the 'rage' of the time as Bill Clinton succinctly described it when he spoke on Thursday. This place did not grow crops of 'bad' people. Things happened that made the conflict happen. Causation – the why of those war years – has not been properly explored. We now need to lift the past out of politics, take it away from those endless negotiations and arguments, give the shaping of some process to others.

What could Bill Clinton and former Methodist President Harold Good, both of whom spoke at yesterday's service, do to help such a process? They could help with their words and wisdom – their different ways of saying and doing things. One from outside of us, the other very much a part of us. Both have helped this process at different times – helped make the impossible possible.

Along the way in the development of that process, prisoners were released. Do we now want a process that sends people to jail, or do we want to find the best ways of achieving the maximum disclosure of information from all the corners of the conflict years, understanding that there will not be absolute truth? We need to end the battles of the past. We need to stop shovelling the hurts of that period on top of generations that did not experience it. We need help – not more political negotiations and disagreements on the legacy question.

The talking at Stormont continues – talking about the implementation of agreements previously made but not honoured. Gerry Adams has said his party is opposed to any extension of Monday's talks deadline. He is saying it is decision time. These talks are not just about Sinn Féin and the DUP, but about the governments – British and Irish. Since Martin McGuinness's resignation as deputy First Minister in January, the politics of this place have changed utterly, including the make-up and arithmetic of the Assembly. The unionist community is nervous. In other communities there is a nervousness about Brexit and its implications. The next steps will need to be as careful and measured as those taken during those remarkable hours in Derry on Thursday.

In the opening to this chapter, I wrote about that faded taxi receipt on which I scribbled those few thoughts from Bill Clinton. It is something I will keep for a long time, to read now as a kind of memo – another reminder that those from outside of us are best placed to find the words that are a bridge from one place to the next – from dark into light. Clinton also acknowledged the courage of Arlene Foster to be in the church: 'I know your life has been marked in painful ways by the Troubles.' Just weeks earlier, McGuinness had pressed the button on the ejector seat that had catapulted Foster out of office, and still she was there in that packed church. This was by no means an easy decision, and to understand it properly you have to read back into the dark. Deric Henderson took us back to that time when the IRA tried to kill her father, and she was on a school bus when a bomb, intended to kill the driver, exploded. The easier decision for Arlene Foster would have been not to attend. In one sentence, Clinton had understood that a harder choice had been made.

Our words leave us stuck in a still divided place: cornered and surrounded by different experiences and interpretations – not able to look from distance as Clinton did on that day in Derry. There is no one opinion or understanding or narrative when it comes to assessing and recording those conflict years. No single agreed script. It is the same in the telling of the story of one of the headline public figures of those times – that young man pushed onto a stage in those earliest days of 'the Troubles'. It was a stage on which he remained in the spotlight for the rest of the days of his life. Martin McGuinness is no longer here to speak for himself. He died – as many others have – before some legacy process was achieved. In the waiting, critical memory is being lost. I have drawn attention to this point many times, but still we wait until it is too late. Important pages are then left for others to write and interpret without the direct input of those involved. Of course, there is no one in war or in politics who knew Martin McGuinness as Gerry Adams did.

GERRY ADAMS:

Martin was a proud Derry man. His core values were shaped by that community, and by his mother Peggy and her home place in Inishowen, just a few miles away in Donegal. This and his experience growing up in the Bogside formed his politics. I met Martin for the first time in 1972. I was 23. He had just turned 22. Internment had been introduced the previous August and Bloody Sunday was fresh in all our minds.

Bloody Sunday had a profound effect on Martin. He knew many of those who died that day. Like many others, especially Derry people, he took the British actions personally. These were dangerous, difficult times. The anger among nationalists and republicans at the violence of the Unionist state to the civil rights campaign, and the actions of the British Army in support of that state, was palpable. In this climate of rage, we and others prepared to meet the British government for secret talks that summer.

Here we are reminded again about how young Adams and McGuinness were at that time – both in their early twenties and already part of secret talks with the British. Clearly, even then, there was an understanding of the need for dialogue, and yet it took so long to get to that point. Try to think of someone you know who is that young and then try to see them in a conflict situation, sitting in secret talks with the British government. It is hard to imagine. How would they cope?

GERRY ADAMS:

When we got together for the first time for a prep meeting Martin and I were the youngest in the group. All men. Myles Shevlin a solicitor was there as an advisor. Martin and I both wanted to know what our agenda for those talks was, what were our proposals, what did we expect to achieve and what was our bottom line. He and I independently formed a view that the approach of our more senior leaders was too formal. While I didn't think this at the time it was a big step for Willie Whitelaw to meet with us. The older members of the delegation saw the 1972 talks as the resumption of the Treaty negotiations and, while it is true that these were the first talks between Irish republicans and a British government since then, the potential for success was limited. More is the pity.

Decades later Martin and I landed at the same airport for another series of meetings with the British government. We were better prepared this time. So were the British. We were more successful and that process continues. In the decades in between and especially as Sinn Féin began to strategise, to grow our political strength and develop our peace strategy, and embrace negotiations as a means of struggle, Martin's instinctive leadership skills grew with experience. This is why he was our chief negotiator.

At the top of the republican leadership, Adams and McGuinness became a forty-five-year double-act. They needed each other. Clearly, they trusted each other, and they had the leadership weight and patience to manage a process without the IRA turning its guns on itself. They won their biggest fight inside that IRA convention of 1997, when the dissidents left but not at the cost of a feud. More than anyone else, Adams will know the fine detail of the McGuinness story, detail that I doubt will ever be shared.

GERRY ADAMS:

His approach to Sinn Féin's electoral strategy, my early efforts, with Fr Reid to engage with the governments, with Irish America, the Catholic Hierarchy and Protestant church and community leaders, and the SDLP, the evolution of strategy and policies, were all grounded in his total commitment to the ideals and principles of Irish Republicanism. He went on to lead the Department of Education as its Minister, shared power with Ian Paisley and then Peter Robinson and Arlene Foster in the Office of OFMDFM. He was often in 10 Downing Street, or the White House or Government Buildings in Dublin. When he met with unionist politicians or loyalist leaders or engaged with civic and political unionism, or met with Queen Elizabeth, or travelled internationally, he did so as an Irish leader reaching out the hand of friendship. He did so confidently as an activist committed to Irish Unity.

He could be a tough negotiator. He had stand-up rows with the like of Mícheál Martin, Peter Mandelson and Charlie Flanagan and others when it was necessary. But he also understood the imperative of flexibility in peace making. He was usually respectful in his dealings with others and made friends with some who were his bitterest enemy. Martin was a decent man, with a ready warm smile, doing his best in often unique and very challenging and difficult conditions.

He was my friend. We enjoyed leisure time together at family weddings and other social events over the years. He rarely took a drink. He stopped in 1970 when he became an activist but for a while in his late fifties, he could be persuaded to sip a wee glass of wine if the company was good. Time with his family was paramount. Wherever he was in Ireland he would try to travel home at night. He and Bernie were made for each other. Their family is a credit to them. He is missed every day. There would be no peace process without him.

The former PSNI Assistant Chief Constable Peter Sheridan – now chief executive of the peace-building organisation Co-operation Ireland – agrees with that last thought, but he understands it is but one part of the McGuinness story. On McGuinness's role at the very top of the IRA, Sheridan adds:

There has to be a level of depravity to have such indifference to human life. Inside the IRA, he was there at the top of the tree, and he couldn't be there, or remain there, if he didn't have that ruthlessness. With politics, he moved. He recognised that violence on its own was not going to succeed and moved into, and became wedded to, the peace process. Without him, it wouldn't have worked.

The McGuinness story is of decades at the top of the IRA. The decision-making that was part of that – the killing, the 'semtex war' made possible by Libyan supplies, the bombs and bullets, that ugliness and bloodiness and bile of conflict. None of that gets written out of the script, and all of it is part of a wider story. When Adams writes that there would have been no peace process without McGuinness, that is also correct. Without his influence at the top of the IRA, it would not have happened. Peter Sheridan acknowledges and accepts that.

When the chance of a peace process presented itself, McGuinness both embraced and developed that opportunity. This becomes the second half of his story, part of that complex legacy. Those who have written in this chapter, understand the two parts. They do not ignore the conflict and his part within it, as we should not ignore the parts of many others. McGuinness tried to make politics work until it became so broken in those arguments of 2016–17, and he became so ill. Beyond his death and funeral, a long negotiation across three years tested the patience of everyone and the credibility and worth of Stormont. By the summer of 2017, the DUP had a different focus and a higher place in politics.

CHAPTER 5

A stage in the London lights – balance of power

June 2017: Unionism found a way off the ropes; it came back from the blows of the McGuinness resignation those five months earlier and the shock of losing its Stormont majority in that 'tsunami of nationalist energy' in March. The UK general election in the early summer of 2017 offered some respite – a result that meant that Stormont could wait. There would be no rush to fix the broken politics of that place. There was now a different focus. Arlene Foster was still party leader, but at Westminster, where things mattered more and most, Nigel Dodds was the DUP's most significant figure. A decision by Prime Minister Theresa May – announced on 18 April – for a snap general election in June meant an early return to the polls. A lesson had been learnt. This time, the numbers would be better for unionism. Within hours, we had the results but, as I wrote at the time, anything but a clear picture. May and politics were in a pickle.

It meant the DUP had a place on a bigger stage – but that stage was far from stable. Theresa May's weakness was the party's strength. When the counting was done in the early hours of Friday, 9 June 2017, the ten DUP seats put the Foster–Dodds leadership into a position of considerable influence; this, after the shambles and the shocks associated with the March assembly elections. There was now a calculation to be made. Was a deal with Theresa May and the Conservatives – some understanding, however formal or informal – more important than the effort of trying to get an agreement with

Sinn Féin to restore the political institutions at Stormont? The choice was London or Belfast. It could not be both.

The Adams–O'Neill leadership was also in a position of strength. Sinn Féin won seven seats. 'Nationalists and republicans have turned their back on Westminster and accept that the centre of political gravity is now on the island of Ireland,' Adams said in a statement that Friday. In other words, this latest vote had endorsed the republican position of not taking seats in Parliament. At this time, the only way the DUP would get a deal with Sinn Féin at Stormont was on the basis of certainty and implementation on issues including an Irish Language Act, marriage equality, a bill of rights and an agreement on a legacy process. The demand that Arlene Foster should step aside as First Minister until the completion of the RHI Inquiry also remained in place.

On this latest result and with these numbers, the DUP had a mandate to sit tight. The almost 300,000 votes would push further away any border poll. It had its confidence back, and space in which to breathe. The question now was what could be squeezed out of some understanding with Theresa May and her party? Was there more to be gained in these talks? This was the calculation that had to be made.

Before now, Sinn Féin had raised concerns about the talks that James Brokenshire had chaired over recent months. Through republican eyes, the Northern Ireland Secretary was seen in the role of player, not facilitator. How much more suspicious and questioning, then, would Sinn Féin be of a government now relying on DUP support? At the time, I thought out loud and wrote and asked, who would rule out another election in the not-too-distant future? Brexit was becoming a bigger mess and the political institutions at Stormont remained in political limbo. The numbers had changed – not the issues. Theresa May spoke unconvincingly of certainty. There was no such certainty – not in London, and not in Belfast.

The story of the wider election was summarised in a headline and three bullet points on the front page of the *Guardian* on 10

June 2017. In a reference to May, its headline read, 'From hubris to humiliation'. Then came those three succinct thoughts:

- PM apologises as her election gamble wipes out majority
- Tories forced to seek deal with DUP to cling on to power
- Labour invigorated as Corbyn campaign exceeds expectations

In a 650-seat parliament, the Conservatives had 318. The value of the DUP's ten seats would add up to a confidence and supply agreement and a major financial package for Northern Ireland. They were needed to prop up a minority government. In London, the lights were on. In Stormont, they were still out. There were predictions that it would end in tears, and in the unfolding Brexit battle at Westminster, we would watch as, at times, the shambles there would take the bad look of this place. On Europe, parliament was paralysed.

Foster in particular, and the DUP generally, needed this result. The party had three MPs elected in Belfast – Gavin Robinson, Nigel Dodds and Emma Little-Pengelly. Elsewhere, big numbers were attached to their wins. Ian Paisley had over 28,000 votes. Sir Jeffrey Donaldson was close to 27,000. This was the unionist vote energised by that scare a few months earlier. The tears would come in 2019 – a punishment for being on the wrong side of the Brexit line. As the London lights dimmed, it was then that the DUP would try to find its way back to Stormont – shown the way in Julian Smith's torchlight. Proof that nothing was going to happen in Belfast until something changed at Westminster. In those two-plus years from the summer of 2017 through to the next UK election in December 2019, the veteran UTV Political Editor Ken Reid had watched the DUP in those London lights – had watched them enjoy that big stage:

KEN REID:

The DUP MPs couldn't believe their luck. A strong Westminster election after the disastrous Stormont poll in March. By a simple twist of electoral fate, they incredibly held the balance of power in London. And boy did they know it. A Confidence and Supply deal seemed to deliver £1 billion of new money. They negotiated for weeks with Nigel Dodds, Jeffrey Donaldson and advisor Tim Johnston spending hours in Downing Street with Theresa May and her officials. Arlene Foster making the occasional trip where she was courted by the lobby and senior Tories, including Boris Johnson. Nigel Dodds became a national figure, Sammy Wilson spent hours in television studios. The other MPs just enjoyed it, but many Tories were not comfortable with the arrangement. Donaldson was the most realistic. The night of the deal, as we walked across Millbank, he told me that it wouldn't last forever. The end of Theresa May proved that to be the case.

In between those general elections of 2017 and 2019, Stormont talked but few listened. The treatment this place needed was on a long waiting list. There were other priorities. Headlines stretched from 'ten days to save Stormont' through to '1,000 days without government'. There was talk of deadlines and red lines and of intensive processes of negotiation. Documents emerged and submerged. Like a submarine, Stormont would occasionally pop its head up, only to drop below the radar again. At times we would sit up only to sit down again. It was a farce, perhaps even a scandal, that this was allowed to pass for politics – that it was tolerated for so long. It continued because too many were prepared to participate and acquiesce in the pantomime; it continued because of that Tory–DUP arrangement. A government in London capable of standing on its own two feet would have closed it down. Why did Sinn Féin not leave the building – not take the decision of the McGuinness resignation to its next step? There were those who thought it should have taken such action, thinking that would lead to an unexpected leadership challenge further up the road.

In the waiting, the Brexit concerns got louder; the legacy battle more angry; this Stormont play more infuriating. In August 2017, Gerry Adams said that without an Irish Language Act there would be no assembly and no executive. Months later, he would be the story and the headline as we watched the next moves in that transition at the top of the republican leadership and listened in Dublin as he set out his plans.

CHAPTER 6

Adams – the person least forgiven

For several decades we have allowed ourselves to get hung up on the question of Gerry Adams' membership and leadership of the IRA. It is something he denies. It is also the wrong question. The answers to Adams are in plain sight. Heard in the orations to the most senior IRA figures and seen in his direct involvement in all of the negotiations involving the business of that organisation, from the 1972 meeting with William Whitelaw right through the major moments of the peace process. An outsider would not be allowed such roles. Would not be allowed inside the closed spaces of the IRA. So, his story involves his association with the IRA – of which he says he is proud – and his political leadership of Sinn Féin. In February 2018 he stepped down as president of that party having given notice of his intention to do so several months earlier. In the story of this place, Adams' name runs throughout the script. For several decades, he has been the republican movement's most senior and influential leader. Those orations, and that involvement in the fine detail of critical negotiations, help us colour in the picture and see it across a wide canvas. I have also asked a number of people to help tell the Adams story.

Peter Hain was in Northern Ireland at a time of headlines. He was here for a sequence of events, all of which will have their place in history – events of such significance that they will be scrutinised and revisited for years to come. During Hain's time here, this place was finding new roads. There were different signposts on the way:

103

the formal ending of the IRA armed campaign (this was the end product of the Hume–Adams initiative that began two decades earlier); the most significant acts of arms decommissioning; the republican endorsement of policing (the importance of which former Chief Constable Sir Hugh Orde captured previously when he wrote that for peace to work, policing had to work); and the making of that political partnership of Paisley and McGuinness at Stormont, which marked the beginning of a decade of those two parties at the top of the executive, before it collapsed in 2017.

In a Blair government, Hain was Secretary of State from 6 May 2005 to 27 June 2007 – a period in which he was able to watch and read Gerry Adams from up close and, from that front seat in politics, assess his influence in the IRA developments of that time. One week, in particular, tells us a lot: the story of those days in late July 2005 as the IRA moved to end its 'long war'. Hain reads back into his memoir and adds some observations as he recalls those days and his conversations and meetings with Adams. The tension in the period is clear – the brinkmanship, people exhausted and exhausting every last opportunity. The chess plays of peace require patience. Being able to imagine and predict the next moves. Adams, in all of his influence, was allowing Hain to see the board – giving him a preview. Firstly, the IRA prisoner Sean Kelly had to be released, and Dublin had to back off a demand for photographic evidence of the decommissioning process; the demilitarisation of the security landscape was also part of the bargaining and demands. As Hain now explains, Adams was in the middle of things. On that chess board, he had control of some of the biggest pieces.

LORD HAIN:

On 21 July 2005 Adams asked me for an urgent meeting over a planned public statement by the IRA ending their armed campaign. It had to be very private, he insisted conspiratorially, with only Political Director Jonathan Phillips amongst my officials joining me. And any report given to Jonathan Powell in Number 10 must not be copied more widely.

Next day a tense-seeming Adams arrived at my Stormont Office with Martin McGuinness, explaining that the IRA were not currying favour with the British. The IRA – he always spoke about it in the third person even though I knew he was a member of its army council – had taken its own decision. But, he insisted, it would be such a decisive, historic move that even for him to discuss it with me beforehand was potentially 'treasonable to the IRA'. Also, [Sinn Féin was demanding a] speedy winding down of the British military presence and its surveillance stations, and the release of Sean Kelly (the 'Shankill bomber' recently rearrested on my authorisation following a disturbance in Belfast). Adams wanted meetings with both British and Irish Prime Ministers the next week and would then show me a copy of the IRA statement the day before it was issued. The meeting was set for [Wednesday] 27 July, having earlier indicated to Tony Blair it [the IRA statement] would be unconditional, with all armed volunteers instructed to pursue only peaceful and democratic activities, and their weapons decommissioned.

Those of us who have been reporting on this political and peace process throughout its many episodes often speak of 'Sinn Féin time', meaning never on time. Their watches and clocks are set in their own zone. Many a carpet has been worn out in the pacing before an expected republican statement. Now, Hain was waiting – waiting on another of those moments of history; and waiting for Gerry.

LORD HAIN:

An hour after the appointed time, I chased Adams. 'You have waited eight hundred years for this moment, so you can wait a few more hours. Don't hassle me,' he said teasingly. Hillsborough Castle was resplendent on a warm summer's afternoon when he eventually arrived in an open neck shirt with rolled up sleeves, sandals and a 'bluetooth' earpiece linked to his mobile phone.

We sat down in the regal décor of the Lady Grey room, Adams complaining of obstructionism from the Irish government: 'My instructions are to show only Tony Blair and Jonathan Powell a copy of the IRA statement,' he said. 'The Irish Government can stew in it. But the statement will not issue from the IRA until Dublin agrees over this outstanding issue between us.' As if on cue the Taoiseach Bertie Ahern rang his mobile, and Adams told him: 'I can't deliver photos of the decommissioning of IRA weapons. We have got to assert the independence of the International Decommissioning agency (IICD). Photos are impossible.'

This was last-minute drama. Adams will have known that he was in control of the board. He had with him the words and statement the IRA would use to formally end its armed campaign, a statement British governments had been waiting on for decades. Was this moment really going to be allowed to fall because of a Dublin demand for photographs of decommissioning? Would Bertie Ahern, a central player with Blair in the Good Friday Agreement negotiations seven years earlier, allow that to happen? The answer was no. As he spoke with Ahern on the phone, Adams shared the planned IRA statement with Hain.

LORD HAIN:

Half-dramatically, he paused, and handed over several typed plain white sheets of paper. They were indeed cathartic: an end to the IRA's armed struggle from four o'clock the following afternoon – [Thursday] 28 July 2005. All armed units were instructed to dump their arms, and pursue purely peaceful and democratic activity, continued criminality excluded too. IRA representatives would also decommission their weapons, in front of independent observers including Protestant and Catholic clerics.

But then came a small sting in the tail. He wouldn't permit photo copies. Instead Jonathan Phillips was forced to copy over 1000 words in long hand, to securely fax to Number 10. That took over an hour. Meanwhile, the tension built. Dublin remained hard line, Minister for Justice Michael McDowell insisting on photos of the decommissioning. I could not get through to Jonathan Powell or Tony Blair stuck in a meeting of COBRA because of intelligence on another Al Qaeda

> London bombing. Sean Kelly's carefully pre-arranged release through
> emails and letters to comply with judicial protocol was threatened
> because Maghaberry Prison would soon close for the night. Adams
> would not budge, sitting in the sun on a bench on the terrace outside,
> taking mobile phone calls, munching fruit and cake supplied by
> Hillsborough staff.

Hain then decided it was his move. Sean Kelly's release from prison
was an important piece of the choreography. In its normal routine,
the jail would close for the night at 8 p.m. Hain had a flight to catch,
and once in the air, he would not be able to authorise Kelly's release.
Adams now had a decision to make.

LORD HAIN:

> My bags were packed, the car engine running, when Adams finally
> spoke to the Taoiseach's adviser in Dublin, obtaining an assurance that
> Bertie Ahern would stand by his previous public position that photos
> were unnecessary. I issued my command to release Sean Kelly through
> and headed to the airport, aware history beckoned the next day.

I obtained a copy of those notes made by Sir Jonathan Phillips, and,
for the first time, they are reproduced in this book. Spread across
four pages, they were purposely written and spaced to be legible
when read by Tony Blair. At the same time, Martin McGuinness was
in Dublin showing the same text to Taoiseach Bertie Ahern. Adams
and McGuinness in different places, doing the same job of closing
out this negotiation.

Hain has taken us behind the scenes – into those critical last
hours of those contacts in the summer of 2005 that determined the
words and actions that would end the war – what the IRA would
say and do, and what the British government must then say and do.
In the choreography and sequencing of this, Adams, sitting inside
Hillsborough Castle, knew precisely what the IRA was prepared to
do and knew what had to be done to bring that into play. Adams
was completing the IRA end of that negotiation, including dictating

who, in the highest positions of the British government, could have pre-publication access to the IRA's planned statement. As already referenced, another important part of this endgame preparation was the effort to secure the release of Sean Kelly. At the time, Robin Masefield was Director General of the Northern Ireland Prison Service. His contribution to this book gives us an insight into how the system prepares and responds in these moments – how the links become the chain. He had been around long enough to know this was not a moment for things to go wrong. In a notebook from that period he logged two sets of initials – GK and LG – the republicans Gerry Kelly and Leo Green. Beside the initials, Masefield noted their contact details, and called one of those numbers when Hain gave the order for Sean Kelly's release. The Director General of the Prison Service then made his way to Maghaberry.

ROBIN MASEFIELD:

It was not the first time I had had a phone call from Jonathan Phillips asking me to do something at short notice involving Sinn Féin, to facilitate the Peace Process. One previous occasion had been a request to go to Chequers first thing the following morning to participate in talks about policing. Those discussions had been in the context of trying – unsuccessfully at that time – to satisfy Sinn Féin that the changes to policing, including the Policing Board, would be fully implemented and that a new beginning was being delivered.

On 26 July, the day before Kelly's release, I had had a contingency planning meeting (over the video-conference facility) with Joe Pilling, the Northern Ireland Office Permanent Secretary, Jonathan Phillips and our senior legal adviser. We agreed that the release would be impracticable once Maghaberry Prison had moved onto its night regime; this effectively meant nothing could be done between 7 p.m. and 8 a.m. [The next day] Jonathan Phillips kindly kept me posted as the talks went on that afternoon; my notes jotted down at the time recorded that by 5 p.m. everything was in place except 'agreement in the South'. Shortly after 6 p.m. Peter Hain had been asked to make the decision, and some time after that I got the go ahead from Jonathan, together with the names of those who would be coming to pick him up. They included Gerry Kelly whom I had met before on various occasions.

I had made arrangements with the prison governor in advance for this eventuality, but I concluded that it would be helpful if I went to Maghaberry myself to ensure there was no slip twixt cup and lip. Sean Kelly's temporary release was processed at the prison's internal reception, and he was then brought out in a prison van, in which I hitched a ride, through the extern gate and onto our designated handover beside the visitors' centre. Maghaberry colleagues were excellent, not least in that it must have been closer to 9 p.m. before he finally left. The following day came the [IRA] announcement. It was momentous at the time and, while there were to be still many checks along the road, it did pave the way for the subsequent restoration of the Executive. And, in 2007, for Sinn Féin to commit to supporting policing and joining the Policing Board.

The 500-plus words of that 'momentous' IRA statement with the 'P. O'Neill' sign-off emerged the following day. (P. O'Neill is the name used by the authorised spokesperson for the IRA leadership. In my period reporting the conflict and the transition to peace, I met with five men in that role.) Steps to stand down the military presence began almost immediately. The peace was being given deeper roots and meaning. Adams – with others – had taken the IRA onto new ground. But Sir Hugh Orde was right in his previous comments. These things don't just stop. All organisations, including the IRA, retained parts of their structure, and when that became obvious, as it did after the McGuigan murder, then there were problems.

Within months, there were questions about the extent of the decommissioning process – an assessment that a range of arms had been retained. In July 2006, the same P. O'Neill of that statement in 2005 gave me another statement, this time detailing an IRA investigation into the circumstances surrounding the killing of Jean McConville, one of 'the disappeared' (see chronology). Almost a year after it ended the armed campaign, this was the IRA still dealing with its past – something that continues right through to today. That organisation met in a convention in 2007, clearing a path for republican endorsement and participation in those policing structures that were referenced earlier by Robin Masefield. And there is a question still about what remains of the IRA structure – including an army council, whatever its role today. It is what makes the past more present; and, at times, our politics less secure. It is the issue that, in 2015, and when he was First Minister, Peter Robinson believes 'held the greatest likelihood of bringing the Executive down'.

Then there is the 'Adams issue' – the questions that get asked of him, more than anybody else, about that past and how it might be answered. On Saturday, 18 November 2017, I travelled to Dublin with my journalist colleagues Eamonn Mallie and David McKittrick (the latter a co-author of the acclaimed *Lost Lives*). It was a journey to hear the Adams speech at his party's Ard Fheis later that evening – to be present at another of those moments in history when his words would talk us and take us towards some chapter end. As Adams spoke from the stage in the RDS, I watched as his aide Richard McAuley turned to the page and the message of this address. It was the reason for our presence – why, earlier, we had taken the road from Belfast to here. Adams announced that he would not be standing for the Dáil in the next Irish election and that this would be his last Ard Fheis as President of Sinn Féin. When he left the stage and came through the press centre, I asked him to sign my copy of the speech. This was one of those points in time, important in the chronology of conflict and peace and this man's part and place within it. I describe a chapter end because, in the story of someone such as Adams, there is never a full stop. His pages – whether in the seventies, eighties or nineties, or in the twenty-plus years since – will be read and reread, written and rewritten, and we will never have his full story.

He is singled out for more attention and more blame and more vitriol than anyone else; the person least forgiven; a hate figure. Yet, the contradiction is that our eventual peace would not have been possible, or made, without him. By the time Peter Hain arrived, the cloud had lifted. It was easier to see. Easier to think. It was altogether different in 1991, when the former Presbyterian Moderator Dr John Dunlop first met Adams. The climate was different. Every day was dark, threatened by the thunderous noise of conflict. It would be three more years to the first of the ceasefires; and it was a time when many, including myself, would have dismissed talk of peace as some fanciful pipe dream. Yet in all that was different, there was something that was the same – that those, such as Dunlop, exploring ways out of the turmoil, went looking for Adams. They knew his influence, knew he had open-door access to the IRA – that he had his own set of keys.

DR JOHN DUNLOP:

It is impossible to live in Northern Ireland and avoid the name and influence of Gerry Adams. His name will be forever associated with the Provisional IRA and the leadership of Sinn Féin. In contributing to this chapter, my initial thoughts turned to a school friend of mine who has spent almost all her adult life as a widow. The IRA killed her husband. Their son never grew up to know his father who was a police officer and a youth leader in the Presbyterian Church. Violence has personal consequences and her story is typical of the widespread violence which left thousands of similarly grief stricken, lonely people from across our communities.

In the 1980s I read two of Gerry Adams' books and came to the conclusion that he didn't understand me or the Presbyterian part of the community to which I belong. Instead of talking behind his back I thought I ought to see if I could meet him. I joined an existing small group of people from protestant churches who were in difficult dialogue with Sinn Féin, using the hospitality of the Clonard Community. That was about 30 long years ago, in the midst of the violence. I tried to convince Gerry Adams and other Sinn Féin people whom I met later in useful conversations, that the problems he and they had were not primarily with London but with Presbyterian people like me, and that violence was making long standing problems worse. For a whole lot of reasons Gerry Adams and Martin McGuinness eventually came to the conclusion that to continue the violence was futile.

These quiet dialogues were important to the making of the eventual peace. Talking adds to understanding; creates possibilities; helps people to find ways out of their trenches; allows them to hear the other. Dunlop, and others from the Protestant churches, began those conversations with republicans, including Adams, before those in the unionist political parties ventured into that space.

DR JOHN DUNLOP:

Sinn Féin was by then, and still is, a tightly controlled strong party. They embarked on that difficult road of political compromise leading eventually to the Good Friday Agreement. They kept most of their organisation on board although by dragging their feet they all but derailed the Peace Process, nearly destroyed John Hume, damaged the SDLP and almost ruined David Trimble and the Ulster Unionist Party.

Political parties include people with different personalities. Although Gerry Adams has always treated me cordially and has made efforts to connect with people in traditions other than his own, his inability to create trust and relate positively to those outside his own community is in sharp contrast to that of Martin McGuinness who, despite his past, displayed impressive inter-personal skills when he built relationships with people across the political divide, especially as deputy First Minister in the Executive. I met him in Derry some months before his illness. At that time, I said something to him to the effect, 'Martin, I choose not to focus on the things which you did or didn't do in the past, but I am interested in what you are doing now.'

I believe the time has come to be generous and care for victims but stop focussing on and enquiring endlessly about all that happened before the Good Friday Agreement, for many of those who know the truth will never tell what they know.

As with McGuinness, there is no one word that describes Adams – no sentence or two, or page or two, that properly tells his story. He is something more than is suggested in some of the usual and typical and lazy headlines. Yes, he denies IRA membership. There is not yet a process that would allow him to speak candidly about these things, and even if there was, he may not do so. This is what I mean by no full stop. In its telling, much of his story is for another time – a time that might never arrive – but there are dots that join up and that give us lines to follow. This is what I mean by his story being in plain sight. He has delivered the orations for all of the big IRA figures: for Joe Cahill in 2004, for Brian Keenan in 2008, for Martin McGuinness in 2017 and then, beyond the date when he stood down as Sinn Féin President, for Kevin McKenna in 2019 and for Bobby Storey in 2020. Adams has not retired or stepped back from that role, and to have such a platform and a place, you have to have knowledge and stripes and standing of your own. If not, why would he be afforded such a stage? Why would someone else not step in – someone of the IRA leadership?

There is much research material in those orations – words that, if carefully read, start to open out the Adams book. At the funeral of Brian Keenan, in May 2008, Adams spoke of their lives being 'inextricably linked' since they first met in 1968 and added, 'It will only be when the history of this period is properly written that the real extent of the key role Brian played can be told. For now, let me say that he was central to securing the support of the IRA leadership and rank and file for a whole series of historic initiatives which made the peace process possible.' Adams knows much about the IRA and its decision making. We might never be told the real extent of his role or the real meaning of those words describing two lives that were 'inextricably linked' across the entire conflict period. These are my words from 26 May 2008 in an article for the *Belfast Telegraph*.

'KEENAN ORATION LEAVES NO DOUBT WHO IS IN CHARGE':

It was much more than a funeral – it was an IRA event and an occasion on which Gerry Adams showed himself both as leader and father of the Republican Movement. Recently much has been made of the 'politically invisible' Adams – the man who has chosen to give Martin McGuinness the lead role at Stormont. And there have been questions. Could he be the next to leave the stage after Blair, Ahern and Paisley?

On Saturday, in the company of those who have been the leaders of Sinn Féin and the IRA, Adams was the man in charge. Addressing mourners in Ballymurphy before Keenan was cremated at Roselawn, it was Adams who was centre stage, he who read the words that defined Brian Keenan's role in the IRA's war and the IRA's peace. It was also an occasion when he chose interesting language to describe his own relationship with Keenan, that most militant of IRA leaders, who in the end was so crucial to the ceasefires, decommissioning, ending the armed campaign and endorsing policing.

Adams described their first meeting in 1968 and how their lives had become 'inextricably linked from that point on'. It was a tease – words chosen and used for a reason – and read back to be heard by those in government, politics and policing, who have used them so many times in the past to describe the relationship between Sinn Féin and the IRA at their highest tiers.

In that republican memorial garden in the heart of west Belfast on Saturday, they were all there, the republican leadership of the war and peace – Storey, Murray, Gillen, Kelly, Ferris, Doherty, Adams and McGuinness. And it was Adams who spoke for them all: 'And for the sceptics within unionism, let me remind them that the recent watershed moments in our history, including the election of Ian Paisley as First Minister, would not have been possible without the work of Brian Keenan and his colleagues,' he said. 'I was one of those who was privileged to work alongside Brian in developing responses to the many challenges that faced us in recent times. On behalf of that small group let me say we will miss him dreadfully.'

That 'small group' is a reference to those including Keenan who changed the republican direction, who took the IRA out of armed struggle and into a process of negotiation and compromises. Keenan, Adams said, 'saw the IRA as an instrument' and 'he believed in the primacy of politics'. Saturday's oration was about giving Brian Keenan his place in republican history.

The IRA was there, but there were no masks and no guns. That army council of the IRA, that is still such a part of the political debate and argument, was present. Its name may change. Its role has certainly changed. But there will continue to be an IRA leadership and an IRA organisation for occasions such as Saturday when its dead are remembered. Adams said of Keenan 'he had a justifiable sense of pride in the IRA's ability to take on and fight the British Army to a standstill'.

> The IRA was also fought to a standstill – and it was out of that military stalemate that the peace was made. Keenan and many others were part of a war in which there were no winners.

If you overthink Adams, allow him to live inside your head, then you will get lost in the maze of this man. Every Adams moment is a page; the oration for Keenan in May 2008 was one example of such, and the address to the Ard Fheis in Dublin in November 2017 becomes another. You have to keep connecting those dots – back and forward. Read his lines, the words he chooses. The Adams story is not about one question and that one answer that never changes. It is about all of his other words – how informed they are. The knowledge he has, and from where that knowledge comes. It is from the inside and from the top tier of the republican leadership, of which he has been a part for fifty years.

It is why John Hume identified him as the republican leader whom he would first have to persuade of an alternative to arms before others would follow, why governments have spent several decades negotiating with him, and why, when words have to be found to honour and remember the IRA's dead, that task falls to him. Of course, in every interview and speech, there are gaps. He leaves us with questions, but so, also, do many others not as fascinating, infuriating or interesting as this republican leader.

What did he mean in the oration for Keenan when he spoke of history 'properly written'? He did not elaborate. Unionists, in the political scrap for the past, accuse republicans of trying to re-write the record. 'You can't re-write history,' one of Adams' senior colleagues, Gerry Kelly, once told me. 'You can give an opinion on it.' Everyone has an opinion on Adams. He is Marmite and dynamite. Loathed and loved. His words – even just his presence in certain settings – capable of causing an explosion of emotions. Two headlines on a photograph of him shaking hands with Prince Charles in 2015 are examples of how he is seen through different eyes. One read, 'Gesture of reconciliation'; the other, 'Charles shakes the hand that's soaked in blood'. The same photograph. Two very different takes.

In the words of a one-time senior IRA figure, who spoke with me for this book on the condition of anonymity, Adams is, 'The single most guarded and Machiavellian figure to emerge in modern republicanism. He understood that external and outward-facing spies and internal and inward-facing spies were essential to any leader hoping to achieve significant victories or advances.' My source asked, 'How will they bury him? What will his ego allow them to say?' He was imagining the oration to Adams and what it might reveal.

For several decades, Roisin McGlone has been at the heart of a number of Belfast's interface communities – part of a project called Interaction, which tried to negotiate and manage the vexed issues of marching versus protest, as well as build relationships with policing. In this, she worked with significant loyalist and republican figures, including the late William 'Plum' Smith and Sean Murray.

ROISIN McGLONE:

After moving from working in north Belfast interfaces back to west Belfast in 1999, it felt like moving to another country. It was not just about me being from west Belfast. It felt much more comfortable being back in the west as an 'activist'. There was also a solid track record of strong women nationalist activists in west Belfast, both in political and community life.

We had all collectively come through the trauma of the 1996–1998 Drumcree parading fallout. This had affected so much of activism in north Belfast; in that deeply divided community, reducing it to reacting to the next 'incident'. It had felt so dark and dangerous in what was the 'patchwork quilt' of sectarian interfaces in north Belfast, with little hope visible. Over 115 families had been displaced from their homes over a few weeks of the summer of 1996.

Think of this period that McGlone is describing – the turmoil of those years in the 1990s. The IRA ceasefire had been announced, had been broken and was then reinstated. The Good Friday Agreement of 1998 had happened, yet on the ground, especially in interface communities, day-to-day living was as difficult and as dangerous as ever. Peace is both a building and a management process. It arrives in different places at different times. In some of those places, it has not yet fully arrived. Peace of mind has yet to be achieved.

ROISIN McGLONE:

Somehow, even though the Falls/Shankill interface was the longest in the North, 'change' felt more doable. There was a consistency about Sinn Féin leadership in west Belfast that had created a stability and willingness to take risks. There is no doubt that Adams' leadership through all of the difficulties had created a safer place for some leading members of Sinn Féin to think in terms of the future and what they and we could do to improve the lives of those most impacted by interface violence.

Meetings across interfaces became commonplace, and by 2004 we had formed a number of influential networks between political activists from the Shankill and the Falls to address interface violence. Many relationships formed in those networks continue to today. When we set about tackling the two most controversial issues of 'parades and protest' and the impact that 'public order policing' had on the interface communities, the environment was right in west Belfast to address these issues. The 'Patten report' envisioned 'Policing with the Community' as a central tenet of policing. Where else to tackle the total breakdown in relationships with police and community than in an area that had felt the brunt of 'public order policing' because of contentious parades and interface violence? Unbelievably, there was a willingness to take risks, which only comes about when political activists have confidence that their leadership will back them.

All of the developments that emanated from this work across the most-difficult interfaces in west Belfast between 2004–2010 came directly from work by ex-combatants in both communities and, on the wider question of policing, through the involvement of some of the most-senior members of Sinn Féin. I do not believe that any of this work could have happened without Adams' leadership.

Join the dots of the observations on recent pages – the different headlines on the Adams/Prince Charles photograph, the comment from the anonymous one-time senior IRA figure and the words written by Roisin McGlone, who has been a member of the Northern Ireland Policing Board and is now the Legacy of Violence Project Manager at the Glencree Peace Centre. They give us jigsaw pieces in the Adams picture.

In the intelligence vaults there will, of course, be the material to write a draft or a version of his story – something pieced together from the means and methods of surveillance and bugging, and from information provided by agents or informants, or those more technically described as covert human intelligence sources (CHIS). Such a version – written by 'the enemy' – would be penned and pieced together from that perspective. It would be incomplete. What are the actions of others that contributed and contribute to the Adams story? Without this information, you have an artist's sketch of Adams and not the finished or final portrait.

At Easter 2010, I listened as he spoke to a republican audience in Milltown Cemetery; I heard him say that he was proud of his association with the IRA and that he was glad the war was over – a war that he said 'should never be glamorised or repeated'. Each word becomes another jigsaw piece in that picture of fifty or so years since the early 1970s. On these occasions, I always look into the crowd to see who is there. His audience included many who were part of the IRA organisation, including some of its most senior figures in the city, among them Bobby Storey, Padraic Wilson and Adams' brother, Paddy.

At the time, the Sinn Féin President was again in the headlines – this time because of claims in a book that he had a role in the execution and disappearing of Jean McConville almost forty years previously. Allegations he continues to deny. That book, *Voices from the Grave*, features interviews with former IRA leader Brendan Hughes, who died in 2008. Adams didn't refer to Hughes by name on that Easter Sunday in 2010, but it was obvious who he was talking about as he recalled moments dating back to the late sixties and early seventies, and the years that followed:

Politics in the dark. January 2020, Tánaiste Simon Coveney and Secretary of State Julian Smith just hours before new light at Stormont. Image courtesy of Kelvin Boyes, Press Eye.

Behind the scenes. Smith and his team at the Northern Ireland Office. Image courtesy of Kelvin Boyes, Press Eye.

Long hours, long years. Simon Coveney at the political negotiations at Stormont. Image courtesy of Kelvin Boyes, Press Eye.

Belfast republican Jake Mac Siacais believes 2021 offers the opportunity to close the book on Stormont – its final chapter. Image © Elle Rowan.

Gerry Adams has stepped off the stage as Sinn Féin President, but he's never far from the headlines. Image © Elle Rowan.

New generation police leaders. Una Jennings. Image courtesy of South Yorkshire Police.
Tim Mairs. Image © Elle Rowan.

Three years without government. Stormont lost in the political woods. Image © Elle
Rowan.

Alliance leader and Justice Minister Naomi Long at the old military site at Kinnegar, Holywood. Image © Elle Rowan.

Stormont shadows: January 2017, Belfast republicans Gerry Kelly, Bobby Storey, Martin Lynch and Sam Baker at Parliament Buildings. Image © Brian Rowan.

Having a laugh. A light moment at Féile an Phobail 2018. Author Brian Rowan, former chief constable Sir George Hamilton, loyalist Winston Irvine and republican Sean Murray. Image courtesy of Mal McCann, *Irish News*.

Quiet conversation: Healing Through Remembering director Kate Turner, Brian Rowan and former chief constable Sir Hugh Orde in a legacy discussion, Belfast 2011. Image courtesy of Healing Through Remembering.

In this book, Kate Turner writes about the republican negotiator Ted Howell: 'While it seemed immediately apparent to me that he is one of those important behind the scenes characters in our society's story, I was surprised to find that many people don't know him or know about him.' Image © Elle Rowan.

Always something to think about. First Minister and DUP leader Arlene Foster at Stormont. Image courtesy of Kelvin Boyes, Press Eye.

As Stormont crumbled in 2017, former Progressive Unionist Party leader and MLA Dawn Purvis advised unionists to end their war. Image © Elle Rowan.

Republican protest. Bobby Storey, Martin McGuinness and Martina Anderson on the Falls Road, Belfast 2014. Image © Brian Rowan.

Mandy McDermott, niece of the late William 'Plum' Smith. Image © Elle Rowan.

Féile first: August 2010, republican leader Martin McGuinness and loyalist William 'Plum' Smith in conversation with the author Brian Rowan. Image courtesy of MT Hurson.

Former Director General of the Northern Ireland Prison Service Robin Masefield. Image © Elle Rowan.

For several decades, Belfast republican Richard McAuley has been on the inside of the Gerry Adams story. Image © Elle Rowan.

One of the headlines of the 2019 UK General Election, Alliance deputy leader and MP Stephen Farry. Image © Elle Rowan.

A note of history. The statement that would end the IRA armed campaign in July 2005. As part of the negotiation, Gerry Adams shared a typed text with the Northern Ireland Office the day before its release, but would not allow photocopies. It then had to be handwritten by NIO Political Director Sir Jonathan Phillips to fax to Downing Street. Sir Jonathan has supplied this image.

Belfast visit: Former Northern Ireland Secretary of State Julian Smith in the city in July 2020 and photographed with author Brian Rowan. Image © Elle Rowan.

Ulster fry: Shankill loyalists Harry Stockman and Winston Irvine had a breakfast meeting with Julian Smith as he moved to put Stormont back together again. Brexit, the Union and legacy all on the plate. Image © Elle Rowan.

Build-up to the New Decade, New Approach agreement. Above Julian Smith's special adviser Lilah Howson-Smith and, below, Smith and NIO Permanent Secretary Sir Jonathan Stephens meet with Arlene Foster. Images courtesy of Kelvin Boyes, Press Eye.

Over the line. January 2020, the deal done and Stormont restored. Above, Julian Smith with Sir Jonathan Stephens watching Sinn Féin's response to the New Decade, New Approach agreement. Image courtesy of Ross Easton. Below, Sinn Féin President Mary Lou McDonald announces a return to the Executive. Image courtesy of Kelvin Boyes, Press Eye.

During this phase of the struggle some of us had to leave our families and homes, go on the run, adapt many ruses, go under false names. We relied totally on the support of the people to protect us. And we, in turn, protected the people as best we could. We did not divulge their names, their roles, their actions. That is still my position. That was the bond of comradeship and loyalty which was forged between us. And let no one think that I will bend to the demands of anti-republican elements or their allies in a hostile section of the media on this issue.

That day, Adams also spoke of how he is singled out: 'I am proud of that Army [the IRA] and my association with it. I am not a militarist and I never have been, but without the IRA the nationalist people of this state would still be on our knees. We would still be second class citizens. So, bear in mind that this relentless campaign against me is not really about me at all. It's about trying to defeat the struggle.' When you read and study the Adams speeches and orations, there is little distance between him and the IRA. Words are carefully crafted, and sentences are constructed and spoken to describe the relationship and association. His connection and connections.

In a blog in this same period, published on 31 March 2010, Adams wrote this about the IRA: 'It was not a perfect organisation and it made many mistakes. Its business was war and, in the madness that is war, the IRA did many things which deeply hurt people. I regret that very much and I have worked with others to ameliorate this.' How might he elaborate on those words if the right conditions and circumstances were created – if it was done for the right reasons of a history 'properly written'? Unless such a wide-ranging process can be shaped, we will never know.

In the absence of that process, think about how conflict is discussed and not discussed – what is said and not said, those we talk about and those we ignore. There are those who condemn prisoner releases as part of an evolving peace process but never speak of internment; who talk about Bloody Friday but not Bloody Sunday – two dates in 1972 when the innocent were slaughtered on the streets of Belfast and Derry. On the other side of this coin, there are those who are comfortable when the conversation is about 'shoot-to-kill' and torture but not so when the focus is 'the disappeared', the 'human bombs' and the interrogations conducted by 'Stakeknife' inside the IRA.

There are those who still argue for investigations and justice and the possibility of jail. Who, in such circumstances, is going to bare their soul? The interview with Gerry Kelly I referenced earlier was about a book he had written, *Playing My Part* – one of those edited and redacted and controlled accounts of his time inside the IRA. The book ends in 1989 when he was released from prison. There is nothing about Gerry Kelly inside the IRA beyond that date – nothing about his role in the leadership of that organisation, about the secret back-channel contacts with the British, or about how the ceasefires, the decommissioning, the end of the armed campaign and the eventual endorsement of policing were achieved. All for another day – and perhaps another book in another time. We have not yet cut or turned the key into such openness.

Adams wrote the foreword to the Kelly book, which includes the following: 'It is a story worth reading. There may, of course, be omissions in how the story is told. How could it be otherwise? I'm sure Gerry [Kelly] has no wish to go back to prison, or to be responsible for others going there. I certainly wouldn't blame him for that.' Within those few sentences is our legacy dilemma and the Adams dilemma – how to achieve maximum information across all the sides when the possibility of jail remains. 'If I'd told the full truth, I might as well have walked into jail,' Gerry Kelly said when I first spoke with him about his book. So, he accepts it is written within those limitations and constraints.

It is also worth reading the Adams oration to the IRA leader Kevin McKenna in 2019, which included:

This August marks 25 years from the first IRA cessation. It was an initiative created by republicans which opened up the potential of the peace process. Kevin had the courage to make the big decisions with others during the conflict. He was also one of those who had the courage to make the big and difficult

decisions during the efforts to make peace. It is in the nature
of these things that the part played by republicans like Kevin
during the long years of war will never be known. The tales
will never be told. Others may boast. Kevin would have none
of that. He had no time for ego trippers, or vanity projects.
He had no time for loose talkers, Walter Mitties or spoofs. He
was the real deal. An honest, decent republican who saw off
Thatcher and her ilk and brought the British government to the
negotiating table.

How do those words fit within a history 'properly written', as
described by Adams during the oration for Brian Keenan those
eleven years earlier? Kevin McKenna was chief of staff on the IRA
army council in the period stretching from the 1980s through to the
1994 ceasefire and beyond – a story, according to Adams, that in its
detail 'will never be known'; a tale that 'will never be told'. Edited
history or history properly written? It is a question that extends
beyond the IRA and republicans to all within and across that conflict
frame. It is not just about Adams and the IRA.

What might this thing called 'truth' look like and read like if it
is ever written? On a page in Adams' book, *Hope and History: Making
Peace in Ireland*, there might be a clue. He is writing about the IRA
bomb on the Shankill Road in October 1993, which resulted in the
death of nine civilians and one of the IRA bombers. The device had
been carried into a fishmonger shop on a busy Saturday afternoon.
At a higher level in that block of buildings, there were offices
often used by the loyalist Ulster Defence Association, including its
Shankill Road leader Johnny Adair. In my reporting of the conflict,
I had spoken with him there, and with other leaders of the loyalist
organisation, on occasions, after they had met as an 'inner council'.

That Saturday, those offices were empty when the bomb
exploded. This is what Adams wrote in his book:

The IRA operation on the Shankill was wrong; there can be no
doubt. The IRA intention was to kill the gang leaders supervising
the deadly killing campaign against Belfast nationalists and

republicans and any available Catholics. But the IRA operational plan had little regard for the civilians in the vicinity, or indeed even for the IRA volunteers involved in the operation. The opportunity of wiping out the UDA leadership blinded the IRA to the consequences of their actions if anything went wrong. In reality, everything went wrong. Ten people died in the bomb blast that day, including four women and two children.

It is a damning criticism of that IRA operation, but it stops short of the truth that some still want and demand. Who made the bomb? Who gave the orders? Who sent the IRA team out that day? The IRA will not turn out that information or those people, and across all the sides, the wider truths will come up short. Might a compilation of the different narratives, written dispassionately and from outside our frames of politics and security and intelligence, provide us with something closer to 'truth' – a history 'properly written'? This, I think, is our best chance and our only chance; but only if politicians will let go of the past and allow that script to be developed by others – by people with pens who have no emotional attachment to the conflict years.

The back and forward of this chapter is what happens when you take an Adams moment or page and you start to think about it, and then you start to connect it with other pages. The more you read, the easier the working out becomes. Why do we need to hear Adams say he was in the IRA? It is a distraction. His significance, his role, his importance, his influence and his part extend far beyond and above that question, and in just following his words, we find the answers. The republican leader who played the big cards in the biggest moments of the many negotiations, and who, in another of his roles, has not had to reach far to find the words to contextualise and remember the IRA's dead, including those such as Keenan, McGuinness and McKenna, who were part of its army council, and Storey, its director of intelligence.

For many years, I have tracked his words, followed the signposts and read between his lines – and gotten him to sign things at key moments in history, such as when the IRA ended its armed campaign and at that speech in Dublin, in November 2017, when he announced it would be his last Ard Fheis as President of Sinn Féin.

When working on this book, I read back to my words at that time. That announcement and page-turn were kept to the end – the last moment in a two-day conference that addressed the detail of politics north and south and that remembered the late Martin McGuinness in a tribute fashioned out of music, poem and words – the latter spoken by Elisha McCallion. I remember the noise, the loud applause, when the Foyle MP said McGuinness had been 'a proud member of the IRA'. 'We miss Martin', Adams added in his speech.

That wintery night was another of those occasions when some questions were answered, but many remain unanswered. When does stepping aside equal stepping away? What about the Adams IRA story – his version of that? Will it ever be told by him? Will we ever arrive at a process that would allow him to do so? There is a chapter in his latest book, *Never Give Up*, under the heading, 'British Secretaries of State I Have Known', and there is a sentence in brackets: '(Whitelaw was also the first that I met, as republicans attempted to negotiate with the British government in the summer of that year [1972], but that's a story for another time.)' Adams wrote a little more about that meeting previously in this book.

It is just one story among many untold stories. We will always be reading between the Adams lines, waiting on 'another time'. Of course, there are those who will only ever see him – as they saw McGuinness – in the actions of the IRA, in the slaughter and destruction of past decades; a hate figure; someone to blame. Such a focus leaves much unseen. It allows others to escape the stage. Adams is part of the story of the conflict and peace of this place. Not all of it.

That Saturday in Dublin, we watched the most significant move yet in that transition at the top of the republican leadership – watched Adams get closer to leaving that leadership to others, including Mary Lou McDonald and Michelle O'Neill. Could Stormont be fixed before Adams stepped away? There was no change in the answer to that question. There would only be if those rights-based issues at the heart of months of negotiations were resolved. 'These issues aren't going away,' Adams emphasised in that speech. We were just months away from the twentieth anniversary of the Good Friday Agreement; Stormont politics and the power-sharing government were still broken.

Just months before this speech, in the summer of 2017, Adams described Richard McAuley as 'the great, innovative, incorrigible and constant presence in my activism'. He did so in the foreword to *Never Give Up*. McAuley has been on the inside of the Adams story and was on the inside of that speechwriting before the Ard Fheis announcement of November that year – a speech that went through weeks of drafting. On the decision not to have the usual advance copies, McAuley explained, 'It was done in the way it was done because Gerry believed that the first people who should know what he was going to do were the activists and the party. It's part of the strong relationship/loyalty that exists between him and the activists and the activists and him.'

In every decade since the 1970s, including in those talks with Whitelaw when Adams was just 23, every initiative that has been about ending the IRA campaign and bringing republicans into political and peace processes has needed his involvement and influence. Think of the 1980s and the Hume–Adams process with then Taoiseach Charles Haughey involved and informed at safe and deniable distance. As we travel into the 1990s, already well developed, it becomes the Hume–Adams–Reynolds initiative (Albert Reynolds, the then Taoiseach). Think also about the big debates on guns, ending the armed campaign and policing that Lord Hain wrote about earlier. Adams has been at the front of all of that; this is the confirmation of the status and stripes that go beyond his being the President of Sinn Féin and an MP and then a TD. He has given us lines to read between, but working them out is not that difficult or complex. I have worked it out in my own head, as I am sure many others have worked him out in their heads. The IRA question, or the specific way that some demand it is answered, has become a silly game of cat-and-mouse. The great television detectives would laugh at our foolishness – our stupidity in chasing a dead-end question when so many other lines are so obvious and open. On this, to borrow a phrase, Adams has played us like a three-pound trout.

After the Ard Fheis of 2017, he would be part of one last big push to get a Stormont agreement before he stepped down as Sinn Féin President, which was due to happen on 10 February 2018. I made a note five days earlier – Monday, 5 February – about a round-table meeting as part of the latest talks. That note includes details of those at the table (Northern Ireland Secretary of State Karen Bradley and senior Northern Ireland Office [NIO] official Sir Jonathan Stephens, Tánaiste Simon Coveney and senior Irish official Fergal Mythen, Arlene Foster and Edwin Poots for the DUP, Mary Lou McDonald and Michelle O'Neill for Sinn Féin, Colum Eastwood and Nichola Mallon for the SDLP, Robin Swann and Steve Aiken for the Ulster Unionists, and Naomi Long and Stephen Farry for Alliance). Others in the room included Adams, his party colleague Conor Murphy and the DUP negotiator Simon Hamilton.

The talk afterwards was of disappointment, frustration and significant gaps. Rather than marking the beginning of any all-party negotiation, the DUP and Sinn Féin were given more time to develop the talks they were having. On a timeframe for this, the Sinn Féin negotiator Conor Murphy said, 'We are talking days.' There were updates from the NIO and from a spokesperson for the Tánaiste, to which I did not pay much attention.

That day, I wrote of politics in the context of a 'groundhog year'. This was despite the typed lines on a page given to me by the NIO director of communications Eamon Deeny, which included, 'Our assessment is that an agreement in the coming days, while not certain, is achievable.' The statement from the spokesperson for the Tánaiste included, 'We share the UK Government's assessment that there is a shared commitment across all parties to see the devolved institutions operating effectively in the interests of all the people of Northern Ireland. Time is short, but the prize is one worth stretching for.'

Sometimes, when you stand too close to something for too long, your vision becomes blurred – you see only what you have become used to. In my eyes, Stormont politics was a garden of weeds – that wasteland and wilderness. A dead place. I read those lines from the NIO and from the spokesperson for the Tánaiste, but they did not compute. Days later, however, I was made to sit up and pay attention. Something was happening, and once again, Adams was in the middle of it.

CHAPTER 7

Nearly fixed, but still broken – 'keep your ears open'

It started with a late-night telephone conversation in February 2018 and ended in a hurried piece of writing in an ice cream shop a couple of weeks later. This is the story of the denial of a draft agreement and then the proof that one existed. Proof, indeed, that there was something happening at Stormont – before it didn't happen. What followed was an acrimonious falling out and a near-two-year delay before the next chance. Eventually, the parties were freed from their purgatory, but only when the governments would no longer tolerate the farce. Enough was enough.

Reporting a negotiation is about so much more than what you are told. It can be about who you see, who is absent, the questions that are not answered, and what you ignore or miss – including those lines I referenced from the NIO and a spokesperson for the Tánaiste just a few days earlier. At times, silence is so much more important than words. It was Friday, 9 February 2018, the eve of Adams stepping down as Sinn Féin President, and I was at Stormont earlier than usual, and with purpose. I had taken a call the night before that included the line, 'Keep your ears open.' This was informed advice. The person who called has been a valuable source for two-plus decades, someone who has talked me through, and guided me through, some of the key developments in the peace process.

All of a sudden, in a politics that had become associated with tumbleweed and turmoil, there were questions – questions that seemed to come from out of the blue. Was there really a chance of politics and politicians climbing out of the mud and the mire of those deep Stormont trenches? Were the DUP and Sinn Féin closer to a deal than we thought, and why now? That Thursday night call – 8 February – stopped short of suggesting that an agreement was over the line, but it nonetheless was the most optimistic assessment I had heard of these negotiations. I was told, 'There is something going on – a different focused approach.'

The concern raised by my source was about the decision-making clout within the DUP – that it was Nigel Dodds at Westminster and the party team there that would have the biggest say on this, not Arlene Foster and the negotiators at Stormont. The caller shared his sense of things – that there was 'a better chance of a breakthrough'. Just hours earlier, the *Belfast Telegraph* political editor Suzanne Breen had reported a more optimistic assessment of the talks.

So, on Friday, 9 February, I made my way to Stormont to see who was about. In the canteen, I spotted one of those so-called 'shadowy figures' in one of the building's most open spaces. He is a man of few words but someone whom I knew would be across the detail of what was happening. I decided to approach him, gave him an outline of what I had heard the night before and then waited for his response. It was no comment, but then he added, 'I'm not denying it.' The few words that followed spoke of 'significant gaps' and of people being 'serious'. I asked did that mean on both sides – meaning the DUP and Sinn Féin – and he said yes. He also smiled by way of confirmation when I asked about those concerns relating to the DUP – as to whether their London and Stormont teams were on the same page. After this conversation, I tweeted that line and advice: 'keep your ears open'.

By lunchtime, there was a completely different vibe to what had become a Stormont ghost house. There was a different pulse – a sense that this dead place was being nursed back to life. A better political heartbeat. Those were my written observations of that day. The then Secretary of State Karen Bradley was in the building with Sir Jonathan Stephens and Mark Larmour, her senior NIO officials. DUP leader Arlene Foster was there with party colleagues. Many of the Sinn Féin MPs and MLAs were present; one of them told me he had been 'summoned'. The Irish government delegation was also there, and the media was now watching more closely, eyes opened as well as ears. This negotiation was, indeed, in a different place.

At times like this, you look for political intelligence – for the people capable of giving you a read from inside the talks – what I call the making of the jigsaw. You need those scraps of information that, when set alongside other detail, can begin to form a picture. What were people noticing in that upstairs corridor of Parliament Buildings, where this negotiation had been happening over a period of days?

An Ulster Unionist source spoke of Gerry Adams and Tim Johnston in a room talking. Johnston is the most significant and influential unelected figure in the DUP; his involvement in this type of negotiation dates back to 2004, when there was the first attempt – much of it at arms-length – to try to establish the first DUP–Sinn Féin executive. His opinion would be critical come any moment of decision. He was also the bridge between the party teams at Stormont and Westminster.

Special advisers from the parties had been sitting and chatting in the corridor. These were indicators of a better mood. That Friday, Labour's NI spokesperson, Owen Smith, was at Stormont. I remember speaking with him outside Parliament Buildings as Eamon Deeny and Rosemary Neill of the NIO communications team arrived; all of this was a confirmation of the gear-change within these talks. Then, there was another piece of information. Sinn Féin was 'pushing for it today' – meaning an agreement. This explained the presence of so many of their MPs and MLAs. If their negotiating team managed to get a deal over the line, then those elected representatives would begin a briefing process across the party structure, talking to the base.

A scheduled all-party and governments meeting on Friday afternoon happened without the DUP and Sinn Féin. It meant their negotiation was continuing and its detail was not yet ready to be shared. Over the next forty-eight hours, I pieced together a ballpark assessment of the negotiation and spoke with two of the DUP's most senior elected representatives – two of their London team. They had doubts that the developing agreement could be sold across the party, and they were right. 'We haven't done anything to prepare people,' one of them told me. The big standoff was still the same standoff: this battle for a stand-alone Irish Language Act.

The NIO official Sir Jonathan Stephens is credited with the formula or fix of trying to advance the Irish language issue alongside two other pieces of legislation – Ulster Scots and 'Respecting Languages and Culture'. I am told this was first rejected by Sinn Féin in the autumn of 2017 and then accepted. That had not been expected, and then, according to a talks' insider, there was 'consternation' and 'shock' within the DUP. The ball was back in their court. This was the 'NIO fudge' referenced in a piece I wrote at the time for eamonnmallie.com – further explained by a source, whom I spoke with during my research for this book: 'We were trying to square the circle; have an Irish Language Act that wasn't an Irish Language Act.' My article is from 11 February 2018 and reads as follows.

'STORMONT: IS THE GLASS HALF FULL?':

The question above is the judgement call for both the DUP and Sinn Féin. Have they enough to take this long negotiation over the line, to end the standoff and to restore the political institutions? Read the speech by the new Sinn Féin Vice President Michelle O'Neill from Saturday and this line in particular: 'As in any negotiation there has been give and take and at this point we have not yet resolved or overcome all our differences to satisfaction.' … 'The mice could still get at it,' one talks insider told this website. It is important to stress and emphasise this point and reality. There is not yet an agreement. No signing on the dotted line; but on Friday there was a different mood and pulse in that building on the political hill – a very clear sense that this negotiation was in a different and a better place. After 13 months of standoff, were we beginning to witness the first real signs of life? Remember also that there was still talk of 'significant gaps' and a job of work yet to be done to persuade people of the worth of what could emerge from these talks. 'We haven't done anything to prepare people,' a senior DUP source told this website. 'Whatever happens, it just can't be bounced on people,' another commented.

This negotiation has been as tight as a drum – not the same worry about leaks that have interrupted and disrupted other phases of these talks. So, for those of us chasing the information, piecing the jigsaw together has been a much more difficult task. The analysis is not complete. There are missing pieces. What follows is what some are suggesting is the ballpark of the discussion: That if agreement is reached DUP leader Arlene Foster will be First Minister (this has been privately understood for months and reported on this website last June). That in the event of a resignation at the top of the Executive, there will be a longer period of time – perhaps stretching into months – to resolve differences (this the sustainability issue the DUP has been emphasising). There is talk of three separate Acts – An Irish Language Act, An Ulster Scots Act and a third covering Culture and Respect … Separate from the planned legacy consultation on the Stormont House Agreement, including the proposed Historical Investigations Unit (HIU) and Independent Commission on Information Retrieval (ICIR), we watch to see if funding is released for legacy inquests and who releases it. (This, I am told, is a continuing discussion). Marriage equality may involve a private members' bill and there is still talk of a review of the Petition of Concern.

This is the talking around these talks. Is it written in Stormont stone? No one is saying that, nor is anyone so certain of success to be trumpeting agreement. Instead, there is the anxious wait now to see if that better sense of the negotiation – in terms of mood and substance and seriousness – can be developed to its next stage. On the languages scenario set out above, one DUP source described it as an 'NIO fudge' – 'there as an item for consideration' – whether acceptable to his party is another question. He had this advice for his colleagues: 'Don't pretend it's something it's not. Then the cover-up gets you, not the content.' In other words, don't pretend that this is not a stand-alone Irish Language Act: 'That wouldn't survive five seconds on Nolan [the Nolan Show on Radio Ulster].'

> This website has been told that in a briefing within the past fortnight, Sinn Féin told representatives of the Irish language community that it would insist 'on an Irish Language Act of substance'. So, any emerging agreement will be read for that detail and for what has been achieved or not achieved on this and on a range of other issues. What is the balance of the give and take? Sinn Féin knows it will have some convincing and persuading to do – that a number of issues have not been progressed to the point of expectations. It was never going to get everything – this the reality of any negotiation … After months of stalemate, there is a last chance for Stormont. Can new light get through those old windows?

As outlined in that piece, the fact that, as far back as June 2017, Sinn Féin was prepared to work in an executive with Arlene Foster, depending on the detail and outcome of this negotiation, tells us that the Stormont collapse was about more than the RHI fallout. In that piece, I also published a tweet from Ian Paisley Jr, the DUP MP – a response to the Michelle O'Neill speech that, in a few words and in a pointed question, said a lot, 'No doubt many will ask who is giving and who is taking?'

A weekend is a very long time in Stormont politics, and it was obvious to me that the mice were indeed getting at whatever agreement might be emerging. Over the weekend, there was news that Prime Minister Theresa May and Taoiseach Leo Varadkar would be at Stormont on Monday. It added to the speculation, to the drama, and it also contributed significantly to the unease of those within the DUP not sighted on the detail of the latest drafting within this negotiation. The draft agreement would unravel. On his blog, Gerry Adams wrote the following, 'The British PM's visit was a clumsy intervention. A visit to Bombardier because there was a convenient recess at Westminster. A visit to the talks was an add-on. Michelle [O'Neill] insisted the Taoiseach needed to be there also. So he was.'

On Monday morning, 12 February, in the Great Hall at Parliament Buildings, one of the DUP's most senior MLAs sat beside me. He, like others, was waiting to see or hear the outline of the developing

DUP–Sinn Féin text that I had been writing about and discussing on radio – that is, about the detail I was aware of at this time. He told me the party officers were in the building, that MLAs were still waiting to be briefed and that he did not expect a deal today. He also told me that he wanted to see something in the text that 'hurts' Sinn Féin: 'If not, count me out.'

What he meant by that comment was that his party could not be humiliated in any agreement. There had to be pain for Sinn Féin, as well – not a republican victory after their decision to collapse the institutions a year previously. He said the previous week he had advised his party leader, Arlene Foster, that people needed to be told what was happening.

What I knew of the text at this time did not suggest a winners and losers type agreement but more a compromise. Even that can be difficult in the politics and the psyche of 'not an inch'. The weight of that compromise would prove too much for the DUP. Within days, these talks would collapse – ending abruptly in a statement tweeted on the DUP leader's account. This, however, would not be the last word on this phase of the negotiation. Developments over the next number of days would end in proof of a draft agreement.

The negotiation collapsed on Wednesday, 14 February 2018. From inside the DUP, I was being kept informed of developments. That morning, in a phone conversation, one of the party's MPs described the talks as 'dead – totally dead'. This was confirmed at 4 p.m. in that statement on the Twitter account of Arlene Foster: 'In our view there is no current prospect of these discussions leading to an Executive being formed.' On the issue of Irish language, the statement added:

> Despite our best efforts, serious and significant gaps remain between ourselves and Sinn Féin especially on the issue of the Irish language. I have made it consistently clear that unionists will not countenance a stand-alone or free-standing Irish Language Act. Sinn Féin's insistence on a stand-alone Irish Language Act means that we have reached an impasse … At the moment, we do not have a fair and balanced package.

At the time, I was in the Great Hall at Parliament Buildings. Kevin Conmy – the Irish joint secretary of the British–Irish Secretariat – was standing nearby and asked about the content of the statement. In what they were seeing and hearing away from the public stage, the governments knew these talks were failing. Now, this development was the confirmation of the DUP's exit from the negotiation. It was 4 p.m. on St Valentine's Day and all was not well. The DUP MP, whom I spoke with on the telephone that morning, sent a text. Two words: 'Told you.'

Eamon Deeny – director of communications at the NIO – turned back from an appointment and made his way to Parliament Buildings. Because of an urgent family matter, Secretary of State Karen Bradley needed to get back home. There was discussion about whether she should speak to the media before leaving. She made some brief comments. After 5 p.m., there was also a statement from Michelle O'Neill, the Vice President of Sinn Féin, which included, 'We had reached an accommodation with the leadership of the DUP. The DUP failed to close the deal. They have now collapsed this process. These issues are not going away. Sinn Féin are now in contact with both governments and we will set out our considered position tomorrow. The DUP should reflect on their position.'

Arlene Foster did not appear at a party news conference that evening. There was a big question to answer on the DUP's explanation of the collapse of these talks. How, after such a prolonged period of negotiation, could there be such different interpretations of the text that had travelled back and forward between the parties? This was a day of missing pieces – a day when the DUP leadership hid behind that four o'clock statement. It felt like they bottled it, buckled at the moment of decision. Why else would you leave the scene? Just days earlier, this negotiation was a page-turn from agreement. During my research for this book, a talks insider commented, 'The failure of 2018 [was that] Arlene Foster didn't have the leadership to bring her party over the line. She was abandoned by Nigel [Dodds].' Both Foster and Dodds denied there was an agreement.

The DUP got away with it because of that London arrangement with the Tories. Any other time, they may well have been called out. Then, they made a mistake. Across a number of interviews, senior party figures dismissed suggestions that an accommodation had been reached within the talks – what Sinn Féin President Mary Lou McDonald had described, on Thursday, 15 February, as a 'draft agreement'.

Arlene Foster told Sky News correspondent David Blevins there was never any power-sharing deal on the table that she could ask colleagues to support. And the party's Westminster leader, Nigel Dodds, issued a statement describing the 'Sinn Féin propaganda machine in full flow'. 'Everyone knows the DUP would never agree to anything which could be described as a stand-alone or free-standing Irish Language Act where one culture is given supremacy over another.'

On Saturday, 17 February, I wrote a piece on eamonnmallie.com exploring this description of a draft agreement. I wrote that it was a document of a dozen pages or more – plus annexes and separate commitments, including on legacy-related matters. Three days later, that thirteen-page paper was given to my colleague Eamonn Mallie. There was a build-up – another interview by one of the DUP's MPs, Sir Jeffrey Donaldson, that again dismissed any suggestion that the party's negotiators had signed up for an Irish Language Act. A source I spoke with that morning said, 'He's going into very dangerous territory. Jeffrey has created a dynamic for publication [of the document].' I did not know that we were just hours away from that happening.

That afternoon, Tuesday, 20 February 2018, I met with Eamonn Mallie in my hometown of Holywood. By now, he had the paper, and in a quiet corner of an ice cream shop on the High Street, we sat and shaped a news script that, by teatime, would bring this story back into the headlines – the story of a thirteen-page draft agreement that had that outline I had reported nine days earlier, including the three elements of a language and culture package and the additional time to rescue Stormont in the event of any future resignation at the top of the executive. The importance of the document was not that it gave us new information about the proposed agreement but that the paper existed.

We also reported that we had definitive proof that on Friday evening, 9 February, named senior Sinn Féin and DUP personnel were corresponding under the heading 'Draft Agreement Text'. This included members of the DUP negotiating team. We later published that proof. So, there were pages of fine detail on 9 February, but just five days later, the talks collapsed. How could there have been such misunderstanding at such a late stage? Arlene Foster had given a hard copy of the document to Michelle O'Neill, and later, a slightly tweaked updated version was emailed from the DUP negotiating team to Sinn Féin under the subject heading 'Draft Agreement Text'.

Eamonn Mallie was travelling to the United States the following day for a conference organised by the peace-building project Co-operation Ireland (also attended by Simon Coveney and Ian Paisley Jnr) So, I handled a series of television and radio interviews that began on Tuesday night and continued through to the BBC and Ulster Television news programmes at teatime on Wednesday, 21 February. That evening, I listened as Arlene Foster attempted, unconvincingly, to downplay the significance of this document and to make it go away:

> We weren't contemplating bringing in an Irish Language Act ... If you look at the so-called Draft Agreement, that's only one of a number of documents that were circulated and put out and about. And, I think, the important thing is that we now reflect on where we got to in relation to all those issues.

The DUP leader's words and sentences were like shovels digging deeper. This document had emerged because its existence had been denied. In any negotiation, the latest paper becomes the most relevant. These documents were not 'out and about' but inside the tightest of cordons, restricted to the DUP and Sinn Féin negotiators. The two governments, of course, would have had a detailed understanding of the negotiation. The text obtained by Mallie was not one of a number of documents but rather *the* document – last updated by the DUP. That party's correspondence with Sinn Féin on 9 February was under the heading 'Draft Agreement Text', no mention of 'so-called'.

Days earlier, one of the DUP's MPs told me that beyond the 9 February text, 'there was to be an agreement on presentation – not to hurt'. In other words, it would be presented by both parties in a way that would not hurt the other. It didn't get that far. On that weekend it began to unravel. I asked was Arlene Foster damaged. My source replied, 'I'm not surprised you're being asked that question.'

By now, it was clear that the DUP negotiators at Stormont had been overruled. 'They got trapped in the process and lost the wider view,' another of the party's MPs later told me. 'They weren't listening.' At this time, Westminster was an easier and safer place for the DUP. They were enjoying those London lights and that higher stage. The March 2017 assembly election had been a disaster. Why, in those circumstances, would they risk anything that could be interpreted as conceding – why would they give an Irish Language Act to Sinn Féin. For all the wordplays in those documents that travelled back and forward, they had not managed to wrap that piece of legislation in enough layers to hide its real appearance. So, Stormont would have to wait. What makes the 'draft agreement' description even more convincing is this – that when a deal was eventually achieved in January 2020, the New Decade, New Approach agreement had its roots and shape in that disputed paper of February 2018.

CHAPTER 8

Stormont breakfast – 'tell me more'

Eventually, things change. It would take almost a further two years to end that gridlock at Stormont – but we know now that people were moving, both in their thinking and in their voting. A number of elections in 2019 changed the political landscape and dynamic, both in London and in Belfast. There was both a mood and a message in the votes – a confirmation in Northern Ireland, or the North, of the rejection of Brexit and, in a wider frame, a protest against what Stormont had become, which was a complete mockery of what functioning politics and government are meant to be. The political sin was the failure of the British government not to shut the building down once it became clear that the institutions would not quickly be restored.

By the summer of 2019, Julian Smith had arrived in Northern Ireland as the new Secretary of State, determined, in his words, 'to up the ante and the pace'. He brought two young advisers with him, Lilah Howson-Smith and Ross Easton. They played significant parts in the developing story; neither of them was stewed or steeped in the politics or the problems of this place. Within a short time, we began to notice something different. They broadened the conversation, and that team started to make things happen. They had no emotional attachment to this place, and they were not of the conflict generation.

They were helped, of course, by the dramatic election results of December 2019. At last, there was a chance to move things. The governments – not the parties – were in charge. There would be a deal or there would be an assembly election. Deal or no deal, I believed that election should have happened. The mandates dating back to 2017 were old, out of date and did not reflect or represent that new mood among voters. An election would have rearranged the Stormont numbers and furniture. One other key factor was the working relationship that would develop between Smith and Simon Coveney. They would lead this negotiation and decide its endpoint.

On Friday, 30 August 2019, there was an opportunity, over coffee, for a few minutes of conversation with the new Northern Ireland Secretary. A media breakfast had been arranged, and in the spacious Conference Room at Stormont House, I waited on my turn for the chance of a few words. Smith – appointed to this job just a few weeks earlier, in July, as part of Boris Johnson's first cabinet – was working his way round the room, pausing for conversation with the groups of journalists present. I was with the BBC correspondents Gareth Gordon and John Campbell and the *News Letter* political editor Sam McBride when he arrived into our company with Rosemary Neill, chief communications officer at the NIO. I waited a few moments and then interjected with a comment along the lines, 'I take it we're not here for a cosy chat'. I then said his department was part of the problem. Smith's response was, tell me more.

What I meant was this: that the NIO was a hostage – perhaps a willing hostage – of that Tory–DUP arrangement at Westminster. As a consequence, it now, more than ever, was viewed with suspicion – even more a player on the unionist side. Certainly not a facilitator. The consequence of this was that since 2017 the talks had been stretched like elastic through numerous deadlines. In this purgatory of politics, there was no clock big enough and no calendar long enough. Days become weeks, then months, then years. Up to now, the talks had failed to find the means and the methods – the will – to remake the political institutions, although, as outlined in the previous chapter, they had come close to doing so in February 2018. Smith would learn from the mistakes of that period.

He, of course, knew the DUP – knew, from his time as Government Chief Whip at Westminster, their importance in that perilous numbers game there. He knew that the confidence and supply agreement gave them a lot of sway and that it would be difficult to dislocate that arrangement in London from the talks in Belfast. For now, they were inextricably linked: the two sides of the one mess – the Brexit standoff and the stalemate at Stormont. Smith, who had that impossible task of trying to get the numbers to work at Westminster, had now been handed the poisoned chalice of this place. He took it willingly and would make a good fist of his time here. One of his special advisers remembers those early days and weeks – the working out of the ways and the geography of this place.

LILAH HOWSON-SMITH:

Our first few days in Northern Ireland were spent travelling from Belfast to Derry-Londonderry – meeting people, understanding the geography of the place, and weighing up the consequences of three years of no government. But none of this really prepared us for a July of staid meetings with the parties in Stormont House. At times, these negotiations could not have felt more remote from the encounters we had during the rest of our time in Northern Ireland.

At the end of July, the parties met Julian and the Tánaiste individually with what felt like long shopping lists of demands and even longer references to documents we were not yet familiar with. Detailed descriptions of what had come before were regularly followed by recriminations about other parties' conduct. That summer, in particular, we were delivered almost childish accounts of who had taken a holiday when and who had told who what. Julian would normally seek to push past these moments, seeing them for what they often were: theatrics. He wanted to acknowledge the genuine issues dividing them, while not accepting a rehash of the last three years as the premise for future discussions. We slowly attempted to inject humour and pragmatism in a way that was often uncomfortable, and frequently unwanted. Talks took Julian and me to conference centres in Manchester, cafes in Dublin, a launch event in East London, and a constituency office in North Belfast, but most surprising was the party leaders' inability to meet by themselves. If we were outsiders only beginning to form our own relationships, we were certainly at a loss at how to get the parties to forge their own bonds.

We understood that their pride was borne out of a desire of mutual respect, a crucial part of the story of power sharing ... but power sharing now required them to turn a new page on those same fractured relationships. This seemed near impossible to achieve through a series of set piece meetings at Stormont. During those first couple of months, we were most comforted by the difference we felt when we met with MLAs or MPs in their own constituencies. At town halls, hospitals, charity buildings and hospices we saw the appetite to solve problems and actually govern, that was so frequently absent from the early months of the talks process. In fact, in these meetings it was surprisingly difficult to get the politicians to discuss the sticking points that had apparently preoccupied negotiations for months – instead regional underachievement, funding for new universities and health reform rightly took centre stage. In the end, it was these real-life concerns that would bring an end to a prolonged period of negotiations.

In those words, you can picture eyes rolling inside those talks – a negotiation of demands and documents that had been recycled more times than the yoghurt pots and milk containers in our bins. The issue of legacy was one such example, with reports and proposals dating back to 2009 and stretching from there through every other phase of this process.

I said something about this at that Friday breakfast in August 2019 – my often-stated position of the need for an amnesty. This is not to suggest some trite drawing of a line; it is to suggest using a statute of limitations across the board to enable a meaningful truth or information process alongside the best practical help for those hurt during the conflict years. I have said many times that you cannot have a peace process that releases prisoners and then a past process that includes jail. That type of U-turn creates all sorts of problems. It contradicts and undermines the peace and political agreements that have taken us to this point.

In the few weeks before the breakfast, I had been back at the BBC compiling television reports twenty-five years after the ceasefire announcements of 1994 – not a look back to that time, but more an assessment of progress since. The scaffolding supporting the political institutions had collapsed. The past was a gaping wound. Brexit had energised the 'New Ireland' conversation. Lord Robin Eames, the retired Church of Ireland Archbishop, had helped deliver the loyalist ceasefire of the 1990s – built, then, on the solid ground of the Union. But what about now? I asked him, could he with any confidence, in 2019, say that the Union is safe: 'I would like to say it is, but I believe that there are danger signs, which I think we all need to be conscious of.'

My reports for the BBC were on 28–29 August 2019. So, I arrived at that breakfast with Smith with these thoughts in my mind: that we were in a political war, a legacy war and the 'Battle of Brexit' – with the border poll conversation louder in our ears. It still felt like the gridlock of 2017. Yet, the results of an election before the end of the year would begin to allow some of the traffic to flow again. Smith, with Coveney, would make sure it moved.

My first impression of Smith was that he was different – a better different from those who had preceded him in the Northern Ireland Office. 'He's the best Tory we've had here in a long time,' is how one of the Northern Ireland party leaders described him. We could all see that he was much more involved, was clearly comfortable in company and conversation. And we watched during his short time here as he tried to make this negotiation a 'personal discussion'. He took it outside the Stormont bubble, wanting to speak with and hear from others.

There were no secrets about what had to be resolved, no new big item on the agenda. Talks of this duration, running through those two-plus-years, become a copy-and-paste type process. Like cogging homework, you can play with the words. Smith speaks of a text that had been 'bobbing around'. Weeks before he and his team arrived, I had read the latest papers. A talks insider had shared documents with me in mid-May, and again on 12 June 2019. That day, I switched my phone off for several hours and travelled outside Belfast to pick up the papers. Leaks had become an issue – something I had been told had already been raised at a leaders' meeting just days earlier.

At Stormont, I sensed the nervousness – the reluctance of a number of politicians to be seen in my company. In the sandwich queue in the canteen, one took a few steps back for fear of being accused of disclosing information about the talks, 'inappropriately,' she added. Others were much more relaxed. It all becomes a distraction. If you can waste time talking about leaks, you can avoid having to make the decisions that matter.

That June batch of papers gave us an idea of how they were trying to shape a summer agreement after the winter attempt the previous year. There were a number of interesting lines, including on the Irish language: 'This paper deliberately focuses on the possible content of legislation, as opposed to the form of legislation that might be agreed in the context of an overall agreement. It is assumed that discussions on form would follow any broad agreement on content.'

The Sinn Féin position was clear. It wanted a stand-alone Irish Language Act. But I was told if the party persisted with that demand, then this negotiation would flounder. Our politics can be so pathetic. The negotiation would eventually deliver the content that you would expect to see in an Irish Language Act, but it had to be called something else – a bit like telling someone that your cat is your dog. This was a shift in the negotiation, a turn in the words and one of the moves towards agreement.

The June 2019 papers also described a party leaders' forum – as a safe space to discuss ongoing issues and give early warning on matters that might cause future political tension or disagreement. In the February 2018 draft agreement, we read of a coalition management committee that would manage areas of disagreement and seek the resolution of any disputes which might arise between executive parties. Here, again, there was mention of an 'early warning system'.

As these papers develop, so old thinking becomes the new proposals under reworked headings. Richard Haass, in his phase of negotiations in 2013 (on flags, parades and the past), spoke of 'ideas that ripen in the public marketplace', while, at that time, Meghan O'Sullivan described a negotiation that had grown from an already 'well developed conversation'. By the time Julian Smith arrived, it had developed and dithered over the course of a further six years. Of course, the talks he would be involved in would have a much wider agenda than the Haass/O'Sullivan negotiation. Brick by brick, it was about trying to rebuild confidence and trust in politics; and not just inside that Stormont bubble, but outside it as well.

Before Smith arrived at Stormont House, one of the numerous phases of negotiation had begun in the spring. The parties had been pressured or pushed back into talks. This followed the dissident IRA murder of a young journalist in Derry – a shooting that happened on Thursday, 18 April 2019. Just hours earlier, I had spoken about the dangers of dwelling in the past – something I wrote about a couple of days later, on 20 April, on eamonnmallie.com.

'IT'S TOO LATE WHEN SOMEONE IS DEAD':

That young face on the front page of every newspaper is a grim reminder – the confirmation of our unfinished peace and of a distance still to travel. I didn't know Lyra McKee, but in my reading of the past couple of days, I know more about her now. She was just 29 – a journalist hit by a bullet fired by a dissident IRA gunman during a riot in Derry. Reporting in the madness of these street battles comes with so much danger. There is no such thing as a safe place to observe or stand.

Just hours before the shooting, I spoke with veteran journalist Deric Henderson at an event in my hometown of Holywood – the theme of the conversation 'Reporting the Troubles' taken from the title of the book co-edited by Henderson and Ivan Little. I spoke these words: 'We as "the conflict generation" are shovelling our experience on the people who come behind us. So, I hear young people talking about things they could only have heard from us, and we need to think about the damage we're doing in all of that.' I asked how do we do the right thing in terms of some legacy process: 'How do we stop shovelling that experience on top of others? That's what I meant [when I said earlier] if we don't do something, we're going to bury ourselves and them in the conflict period.'

Just hours later, Lyra McKee was dead. Like many, I read the news in disbelief. This is 2019 – 25 years after the ceasefires of 1994 – and the headlines are about the murder of a young woman; a story illustrated in the pictures of rioting, petrol bombs, burning vehicles and gunfire. Who directed that riot in Derry – manipulated the young people in that situation and ordered a gunman on to that stage? There are those who can't live with the 'peace' and, so, people have to die – on this night, and in this place, it was Lyra McKee.

Political leaders issued a joint statement and came to speak with and stand with the people of the Creggan. In this, there is hope; some light in the darkness that, perhaps this time, those many dissident organisations might go away – because they have been shamed into doing so. We witnessed such a retreat after the Omagh bomb in 1998. Yet, there can be no certainty about this. Denis Bradley, who co-chaired the first legacy consultation process here more than a decade ago, is right: 'Those hopes have been raised before and have been dashed before.' He was writing in the *Irish Times*, writing with all the experience of years of watching and listening.

There is no security or intelligence initiative that will extinguish the dissident threat. In my opinion, MI5 is part of the problem, their continuing presence on the security landscape providing part of the excuse that dissidents use when arguing that nothing has changed. For years, I have said there is a need for an initiative in which the nationalist leadership speaks directly with the dissidents; a joined-up initiative that needs the weight of Irish Government involvement, the political and church leaderships and those of community influence, including the GAA. The purpose and focus of any such dialogue should be a demand that says, Stop.

More than 30 years ago, John Hume made that same demand of the IRA. People, including journalists, suggested he was wasting his time, but he with others succeeded in delivering the ceasefire and in shaping the political process that gave us the Good Friday

Agreement. Those joined up political and policing steps taken on Friday are important, but they are not enough. There is no time for waiting. It is too late when someone is dead, and already it is too late for Lyra. As for any legacy process, what should its principal purpose be – to ensure that the conflict is not repeated, that it never happens again.

Days later, on 24 April, Prime Minister Theresa May, Taoiseach Leo Varadkar, Irish President Michael D. Higgins, Tánaiste Simon Coveney, Secretary of State Karen Bradley and the Northern Ireland party leaders attended the funeral at St Anne's Cathedral in Belfast. Fr Martin Magill commended those who stood together with the community in Creggan in Derry on Good Friday. Then, there was a standing ovation, when, with biting words, he asked, 'Why in God's name does it take the death of a 29-year-old woman with her whole life in front of her to get us to this point?' Before the funeral, Magill had discussed those words with the former Methodist President Harold Good, from whom he had asked some advice. When writing this book, I asked Fr Magill to think back on that period and to share his thoughts here.

FATHER MARTIN MAGILL:

I couldn't believe it when listening to the radio news on Good Friday morning, 19 April 2019, to hear that Lyra McKee had been killed the previous evening in Derry. I had met Lyra on a number of occasions and had last heard from her a few weeks previously. Later that afternoon I was contacted by a member of Lyra's family to ask if I would take part in her funeral service.

In preparing for Lyra's funeral in St Anne's Cathedral, I was in regular contact with Dean Stephen Forde who invited me to give a reflection. On Easter Sunday afternoon Stephen and I called to the wake for Lyra and spent time with her family to prepare for the service. Over the following days, Stephen and I were in daily contact. In the latter part of Easter Monday, he was able to tell me that a number of political leaders were planning to attend the funeral. It was now becoming clear that this would be a very different funeral to those at which I normally officiate.

Magill is always tuned in to the peace process. He is well informed, watches closely, keeps in contact. So, he knows the dissident republican threat. We hear him speaking out on the so-called punishment beatings and shootings, on that sick street justice that has never been eradicated. He has been in some of those parishes of north and west Belfast where people still wait for peace to arrive. And he has a network of contacts and friends across the communities. Alongside the Presbyterian minister Steve Stockman and a wider committee, he is an organiser of Belfast's Four Corners Festival. It is what its title suggests – a programme of events that stretches and reaches out across the city and encourages difficult and challenging conversations.

FATHER MARTIN MAGILL:

With the daily media coverage of Lyra's death and lead up to the service, I decided to take advice from some trusted friends about what I should say. On Easter Monday evening, I rang Rev Harold Good and asked if he were in my position what would he say. Harold suggested a question – 'why in the name of God does it take the death of a young woman to bring our politicians to stand together?' This was a reference to the political leaders of the local parties standing side by side in the Creggan in Derry, close to where Lyra had been shot.

Harold Good is someone I know well, and someone to whom many turn for advice. He was one of the churchmen who began the early exploration of the possibilities for peace in direct conversation with republican leaders; he became a friend of Martin McGuinness and spoke at his funeral. Good, also, is tuned-in, and he will have known the importance of that question he suggested to Magill – the grit within it, particularly at a time of political standoff and growing disillusionment with Stormont. The funeral was an opportunity to speak directly to those who would have to try to lift politics up again.

FATHER MARTIN MAGILL:

By Easter Tuesday afternoon, Stephen and I now knew that Prime Minister Theresa May as well as President Michael D Higgins and An Taoiseach Leo Varadkar were all planning to attend Lyra's funeral along with the leaders of the local parties in Northern Ireland. In writing the address, conscious of the influential congregation, I decided to address several issues including how young people were still being recruited into paramilitary organisations, quoting one of Lyra's friends who powerfully made the point that the young people in deprived areas needed jobs, education and training and not a gun put in their hands. I also chose to address some of the underlying conditions which made it easier for the recruitment of young people by referencing the first report of the Independent Reporting Commission which had examined in depth paramilitary style attacks and found a clear correlation between these attacks and areas of social deprivation. Aware also from Dean Stephen Forde that the service was being streamed I raised the contentious issue of 'touting' and encouraged those with information about Lyra's killing to bring it forward.

When I stood up to give my address, I had no idea about the reaction I would get. I was taken aback when the applause started and people began to stand up. I wasn't aware how the politicians were reacting because I was trying to work out how I would continue with the rest of my address. I kept asking myself as the applause continued: 'now what do I do?' and 'how am I going to finish the rest of what I had written?' After silence returned to the cathedral, I repeated a few words and continued with the rest of the address.

You see in the pictures from inside the Cathedral that, momentarily, the politicians paused as they also worked out what to do. They were lifted to their feet by that response from around them and, within a fortnight, they were back in talks.

The date for that spring phase of negotiations was set for 7 May 2019, preceded by local elections that changed the face of Belfast City Council. Alliance was the story, its success summarised in the lines of a tweet by party leader Naomi Long: 'Best election in 42 years, 11.6 per cent of the vote, 53 seats and representation on ten out of eleven councils.' At the time, party deputy leader Stephen Farry spoke to me of multiple reasons behind this surge, including 'people re-assessing who they are post-Brexit'. Within weeks, Long would be the headline in the European election, and before the year was done, Farry was one of the big stories of the general election. In May, the Green Party also had a good set of results – nothing like the success of Alliance, but eight councillors elected, including four in Belfast.

The DUP and Sinn Féin were still the 'big two' parties with 100-plus seats each across the councils. So, any deal would still depend on them. The DUP was arguing for the immediate restoration of the political institutions and talks in parallel. Sinn Féin insisted on the negotiations happening first. So, these new talks were happening on old ground – the choice, in the words of one source, 'politics or a wasteland'. There would be working groups and more of those recycled papers dressed up in new words. There was nothing certain about these talks, nothing certain about Stormont and nothing certain about anything within our politics at this time.

In late May, there was another big moment in the result of the European election. There were three seats in Northern Ireland – two of them, to this point, the property of unionists. This time Naomi Long (with 18.5 per cent of first preference votes) took a seat; she was elected with Diane Dodds of the DUP and Martina Anderson of Sinn Féin. The numbers and names told the story of the consequences of Brexit. As Green Party leader Clare Bailey explains, it has broken the voting mould:

By the time of the European elections in 2019 people had begun to take this as an opportunity to make themselves heard. Young and old had mobilised campaign groups to return anti-Brexit MEPs and the result was a stunning victory for the Alliance Party returning their first ever MEP. NI now had 2 out of the 3 MEP seats held by anti-Brexit parties. It is hard to put into words the sense of jubilation across NI as people, quite rightly, owned this as their victory. This was following the local council elections a few weeks earlier. The results from that election caused more rumbles where we saw the electorate vote for new candidates and expand political representation particularly on the left and the middle ground.

The European election was the most tactical and thought-through that I had witnessed in my lifetime – the working out in the heads of voters how to get a second Remain candidate elected. We knew that Anderson and Dodds would be safe. All the talk was about that third seat. Could it be won by Long or the SDLP leader, Colum Eastwood? The Ulster Unionist vote collapsed; it was the first time since 1979 that the party failed to win a seat. The surge in the local elections of the non-aligned/other vote was becoming a trend – something that would be further confirmed late in 2019. There is, of course, a wider significance. On their own, neither Orange nor Green can win any border poll. The result will be determined by this third block – its mood and mind on that question of Union versus unity whenever a vote occurs.

The developing and fascinating story of 2019 was the price that was being paid for the deadlock at Stormont – and also for Brexit. The council, European and general elections were three chapters coming together to tell a story of change. One significant result can be dismissed as some protest vote, but this was different. It was a trend that continued through all three sets of results. The political ground was shifting and this place was moving beyond its story of two tribes. Come December, Alliance deputy leader Stephen Farry would be elected as an MP. Here, I have asked him to share his thoughts on what was a remarkable breakthrough year for his party.

STEPHEN FARRY:

There has always been people in Northern Ireland that did not fit or moved away from the traditional binary conceptions of identity in the 'two traditions' or 'two communities'. Today, more and more people are expressing open, mixed and multiple identities. This is especially prevalent amongst young people. The acceleration of this trend and the Alliance electoral growth over the past decade including the surge of 2019 align with each other but don't entirely overlap. That Alliance success also reflects successfully channelling frustrations around the politics of deadlock and delay around the prolonged Stormont impasse, and the desire to see change, reform and delivery, and having called Brexit correctly. The party also adopted a stance on Brexit that was in tune with the majority opinion in Northern Ireland. Some of these factors may prove to be time specific and therefore point to a need to avoid complacency and refresh and update our message. Nevertheless, the party has proven that in a political context usually framed around the constitutional question and a clash of identities that a liberal and cross community party can not only survive but flourish.

Alliance had waited a very long time for these results; then, like buses, three arrived almost at the same time. In their voting, a growing and significant number of people had bought tickets for a different journey, the destination of which is still not clear. We often talk about the 'big two' parties, but there is now a growing third party – much more obvious and relevant in the picture, and on the heels of that 'big two'.

STEPHEN FARRY:

The central message remains building reconciliation and creating an integrated society, based on fairness, rights and equality. This cannot be an inward-looking project. Alliance is conscious of calls for wider change across these islands. We recognise that Brexit and other factors have energised the debate around the constitutional question. Given the nature of Alliance, some may suggest that this would be a particular challenge. But on the contrary, these are debates in which we can engage with confidence. Alliance is not a party that is defined by the constitutional question. But we are not an amalgamation of unionists and nationalists in an uneasy co-existence. While there may be some members who prefer the union, and some who prefer a united Ireland and indeed many who are open to persuasion, we are not only united, but defined, by our shared commitment to make this society work, to overcome division and to build a better future.

We don't believe that there is currently the case for a border poll, and nor are we pursuing one, but we do recognise that there is a very fluid situation and multiple active debates are underway, not only about a united or agreed Ireland but also the future nature and shape of the union of the United Kingdom. We can with confidence, and without prejudice to any outcome, engage in civilised, rational and evidence-based discussions. Propositions need to be tested and at times challenged, and other concepts and mechanisms need to be much more developed. In all respects, we will be guided by our vision and values and always advocate what we think is right for Northern Ireland. The voices of that widening centre ground may well prove pivotal in determining the future direction of travel and any change.

This is the key point: such is its influence now, that third block will have a critical role in determining the future direction of travel. Some in our politics have not yet wakened up to this new reality.

STEPHEN FARRY:

While Alliance fully acknowledges and respects the framework for constitutional change under the Good Friday Agreement, it may be opportune to consider other outcomes beyond a binary choice that reflect the shared and interdependent nature of a diverse Northern Ireland and respect the web of relationships across these islands. And without prejudice to the possibility of political and constitutional change, there is considerable scope to radically upscale the nature of practical co-operation across the island on social, economic and environmental issues. This can give practical effect to a shared Ireland. On top of that the outworking of the Ireland/Northern Ireland Protocol under Brexit may reshape the nature of interactions on the island. Wherever lines are drawn on maps, promoting reconciliation and developing a more integrated society remain the core challenges for this place, and in turn the spirit of partnership and co-operation across these islands, built on the Good Friday Agreement, must be preserved and indeed enhanced.

Those spring negotiations continued into the summer, towards July, and then into another row at that time about the seriousness of the talks. Away from Stormont, golf offered some better headlines. For a few days, 'The Open' championship at Royal Portrush became the story from this place and of this place – how it can shine. Rory McIlroy, described in commentary by Paul McGinley as the brightest in the class but with a tendency to daydream, failed to make the cut. The occasion got the better of him. Shane Lowry was the story of the championship – an Irish winner of this prestigious title in a week when politics was forgotten.

Within days, the new Conservative Party leader, Boris Johnson, was in Downing Street and Julian Smith was here. Before then, there had been some chatter about a possible deal – that the DUP, including the party's Chief Executive, Tim Johnston, were more seriously engaged with Sinn Féin. I checked to see if the Stormont statues were moving. If they were, it was not obvious. We were still some months away from a breakthrough.

That 'something different' that I had sensed in my first conversation with Julian Smith was something that others would soon share with me as part of their observations. Importantly, he knew his high rank and position in this negotiation – that he had to take control and charge of it and, somehow, turn this talking shop into a deal. I was hearing that he was more engaged, that he was not a Boris cheerleader (something that would become clear), that he was intelligent, that he gets it, that he cared and that he was genuinely sound.

We were now in October 2019, in that weekend that would stretch from Friday, 11 October to Sunday, 13 October – this end date marking 1,000 days without government at Stormont. This is what I meant when I wrote earlier about no calendar being long enough – those 1,000 days becoming the story of misery, suffering and the pathetic nature of politics in purgatory. That weekend, I followed a series of Smith tweets in which he described positive discussions and constructive meetings with various political leaders. One of those tweets referenced an enjoyable late-night meeting in Derry/Londonderry with the SDLP leader Colum Eastwood. They had a few pints together upstairs in the Grand Central Bar, owned by Eastwood's wife, Rachael. Lilah Howson-Smith was also there. Eastwood poured the pints – a brew exclusive to the pub. Its brand name is 'Dopey Dick', the nickname given to an orca whale that lost itself in the River Foyle in 1977. This is another example of that 'different' that I described earlier – part of Smith's ability to step outside the usual frames of negotiation and step inside spaces that are much less formal.

COLUM EASTWOOD:

One Friday afternoon in October I got a WhatsApp message from Julian Smith. That wasn't odd for Julian. But I've dealt with a few Secretaries of State and he's the first one to give me his mobile number. From the outset, I got the sense from him that he wanted to understand this place. He was in a hurry to make progress. Our engagement with him felt very different. So, he messaged me to see if I was free later for a drink. That was definitely different.

We arranged to meet in my wife's pub, The Grand Central Bar, in Derry. I got there early to see who was around. You wouldn't know who you would find in there on a Friday night. Then came two guys in Barbour jackets. I knew straight away who they were. So, I brought them upstairs. I advised them that the best place for a British Secretary of State to drink in Derry city centre was probably upstairs in the lounge, out of the way. They readily agreed. When Julian arrived, I brought him and his advisor, Lilah, upstairs and I started pouring the pints.

In his opening thoughts, Eastwood also writes of a 'different' Secretary of State, and of someone in a hurry to make progress. This was something that became part of the conversation in those early months of Smith's term – that with him involved, there was at least a chance that the negotiations would get somewhere. He was a deal-maker, and not someone here to drag his heels or allow anyone else to do so.

COLUM EASTWOOD:

The latest Brexit deadline was close and there was a sense that there would be a financial package for Northern Ireland as a result. He didn't need any help in understanding the potentially devastating impact of Brexit on Northern Ireland and he was prepared to ruffle feathers in his own government to try to get them to realise it too. We talked about Brexit. We talked about the circumstances that could encourage a return to Stormont and we talked about the need for a new devolved government to begin delivering for places like Derry. I had a list of asks. I always do, and he seemed willing to push for some of them in the talks.

Many of the policy objectives that ended up in New Decade, New Approach [published in January 2020] were discussed that night. He immediately grasped the significance of the potential for change that an expanded Magee University could have. To his credit, he supported our position on the proposed Medical School for Magee in the talks. He also made provision for financial support for a new addiction centre run by Northlands.

I was grateful that we seemed to have a listening ear from a British Secretary of State for some of our key policy asks, but, more importantly, I was encouraged that we had someone in that position interested in trying to understand how this place works. He was getting out of the comfort zone that most Secretaries of State stay within. He was trying to understand where nationalists were coming from and I appreciated that. He was also trying to go downstairs to the packed bar to listen to the singer/songwriter who was playing. I politely explained to him that he had a bit of learning to do yet if he thought that was a good idea.

There is a Friday night ordinariness about all of this, especially in this place – that mix of a pint and talking politics. Yet it was not ordinary at all. It was a reaching out from that problem place that the Northern Ireland Office had become – steps being taken by Smith and his new team that recognised that it is in building relationships that work gets done; also recognising the different parts of the Northern Ireland community. In conversation with me for this book, Smith described himself as a 'committed unionist', but he also understands the importance of being respectful of all sides – the nationalist vote and the non-aligned vote. He also understood the security implications of that visit to Derry on a Friday night – but, also, the importance of trying to 'move on'. Inside the pub, the men in Barbour jackets drank tea.

In the words he has written on that meeting, Eastwood acknowledges the significance of the steps taken that night. Smith had travelled to the city where, just months earlier, the young journalist Lyra McKee lost her life to a dissident IRA bullet – to a city where that threat is always there. It was a different step. Another example of Smith and his team finding the right step. What we also began to see was a British–Irish government-shaped process that would end in January 2020 with that Smith and Coveney paper – New Decade, New Approach – offered to the parties more or less on take-it-or-leave-it terms.

Later, we will read how Smith reached out into the loyalist community. 'I wanted to deal directly with people, partly to make up for the gap,' he told me in conversation in late July 2020, some months after he had left Northern Ireland. What he was describing was the absence of loyalist representation at Stormont since the days of Billy Hutchinson, David Ervine and, then, Dawn Purvis. Earlier, Lilah Howson-Smith mentioned meetings in Dublin – including, I understand, in a café with Mary Lou McDonald and Conor Murphy, elsewhere in the city with the Fianna Fáil leader Micheál Martin and then in Government Buildings with Leo Varadkar and Simon Coveney.

Coveney had been around these talks for a longer period of time – since the early summer of 2017, when he became foreign minister. I remember his first news conference at Stormont Castle; it was an occasion when he took questions – not in the usual pre-arranged sequence or order, which so often, and too often, is the play and the preference of government ministers and their press teams, but as they were asked spontaneously. He then took time to set out his thinking, knew the issues and, importantly, also knew his rank in these talks – that of the Irish government being a co-guarantor of the Good Friday Agreement. I am not suggesting that he stormed in with hobnail boots, but nor was he there to tiptoe round the unionists and the British government. At times, he would anger them, and, at times, that needed to happen.

My impression is that in his time, Smith understood Coveney's role and approach, much more than James Brokenshire and Karen Bradley did during their unremarkable periods at the Northern Ireland Office. Brokenshire was there when the institutions collapsed, and Bradley was Secretary of State at the time of the failed draft agreement. Apart from during those few days in February 2018, I never really believed that Stormont could be put back together again; I never believed that either Brokenshire or Bradley could shape a deal and then put it up to the DUP.

They never really found their feet or the words and the ways for this place. Their steps and commentary were never certain. In the bigger picture, Westminster was always more important than Stormont, and government in London depended on keeping the DUP onside. In fairness, it meant there was little room for Brokenshire and Bradley to do anything.

So, the challenge for Smith and Coveney was to somehow reconvince the most sceptical of audiences that confidence could be restored and that these talks were worth one more effort. Before this Smith–Coveney initiative, I had given up on Stormont. I would not have bet fifty pence on the institutions being restored before the centenary of Northern Ireland in 2021, nor would I have cared. Parliament Buildings had become expensive office space with little purpose. The fear, of course, was a complete collapse and a return to direct rule from Westminster or some joint British–Irish initiative. In one news conference, back in September 2017, Coveney had reminded everyone that there was no such thing as British-only direct rule – one of those occasions when he refused to tiptoe over the political eggshell or around some of the egos in the Northern Ireland Office.

There was a terse response in a statement from the UK government: 'We will never countenance any arrangement, such as joint authority, inconsistent with the principle of consent in the agreement.' Coveney had not mentioned joint authority but was simply explaining and pointing up the role of the Irish government as a guardian – that co-guarantor – of the agreement and arrangements dating back to Good Friday 1998. His comments that day stressed the importance of getting the executive back in place at Stormont. This was his focus. The NIO must have known this. But what we were witnessing was a dancing by some to the tune of the DUP as part of that Westminster arrangement. Policy by WhatsApp, one source called it – meaning decisions and statements based on the latest DUP message.

From the summer of 2019, Smith and Coveney were leading a last-chance negotiation. That is how I viewed this latest phase of talks. On 13 October 2019, I was at Stormont to observe a rally under the banner 'We Deserve Better' – a people's protest about the shambles of Stormont. My diary note for that day reads, 'Miserable weather matching political mood'.

It became more miserable with Brexit dominating and determining everything. Boris Johnson walked his own path without the DUP, making a deal that did not have their support. Others, with better vision, saw all of this coming. There had been a string of statements from the Ulster Unionist Party predicting a border in the Irish Sea. Lord Empey said, 'I believe that those in Northern Ireland who voted to leave the EU never imagined that goods coming from Scotland, England and Wales would have to be checked before they came into Northern Ireland; they never foresaw and were promised no border in the Irish Sea.' Party leader Robin Swann said the Brexit deal placed Northern Ireland on the window ledge of the Union.

The DUP was the target of those statements. Their influence and relevance at Westminster, their closeness to the London end of the negotiation, and their part in the confidence and supply agreement with the Conservatives had failed to stop Johnson. He ignored them. Did his own thing and left them to carry the can back home – to pay a price they would never have imagined. Days before the Johnson deal, I was told of meetings involving the DUP leader Arlene Foster and colleagues with senior loyalists in Belfast; loyalists told me that these were conversations primarily about Brexit, but also the likelihood of a general election. 'I think we're fucked,' one of them told me. 'If Sinn Féin think it's all right, loyalists will think it's all wrong.' They were waiting for what they knew was coming, what they could see at a distance from this negotiation, that to get his deal, Johnson would throw Northern Ireland under the bus.

As this story developed, a former President of the Methodist Church, Brian Anderson, in an interview with Judith Hill of Ulster Television, spoke of parts of the loyalist/unionist community being 'constitutionally unnerved'. Some days earlier, a week or so before the UK–EU deal, another senior cleric had predicted, 'If hardy comes to hardy, they'll chuck us over.' It was an accurate reading of Johnson, seeing through his woolly thinking and words, and finding the real order of things – the emphasis on Brexit over the Union. It was in this period of angst that Smith and his team began a direct engagement with loyalists and others across the wider unionist community.

All of this was happening as another Northern Ireland talks deadline approached. That date – 21 October – brought another of those days of farce at Stormont, with a meaningless assembly recall that served up heated words and cold politics. New laws on equal marriage and access to abortion would be progressed at Westminster – a statement, in many senses, that change would no longer wait for, or be dictated by, this toy parliament in Belfast.

In the inability of this place to function, there was a stand-out line from the then Ulster Unionist leader Robin Swann at one of the many news conferences in the Great Hall that afternoon: 'Some may now ask, is Stormont worth saving?' Above the noise and the chaos of the latest political play, it was the question of the day and of those times. This was also the month when Westminster was finally broken. A dead parliament strangled in the knots of the Brexit argument.

On 29 October, MPs voted for a general election that would happen on 12 December; this representing the only possible way out of the stalemates both at Westminster and Stormont. My long-held view was that nothing would change in Belfast until the numbers changed in London. The backdrop to polling day was the Brexit saga: the broken parties, a divided Britain and a dis-United Kingdom; the machinations and manoeuvres that had finished Theresa May as Prime Minister and that had given Boris Johnson the place and position that were his political destiny of Downing Street.

There was another significant development late into 2019. Michelle O'Neill faced a challenge for the position of Sinn Féin Vice President, which she won in a party vote in November. The story had developed over a period of some months, easing its way into the news in late August–early September. John O'Dowd had stepped out of the usual huddle of party decision-making. It was not an organised coup, or something choreographed, but it was O'Dowd making a statement about lack of debate and, in this challenge, trying to open out a discussion on the next phase of the peace process.

I was told that in internal discussions that pre-dated this decision, he had reminded the party that its best assembly result was when it brought the political institutions down, and that he had argued that they should have taken their leadership, party management and press office out of Stormont at that time. In then going public, O'Dowd had broken the Sinn Féin way of doing things. It was a serious challenge and statement from one of the party's senior and significant figures. When it happened, Michelle O'Neill won the vote – 493 to 241. A comfortable win, but numbers that spoke to significant support for the O'Dowd arguments and position.

In her speech at the Ard Fheis, Michelle O'Neill had something to say on the Stormont negotiations: 'I stand ready to form a credible Executive. A new Assembly and a new kind of politics in the New Year is what I'm working towards.' That same weekend, Julian Smith pointed to an assembly election in the event of no deal by his 13 January 2020 deadline. Things were about to get serious.

CHAPTER 9

No more road – election then agreement

Late into 2019, Julian Smith started rolling the ground – smoothing it for that moment when he might have to present and explain an agreement and sell it to the widest possible audience. He had been briefed on the events of February 2018 – the fatal flaw in a negotiation that had been brought to the point of near agreement only for it to collapse at the last minute. The DUP had not prepared its ground. So, this time, Smith did it for them.

While writing this book, I learned of a series of meetings he had held from late October 2019 into the turn of the New Year; they were a direct engagement with loyalists and others in the unionist community, including from the loyal orders. Three of those meetings were at Stormont House. There was then a breakfast on the Shankill Road and, less than a fortnight later, a gathering at Hillsborough Castle on 1 January 2020. Jackie McDonald was there; Harry Stockman and Winston Irvine – all of them senior figures in the loyalist community. In this series of meetings and conversations, the talking points were Brexit and the Union – also, the question of dealing with the past.

One source, with direct knowledge and involvement, described 'set-piece engagements'. On Brexit and the question of an Irish Sea border, they wanted to talk about the promised 'unfettered' trade between Northern Ireland and Great Britain – the question: 'What exactly does that mean?' And on another issue they asked, 'What are the tangible, concrete ideas for strengthening the four nations of the Union?' Legacy and confidence-building, in respect of loyalist/ unionist communities, were also in the mix of this engagement.

The breakfast meeting on 19 December 2019 was on the Shankill Road at the offices of ACT (Action for Community Transformation). Loyalists have shared some photographs of that visit with me. It is a typically dark December morning – just six days to Christmas – and the clock inside the nearby café, Mikala's Kitchen, where breakfast was prepared and delivered to the meeting, has not yet reached 8 a.m. Smith had gone there to thank the staff, his 7 a.m. meeting in the ACT offices now over. He and his adviser Lilah Howson-Smith had met with Irvine, Stockman, Dr William Mitchell and – a fourth loyalist from the east of the city – Rab McCartney. Every minute was being squeezed out of long days in an effort to create the circumstances for an agreement. Hours later, in the pouring rain outside Stormont House, Smith and Coveney said the governments were ready to publish a text as the basis for a deal. The delay was blamed on the DUP. Their days of influence gone – the political now a very different place, and this public rebuke a confirmation of that. There would be a breathing space over Christmas, but that was it. The two governments were now going to move this at their pace.

In that December 2019–January 2020 period, politics raced from a standstill into something more in keeping with a sprint. The general election results rearranged the landscape both in London and in Belfast. The Tories and Johnson, with 365 seats, had a big majority. On Friday, 13 December, when the counting was over, no time was allocated or allowed for moping about in the debris of the results. There were many casualties in the numbers. None bigger than the DUP Westminster leader, Nigel Dodds. One source described the DUP as 'deeply traumatised' by what had happened to them electorally – what had happened to Nigel. It had been a day of reckoning – the ending in tears that had been predicted at the time of the confidence and supply agreement with the Conservative Party in 2017.

Emma Little-Pengelly also lost her seat in South Belfast. In this constituency, the Green Party leader and MLA Clare Bailey endorsed the SDLP candidate Claire Hanna. It was a decision that was all about Brexit – that issue that has shifted, and is shifting, the sands of politics here. Sinn Féin also stayed out of this race. Hanna had 27,079 votes; Little-Pengelly, 11,678. Any suggestion that this was an Orange versus Green battle does not stand up to scrutiny. Those numbers do not fit within such a frame but are an extension of, and an explanation of, that Brexit play that is pulling our politics and our people and their votes in different directions. Clare Bailey understood that changing mood and knew that Brexit would be a major factor in this election.

CLARE BAILEY:

That was not just my sense. My phone was ringing off the hook. People were calling to my office. Community campaign groups were being formed. What they all wanted was a single agreed anti-Brexit candidate that could win the seat back at this critical time. It was important for the people to have an MP reflective of the majority view from the constituency. But I think it was important in a psychological sense also. People had seen the power of their vote begin to change the landscape and they were not for stopping now.

This is a reference back to the earlier council and European elections of 2019 – how one of those elections changed the face of Belfast City Council, and how, in the second, Naomi Long won a seat in a result that once again expressed the Remain view of the 2016 referendum here. Bailey believed that mood would continue into this next election and that the field had to be cleared for Hanna.

CLARE BAILEY:

For me, maximising the pro-Remain vote meant not standing in South Belfast. The Green Party NI had built from very small beginnings in the constituency, but we had worked so hard for any electoral success that we had achieved. We had also come off big gains in the local government elections and like any political party we were keen to continue that growth. Making the call not to stand in South Belfast was not an easy decision, it was a high risk, but I knew that these were extraordinary times that called for an extraordinary response. The chats with constituents asking me to do everything possible to send a pro-Remain voice to Westminster sealed it for me. During that period, anytime I ventured out for a coffee, a pint or to shop I was urged to do what I could to make sure South Belfast returned a 'Remainer'. People I knew, and people I didn't know, brought it up. The message was coming at me from all directions.

Bailey had worked out that Hanna had the best chance of unseating Little-Pengelly. The Green Party leader had discussed this widely – with her members and with some of the other parties. When she settled on her decision, she signed Hanna's nomination papers, spoke at her campaign launch and explained her thinking to as many Green voters as possible. It was not easy. The party had worked hard for its success in the constituency, something Bailey does not take for granted, but she believed that in this moment, and in this election, it was the right thing to do.

CLARE BAILEY:

The Westminster 2019 election was extraordinary and people understood that. We have a savvy electorate here in Northern Ireland and they are politically astute. The majority of people are also aware of the important contribution that the European Union has made to our lives, our peace, economy, environment and community relations. Yes, this place is tribal and sectarianism is entrenched, but sometimes a situation demonstrates a different facet of who we are. Returning a pro-Remain MP in South Belfast and in other constituencies like North Down showed that sometimes we can manage to transcend tribal politics.

The Green Party decision extended further than South Belfast. It pulled out of all four constituencies in the city, as well as in North Down, where the Alliance Party deputy leader Stephen Farry had the most remarkable victory, winning a seat that the DUP must surely have believed was theirs. I was in a BBC studio overnight, sharing jigsaw pieces of information with presenter William Crawley as this Friday the 13th story developed, including an unofficial tally from the count that John Finucane of Sinn Féin was about 2,000 votes ahead of Dodds. The SDLP leader Colum Eastwood won in Foyle; it was the seat of his predecessors, John Hume and Mark Durkan, that Sinn Féin had snatched in 2017. Michelle Gildernew of Sinn Féin held on in Fermanagh South Tyrone, but only just; the Ulster Unionist Tom Elliott was just a few dozen votes behind. Across the constituencies, Alliance had a 16.8 per cent share of the vote; that third pillar in politics was now much more visible and much more significant.

Dodds losing the seat he had held since 2001 was one of those earthquake moments. Think of his profile at Westminster and across the media throughout those Brexit days, something the veteran political editor Ken Reid referenced earlier in this book. He was big picture – part of everything. Now, he was on different ground and in a different place. The numbers in 2017 were close – the gap just a little over two thousand votes. There was a token SDLP candidate in the field in 2017. This time the party was absent. On the eve of voting, someone watching the Dodds campaign very closely from within the loyalist/unionist community gave me this read out, some of which I would use in my election commentary on the BBC.

'There are people who won't go in and hold their noses and vote DUP,' my source said. 'There is a sizeable pro-Remain unionist vote who remain committed to that position,' he continued. His observation was that Sinn Féin's 'ground game' was better – 'far more effective' – and this would be 'important to getting the vote out'. 'Nigel is a big scalp,' he continued. So, the 'motivating factor' is stronger. Then he said, 'If I had to call North Belfast, I'd call Finucane. Nigel is stressed. A worried man; not coping well [and] sees the writing on the wall. I've been up close,' my source said.

On the eve of the election, another unionist called me, this time from outside Belfast. He had spoken to someone in the city, who was concerned that Dodds could lose the seat. 'Someone who would know?' I asked. 'Yes,' was his response. What I meant in my question was this: was he talking with someone who was close enough to be able to read this accurately? His own assessment was that Dodds was still favourite, but he was watching this from further away.

For Sinn Féin, the fact that the SDLP had stepped aside did not mean job done. It was a long process and argument to persuade traditional SDLP voters to go with Finucane. 'Trench warfare on abstentionism' was how veteran republican Jim Gibney described the experience on the doorsteps; this was to do with Sinn Féin not taking its seats at Westminster and about Stormont not functioning. Forty-eight hours before polling day, he had detected a shift and a change: 'They are coming out for John.' Some of them would do so grudgingly as reluctant tactical voters. On the day, Gibney described a 'major operation' in North Belfast on the part of Sinn Féin: 'methodical, combing streets, knocking doors with scores of people involved'. The vote was 'out in big numbers'. 'The people up here can't believe it,' he told me, 'smiles all round.'

This was the 'ground game' identified earlier and anticipated by one of my sources in the loyalist/unionist community. Hours later, it was Gibney who gave me that unofficial tally he had received from the count, which had Finucane winning the seat by around 2,000 votes. In studio, I shared this information with the presenter William Crawley. Later, the official figures had Finucane on 23,078 – Dodds, 21,135. It was the story of stories on this election night. It also helped cover up some of the cracks, including the Foyle result, which was a disaster for Sinn Féin. Eastwood had 26,881 votes (the highest ever for the SDLP in the constituency) – Elisha McCallion, 9,771 (the lowest Sinn Féin vote since 1992). One observer spoke of Eastwood winning the seat with a majority that could have filled the local Brandywell soccer stadium several times.

Those results were the backdrop to the next push within the Stormont negotiation. Before Christmas, the governments had given the parties that last chance to complete a deal of their own making. Soon, Smith and Coveney would take control of the talks, and the timing of the text's publication. What developed from here became a significant British–Irish moment made possible by politics and advice that could see beyond the often-heard talk of 'keeping Dublin in its place'. Julian Smith would not have got this done without Simon Coveney and vice versa. Both were in the right place at the right time. Both, as I wrote earlier, understood their rank above the parties. Twenty-seven days after the election results, the two governments published their terms for agreement. Smith's final deadline of 13 January was just days away and, this time, it was for real.

On that hill at Stormont, you can feel the wind. It gets into your bones. Thursday, 9 January 2020 was one such night. It had been raining. It was dark. Too miserable and too cold to be outside. There had been a WhatsApp message – an operational note to be in place at 9.15 p.m. for a news conference 15 minutes later. That steep hill would be the stage for a piece of winter theatre, its significance hidden in those few lines that had pinged on our phones in the warmth of the Great Hall in Parliament Buildings as that night got longer. We were told the Secretary of State and Tánaiste would give 'a short update on the talks process'. When it happened, it was something much more important than that; this was the outworking of a decision that had been taken two days earlier.

This is when the governments had agreed their next move. 'Tuesday [7 January] was the day we decided we are going to go,' an insider explained – meaning the text would be published and the parties would be tested. The only question now was timing. It nearly happened on Wednesday, but the Secretary of State paused for twenty-four hours after a meeting with Arlene Foster and the DUP Chief Executive, Tim Johnston. I was told that it was Johnston who asked for the delay. Smith described this as an 'important moment – important I listened to him'.

On Thursday night, that quickly arranged stage had two lecterns. There was talk about how to light them; and there was talk also about a deal. One of Julian Smith's advisers, Ross Easton, was on the hill – quietly whispering and setting the scene before the main act. Rosemary Neill, chief communications officer at the NIO, was also there. There would be a build-up. Smith and Coveney would walk towards us, the lights of Parliament Buildings as their backdrop. A dead place coming back to life. There was no more time. And it was time.

JULIAN SMITH:

It was 9.20 p.m. on Thursday, 9 January 2020 and we had lost Simon Coveney. We were due to launch 'New Decade, New Approach' at 9.45 p.m. We finally located Simon who was in the Alliance assigned room at Stormont House trying to persuade party leader Naomi Long to sign up to the deal. 'Just get him, we need to go', I shouted to my Special Advisor Lilah Howson-Smith. Having been at my side for seven months, negotiating and providing pitch perfect advice, Lilah rightly chose not to execute this particular request, suggesting that pulling the Irish foreign minister out of a meeting was above her pay grade. I slammed on the door myself, gave a lame excuse for interrupting the meeting and got Simon out without revealing to the room what we were about to do. We were about to launch the New Decade, New Approach deal in front of an illuminated Stormont, late at night without the prior sign-off of the still bickering parties. It was a bounce, and we had to surprise; move hard and fast and not lose time. As the parties couldn't agree things up front – we had decided to lay it out and dare them to reject it.

For three years, words had been running in circles on the pages of one text and then another. It became a dizzy play, chasing after one sentence and losing another. In all of this, the process lost itself. I think we, as journalists, became part of the problem – lining up for the endless news conferences that said the same thing and said nothing. We gave a sense and a semblance of importance to something very pathetic. It needed this Smith–Coveney moment to save us all from this sham – and from the shame of Stormont.

JULIAN SMITH:

The Civil Service teams had finalised the last of the text changes. We had fine-tuned the text to as close as possible to what we thought each of the parties could live with. Now there was an added pressure.

Ross Easton and the NIO press team had Northern Ireland's leading journalists on the Stormont hill on one of the coldest days of the year – and they were freezing. The decision to launch the document had come earlier that day when we were going round in circles, and Simon Coveney and I agreed that we needed to pitch the New Decade, New Approach that night, or the text that the parties had seen in one form or other would have been picked over, analysed minutely and rejected by one party or another.

In my research for this book, I spoke with an informed talks insider – a source who knows the detail of the planning of those key days in January 2020. He knew exactly how far the governments would allow the parties to run before Smith and Coveney would make public their terms for an agreement. The governments knew this moment might well arrive, a point in the talks when they would have to test and challenge the parties. It is why Smith had been spending time with others 'rolling the pitch'. Now that time had arrived on the Stormont hill in the freezing cold of 9 January.

JULIAN SMITH:

Northern Ireland had been without government for over three years. We couldn't afford any more delay, for the sake of frustrated and patient voters. Three years had been wasted in which vital social, economic and political decisions were being made without direction from political leaders despite the fact that they continued to be paid. And three years had passed without a key leg of the Good Friday Agreement functioning. I was the third Secretary of State to oversee talks since the Assembly and Executive collapsed in January 2017. The talks had ebbed and flowed, nearly successful in February 2018 and also again in June 2019, but never getting over the line.

In July 2019, when I arrived at Stormont House, I had been determined to up the ante and the pace. With a negotiating text that had been in play for some time and a new civil service team led by the excellent veteran Permanent Secretary Sir Jonathan Stephens and Mark Larmour in Belfast, augmented by the former members of the

Cabinet Office's Europe Unit, Brendan Threlfall, Mark Davies and Paul Flynn, and two highly talented Special Advisors – Lilah Howson-Smith and Ross Easton, we took a more direct approach.

Everyone noticed that new approach and energy. There were not enough hours in the day as Smith worked with his team and with Coveney to get this done. Sleep was a bonus. All of us who had watched these talks over three long years knew that deadlines always moved, but there was a 'different' sense this time. Smith was serious about the 13 January date. Answering questions from me and others, he made that clear. If there was no agreement, he would send the parties to an assembly election.

JULIAN SMITH:

I wanted to inspire trust and to force the parties to engage. At first it was slow with the DUP and Sinn Féin at different times more or less dynamically engaged. The smaller parties were less reticent but increasingly frustrated that Sinn Féin and the DUP wouldn't knuckle down and work through their differences. Things came to a head with the health strike and the 2019 General Election. The first nurses strike in a hundred years and the clear message from voters that they wanted power-sharing back to fix nurses pay and other issues. Now the Conservatives no longer needed the DUP to win votes at Westminster, there were greater reasons for that party to engage at Stormont; and equally with an Irish election in sight, Sinn Féin needed to show that it could govern responsibly at Stormont if it wanted to be trusted in Dublin.

Whilst there were incentives to get agreement, success was far from inevitable. Immediately after the UK General Election on 13 December, I made another talks push but as well as not talking to each other, the support base of the main parties were still not in the right place to put their leaderships under pressure to come to an agreement.

The final push came on 1 January 2020. The UK team arrived at Hillsborough with everyone clear we were staying until we got the job done. If a new executive was not formed by 13 January, I would have been forced to call new Assembly elections. That fact – and the fear of what would happen at the ballot box – plus the changed circumstances following the General Election, would ensure we had sufficient heat under this round of talks to get everyone focused on a deal. Whilst the UK and Irish Governments had to force the issue on the evening of 9 January, by that time it seemed more likely than not that it made sense for all concerned to get Stormont back up and running. But as we pitched New Decade, New Approach into the dark night of 9 January, it was far from clear that our strategy would succeed.

It really was a 'bounce', to use Smith's description. The Coveney–Alliance meeting has been described to me by someone present as 'heated': 'The worst bit was we were having a conversation about the possibility of changes being made [to the text].' Party leader Naomi Long, the assembly team and former Justice Minister and MLA David Ford were there – also present were party staff. Throughout the day, new MP Stephen Farry kept in contact with the negotiation by phone from London. Part of the heated discussion was on the issue of identity and the use of the term 'other'. My source spoke of 'extreme displeasure', adding, 'Nobody describes themselves as other.' On Smith interrupting the meeting, I was told he 'just popped his head in' to 'borrow [Simon] for a second'. What followed was that news conference in front of the 'illuminated' Parliament Buildings and the publication of bound copies of an agreement. 'Part of my brain was, "they couldn't be that sneaky",' my source added.

There was a mood to the negotiation that Thursday and in the hours leading to the publication of New Decade, New Approach – a building anger that could be heard in a series of news conferences that afternoon, and which I summarised in a tweet just before six that evening: 'STORMONT: 5-party talks process now looks like a 2-party negotiation. Alliance, SDLP and UUP yet to see governments text. Approach ignores the changing numbers and trends in recent elections. If governments want a 5-party Executive, they should wise up.'

The governments, we know now, had set their course two days earlier, on Tuesday. This was when they decided they were going to publish their document, and that the parties would not be allowed more time to argue over the text. It had been with them in various forms and iterations since the autumn of 2017, through the draft agreement of 2018 to this final version in 2020. 'The parties hadn't signed off and we weren't seeking their permission [to publish New Decade, New Approach],' an insider told me. One 'guesstimate' suggests something in the region of one hundred meetings with the parties from the summer of 2019 through to December, and around fifty meetings in that intensive period of talks in the early days of January 2020. 'Up to the last minutes, they were looking for more, more, more,' a source commented. He said a priority of the negotiation and the emphasis of the talks had been on achieving a five-party executive, but he accepted that the two 'big parties' 'eat up all the oxygen and time'.

'It was the same deal,' that source explained when I spoke with him in July 2020. Commas and paragraphs had been moved, *Roget's Thesaurus* exhausted. The decision now was more about politics than substance. The playing with words – that game of clever dictionary – was over. The governments had settled on a text and a title: New Decade, New Approach. As Smith and Coveney spoke, we could see the document in a box, waiting to be circulated as the hard-copy confirmation of their deal. The waiting now – as Smith explained – was for those who would have to form an executive. As to whether the governments would get buy-in from all the parties, one insider said, 'There were varying degrees of confidence.' 'It was not certain,' my source continued. 'Fundamentally, it was a call: It's now or never. There was no point in adding more time.'

Coveney had been working and waiting longer than Smith for this moment and this platform. Stormont politics were a laughing-stock. The talks had gone on for far too long. Credibility had been exhausted.

SIMON COVENEY:

We were running out of road. It was three years since the Assembly and Executive had been functioning. Three years which had seen push after push to restore them but also periods where it was not possible to build any substantial momentum. There were, as there always are, voices of pessimism and fatalism that said that the institutions at the heart of the Good Friday Agreement would not return. They said political polarisation was now too entrenched and the parties saw other paths to achieve their goals. Brexit simultaneously made the need for devolved power-sharing Government more urgent and more difficult to achieve.

The killing of Lyra McKee broke that cycle. The words of Father Martin Magill in St Anne's Cathedral crystallised the truth, which was the opposite of that cynicism: ordinary people wanted the institutions of the Good Friday Agreement back. Like Lyra, they wanted their politicians to work together. They wanted their politicians, including both Governments, to fulfil their responsibilities. Like Lyra, they were not complacent about the achievements of the peace process and they were not fatalistic about the future.

That tragedy gave the Prime Minister and the Taoiseach the moment to relaunch intensive talks over the summer of 2019 chaired by myself and the Secretary of State, Karen Bradley. There were times then that it seemed possible that we could land a deal, including on the most contentious issues. Wider political circumstances were against it but very valuable groundwork was laid in all-party sessions clearing the way. That meant that when the window of opportunity arrived, no time would be wasted in bringing it to a rapid and positive conclusion.

What was needed was leadership and we were seeing it now. Not two governments being played by two parties, but two governments determining the path. I wrote earlier about the importance of rank. In this phase of the talks, we noticed the change. Smith wrote about it earlier. The UK general election results meant the votes of the DUP were no longer needed at Westminster. They were now being offered a way back to Stormont or another day before the electorate – another election while still trying to manage the trauma of December and what had happened to them on Friday the 13th.

SIMON COVENEY:

The appointment of Julian Smith as Secretary of State for Northern Ireland was an important one. He showed drive and imagination and a real personal commitment to wide and direct engagement with people across the spectrum in Northern Ireland. For decades now, the dynamic of partnership between the British and Irish Governments has been a distinctive and crucial feature of the peace process and the stewardship of the Good Friday Agreement. I saw that we shared a determination to live up to that record – and could work together to push for a breakthrough.

The autumn was dominated by the UK elections but as soon as they concluded, we had our window and we took it. Myself and Julian chaired an intense drive that narrowly missed succeeding before Christmas and we then picked it up immediately in the New Year. The parties wanted to reach agreement but that was not enough by itself. Very early on, myself and Julian realised that there would come a point when we would have to make a call and put a complete document on the table. It would be the outcome of the work of all the parties but, in its compromises, we knew that every party would have real difficulties with it. No party was signed up in advance. There was a very real possibility that one, or more, or all, would take it to their membership and see it rejected.

Would they have rejected it knowing that the consequence of any such decision would be an election? Now that they had lost their influence at Westminster, the DUP needed Stormont. They had nowhere else to go, and a Northern Ireland Centenary celebration in 2021 without a working parliament would be a damp-squib occasion. Sinn Féin also needed back in. Three years into this political crisis, many voters had forgotten how it had started and were determined that it should end. The health strikes and the fact that politicians were still being paid added to a sense of 'enough is enough'. Smith and Coveney knew the pulse and the mood of the moment – that it was the right time, or the best time, to push for an agreement. This was their window of opportunity.

SIMON COVENEY:

On Thursday 9 January, there were still serious voices calling for more time, more process. We didn't think it would help. In fact, we thought delay could be fatal to the credibility of the process and the participants. So, we made the call and we published. The parties considered it and, in the end, all five main parties accepted it and power-sharing was restored. It wasn't easy for any of them. All the party leaders showed courage and vision in doing it. I don't know what would have happened if it had gone the other way. Assembly elections would had to have been held, as it had been made clear that they would. I don't know that an election campaign would have set the scene for the kind of compromises needed. Politics in Northern Ireland, like everywhere else, would have been hit by the tsunami of the Covid-19 pandemic. The situation of civil servants making decisions in Northern Ireland in the absence of Ministers would have been entirely unsustainable. We would have been into completely uncharted territory, and still drifting further and further from the solid course the Good Friday Agreement had given us.

It is important to be impatient with politics and easy to be dismissive. But what I saw in those endless hours in those small rooms in Stormont was a whole lot of dedicated people who wanted to represent their voters and their communities, and to deliver a better future for people in Northern Ireland. For all the differences in perspective, I trust in that spirit to continue to see us through all the tremendous challenges we face.

The governments had taken a calculated risk. We read both in Coveney's and Smith's words a sense that they knew that the parties had nowhere else to go; that they had indeed run out of road. Had they rejected the proposed deal, then the prospect of another election was large in the frame, and given the voting trend throughout 2019, how many of the parties would have wanted that? Alliance and not many others. Smith and Coveney knew what they were doing. Stormont was buzzing the next day. At lunchtime, Smith was in the canteen. I had just arrived there after a BBC interview, and I caught a few words with him as he left. He was taking nothing for granted. Months later, in August 2020, his SpAd Ross Easton sent me a photograph he took later that afternoon: inside Stormont House, the Secretary of State and Sir Jonathan Stephens, the Permanent Secretary at the NIO, are watching the Sinn Féin news conference up the hill in the Great Hall at Parliament Buildings. It was that party's response to the events of the night before and the publication of the governments' deal.

ROSS EASTON:

We were gathered in the Secretary of State's office as Mary Lou McDonald appeared on the television screen in front of us. An hour or two before, I had heard through the grapevine that Sinn Féin was preparing to hold a press conference but the timings, and certainly the detail, were somewhat unclear. Surely this would be good news, but there was no room for complacency as we sat down to watch what was about to unfold.

As Julian's special adviser focusing on media relations, it was typical to see me glued to my iPhone at the back of a room somewhere and up until that point, today had been no exception. I had been scanning Twitter, email and WhatsApp almost simultaneously trying to keep abreast of what was happening, looking for clues as to what might be about to come and catch us out. Did I need to help prepare for the worst or were we about to witness the restoration of power-sharing in Northern Ireland once more?

Julian had arrived in the role with a determination to get the job done. Unlike Lilah, I hadn't worked with him before and was having to quickly learn his style. His charismatic enthusiasm and infectious drive stood out, yet his business-like mindset meant he was a tough negotiator and instinctively seemed to know the right approach to take (before becoming an MP he ran his own business).

'It's time to get Stormont back up and running' was the simple phrase we had coined in the first few weeks of him being in office. I've worked my socks off in jobs before but working with Julian was a whole new ball game. Every hour was spent doing something which contributed to getting Stormont back up and running. Even on the sole occasion we managed to go for a run together around Hillsborough Castle, the time was largely spent discussing the talks. (A reason I firmly blame for him beating my pace, by the way.)

I first met Ross Easton at that media breakfast in Stormont House back in August 2019. He gave me his card, and we spoke several times as this negotiation developed. Those conversations were straightforward; none of the bullshit of lines to be attributed to a senior UK government source. With the detail he could share, he was matter-of-fact. In a conversation at Parliament Buildings on Tuesday, 7 January, he put us on standby for a possible press briefing the next day. It became a day of waiting and pacing in the Great Hall, but with no product. I note in my diary, 'At Stormont for a period. Expecting media briefing on governments' text. This didn't materialise.' We know now that the delay was that 24-hour pause that Smith agreed with the DUP. Wednesday the 8th became Thursday the 9th – just four days left in this talks' deadline of the 13th.

ROSS EASTON:

The weeks leading up to 13 January 2020 were some of the most gruelling. I had arrived in Northern Ireland on a freezing cold and damp New Year's Day (Julian was already there), and the next two weeks were flat out with talks, meetings and impromptu engagements. The healthcare system was on its knees, and nurses had gone on strike for the first time in more than 100 years. Brexit was looming (and, as it happens, unbeknownst to the world, so was a global pandemic). Northern Ireland needed a devolved government.

As the meetings intensified, I saw the clock on Julian's Stormont office wall strike 12.40 a.m. one morning, and after a brief sleep at Hillsborough Castle, I saw it strike 7.30 a.m. a few hours later. It was clear Julian was unwavering in the final few weeks of talks and was not going to lose a minute of time in trying to get the deal over the line.

The night before the Sinn Féin press conference, Julian and Simon Coveney had given a press conference of their own, late in the evening in which – in somewhat dramatic fashion – they had emerged from the darkness in the freezing cold, walking side-by-side to present 'New Decade, New Approach'. This was the moment the chips went down; the deal had been laid upon the table for the people of Northern Ireland to see, it was now up to the political parties to decide what happened next.

That Friday afternoon, I was in that packed Great Hall for the Sinn Féin news conference. There was a lectern in place for Mary Lou McDonald, an indication that there would be a prepared speech or statement, as well as questions from the media. Pearse Doherty was on her right-hand side, with Michelle O'Neill to the left. Declan Kearney and Conor Murphy were prominent inside this picture frame. Gerry Adams was there, standing close to Matt Carthy, Caoimhe Archibald and Carál Ní Chuilín; the tall figures of John Finucane and John O'Dowd were several rows back. The party had some dozens of its elected representatives from north and south in the Great Hall; they were there to hear an acceptance of the Smith–Coveney agreement as a basis to re-enter the political institutions. All of the major news organisations were present. That three-year standoff at Stormont was over.

ROSS EASTON:

As Mary Lou began to speak, Julian sat in his office, poker-faced, calm and unassuming but glued to the television screen. As it became clear power-sharing was to resume, the room seemed to breathe a collective sigh of relief and the tense silence was broken as a round of applause went up from various rooms in Stormont House. Julian quietly stood up and with a beaming smile on his face, shook hands with Sir Jonathan Stephens, the Permanent Secretary of the Northern Ireland Office who had worked tirelessly with several Secretaries of State to help get to this point. 'Well done,' Julian said warmly. It was Sir Jonathan's final achievement as Permanent Secretary before he was due to retire. True to character, Julian wanted to recognise Jonathan's efforts first and foremost.

Three months before the deal was done, in October 2019, I had snapped a photograph of Parliament Buildings during a rare break in that day's agenda in which I'd gone for a walk around the Stormont Estate. With a crisp, bright blue sky above and dramatic clouds spiralling towards the camera lens, the building looked impressive and yet stood empty. The media had retired for lunch and there were only a few dog walkers and tourists taking photographs outside. As I listened to the peace, I thought about the history of the place.

After spending an hour thanking his team for their hard work, Julian tweeted the photograph I had taken on that day. With it he wrote, 'A devolved government can now start delivering the reforms needed in our public services. After three years, it's time to get back to work – for the people of Northern Ireland.'

In the end it all seemed so simple. There were no shocks or surprises in the words and lines of New Decade, New Approach. We had read much of it in that forest of papers that had grown in these endless talks – the same papers and words and forest in which the parties and politics had become lost over the past three years. On the Irish language, we had known for a while that this would fit into some overarching package – not a stand-alone act, but legislation that would stand beside and inside some wider frame. The Irish government had insisted that this should be published as part of New Decade, New Approach, including the agreement on an Irish Language Commissioner. This was part of the closing discussions between Smith and Coveney in the days leading to their news conference.

The June documents I had read had moved the emphasis to the content of legislation rather than form: what it would entail rather than what it would be called. All of this was to spare the blushes of the DUP. There was not an Irish Language Act, but there was an Irish Language Act, except it was called something else. The cat had become the dog, and that 'crocodile' comment of 2017 had contributed to this moment.

On the issue of the future sustainability of the political institutions, we had read the proposals through a number of papers over a period of some months. There would be more time – several months – to resolve matters in the event of a resignation at the top of the executive, and the new party leaders' forum, which would act as an early warning of any issues that could cause political tension or disagreements, was also part of the deal. This too had been set out in those papers during the early summer.

Smith's big selling point, and the pressure point for the parties, was on the priorities for a restored executive – headlining health and including moves to immediately settle the ongoing pay dispute and to introduce a new action plan on waiting times. It was probably this, more than anything else, that the governments were daring the parties to reject. The publication of a text also gave those parties something to hide behind, particularly on issues that had not delivered all they wanted or on which they had to give more. They could argue that it was not their deal but something determined by Smith and Coveney.

On Saturday, 11 January, with two days left in the deadline, the new executive was in place: Arlene Foster as First Minister and Michelle O'Neill as deputy First Minister, and all five parties back round the table. The Ulster Unionists were late and last with their decision, party leader Steve Aiken announcing it just before the assembly sitting that weekend. Robin Swann would be the new Health Minister. By Monday, Boris Johnson had come running to take a bow on the stage, to steal a slice of the success and to muddle his way through some reworking of Tony Blair's 'hand of history' quote from 1998. Just weeks later, in a Cabinet reshuffle, Smith was sacked; the shallowness of Johnson and the influence of Dominic Cummings were both evident in that decision. On a number of issues – including his concerns on proroguing parliament and his refusal to play along with no-deal and security co-operation threats on Brexit – Smith had, in some of the headlines of that time, clashed or broken ranks with Johnson, whom he had supported in the Tory leadership contest. As far as the former NI Secretary is concerned, these were policy issues, not personal issues.

This was all part of his being different. It is why, in a short space of time here, he made such an impression – why he is missed. You read on social media how he connected with this place, its people and its issues, and how they connected with him. Not just him, but that young team that arrived with him in the summer of 2019. I witnessed it on a short walk with him in Belfast at the end of July 2020, when he was back for a visit: how he was greeted, how he was introduced to others. He was given a bag of dulse and was not sure what to do with it, later tweeting it alongside some Tayto crisps and asking for advice on his choice of snacks. Small things matter.

On that Johnson visit to Stormont on Monday, 13 January 2020, he stood in the Great Hall alongside the Belfast republican Alex Maskey. In this one image we could see the change of the past thirty-plus years. When Maskey was elected to Belfast City Council in the early 1980s, the roof almost caved in. Now he was Speaker in the Stormont Assembly, in that picture frame with the British Prime Minister, and no one in that Great Hall at Parliament Buildings batted an eyelid.

It should never have taken this long. Those days in January 2020 represented a success story for Smith and Coveney, but those three years of wasteland are another stain on the political history of this place. Think of those big moments and decisions of the 1990s and the political agreements that followed. Then, think of what had to be resolved in this negotiation and how long that took. This really should be Stormont's last chance. If it fails again, then it should fail forever. The day after the Johnson visit, attention switched to Dublin and the announcement of an Irish election on 8 February. Politics there would be turned upside down.

Sinn Féin and its leader, Mary Lou McDonald, were the story of the polls and the story of the results. The percentage share of first preference votes read Sinn Féin 24.5 per cent, Fianna Fáil 22.2 per cent and Fine Gael 20.9 per cent. On seats, Fianna Fáil had 38, Sinn Féin 37 and Fine Gael 35. The decision to fight Sinn Féin on the Northern question – on the IRA past and on stories of 'shadowy figures' – backfired. The months of talking that followed were about keeping Sinn Féin out of government, which was both short-sighted and short-term, and an approach that screamed of double standards: what is good for the North is not good for the South. Not once in all of the negotiations relating to Stormont was there ever any suggestion from Dublin that Sinn Féin should not be part of the executive. A programme for government was agreed between Fianna Fáil, Fine Gael and the Green Party. Micheál Martin would serve as Taoiseach until December 2022 and then Leo Varadkar. Simon Coveney remained as Foreign Minister.

Weeks later, when it was eventually published in March, the RHI report arrived and left us almost in a whisper. By now, our attention had shifted to more important things: to the pandemic that was the new war and the new fear – the tsunami, as described by Simon Coveney.

CHAPTER 10

'Project Dignity' – politics and pandemic

This is a chapter about fear, not the detail of the health responses to Covid-19 or the arguments over equipment and testing and timing – or how prepared or not prepared we were. All of that is for another day, when there has been proper time to reflect on decisions and those moments of indecision. This is a story that takes us inside the emergency mortuary at Holywood in County Down, which was constructed as part of worst-case planning and as a response to predictions that we could be overwhelmed by the numbers of dead. A story that also takes us inside the thinking of Health Minister Robin Swann, who sat in the day-to-day places of decision-making as this pandemic arrived and reminded us of how delicate our world is and how fragile we are within it. We were back in time – back in fear and living with a different terror. As the story develops, we arrive at the funeral of the republican Bobby Storey, a day that becomes the next test of our politics – and of that relationship at the top of the Stormont Executive.

The coronavirus invaded our minds; it got into every corner of our thinking. We were afraid of every cough and sneeze; afraid of this thing we could not see. Yet its threat was obvious. It was there in the pictures we watched from inside intensive care units in China, across Europe and, then, as the virus arrived in Britain and Ireland. It was raging against the world. We all had to learn a new language of lockdown and social distancing and the new meanings of bubbles, cocooning and shielding. We had to pay attention to the

'R' number and to those directional arrows and distance markings that became the new rules of shopping.

We walked on roads to avoid others on the pavements. We washed our hands until they cracked, and then cracked some more. Rice, pasta, soap and toilet paper became the new pots of gold. Working from home became a bigger thing. Exercise – a walk – was restricted to once a day. Streets were empty; they were eerie. In the silence, we heard more. There is a beautiful line in an Imelda May poem about 'hearing the birds again now that the traffic has been turned down'. I wrote at the time about having to learn the discipline of distance and, in that, coming to better value the closeness that had been taken from us. Covid-19 made us listen, hear everything, read everything, until we could listen no more. Like the conflict years, it became too much. I switched the radio and the television off.

My daily walk was at Kinnegar in Holywood, along a stretch of road and along the line of a high fence with coiled barbed wire on top. The Ministry of Defence property signs detail the parking and photography restrictions. They are reminders of the 'old war'. There are ramps leading to a checkpoint, and then, about 250 steps beyond, as you walk towards Belfast, I came across an open gate and heard work going on inside. The open space here is dressed in a coat of weeds and shells, the old army base showing its age and how large swathes of it have fallen into disuse – evidence that a previous threat has gone. At this point on the fence, those MoD signs – fewer in number – have been dulled or dimmed, and further into the site there are the sheds of that emergency mortuary. This was the work of 'Project Dignity'. In the restored executive of January 2020, Alliance leader and Justice Minister Naomi Long had a seat at that top table.

NAOMI LONG:

When I became Justice Minister, I knew the issues that would come across my desk would be hugely significant. I knew they would have an impact on people's lives, often when they are at their most vulnerable. I was fully prepared for that. What I wasn't prepared for, and what none of us could have foreseen, was that within two short months my department would be faced with the prospect of finding a suitable site to establish a temporary mortuary capable of coping with large numbers of people who could lose their lives due to the pandemic.

When Health Minister Robin Swann told the media that the scale of the potential death toll surge facing Northern Ireland was of 'Biblical proportions', these weren't empty words. This was the context in which we had been working; and I think it's all too easy now for people to forget how stark and how real that prospect was. There was silence in the room when my officials were told that based on the initial modelling the reasonable worst-case scenario around Covid-19 meant that up to 15,000 people could lose their lives over a short period of time. It was a jaw dropping moment. The magnitude of it was difficult to comprehend for anyone hearing it for the first time. After all, we are all human and as a society we do not like talking about death but here we were, dealing with the very real prospect of a pandemic leading to loss in our community on a scale we had never experienced.

There was a question then of where to place this mortuary. In Northern Ireland, or the North, it's a question that becomes more difficult because of our history. That coat of weeds and shells that I described earlier tells the story of the old military site at Kinnegar in Holywood. There is an armed guard at one of the gates, but this is not one of those heavily fortified bases identified with the conflict period. It is situated on the lough shore, in a place of peace and quiet. It can be beautifully calm. At some point it will be developed into something else – more fitting with the scene in which it is situated, and as part of our evolving peace. All of this made the decision on the temporary mortuary easier, but not easy.

NAOMI LONG:

We immediately faced the sensitive and difficult balancing act of finding a suitable site for a temporary mortuary facility while not increasing public fear and speculation because, at that point, the magnitude of the potential death toll had not been fully comprehended. Essentially,

> we did not want to create unnecessary anxiety but we had to ensure
> that we were as prepared as we could be; and so 'Project Dignity' was
> born. The work stream was aptly titled because respect and dignity for
> the deceased, and for their loved ones, was at the heart of everything
> we sought to do.

I find people don't want to speak the word 'morgue'. They whisper
it. Yet, there is a fascination about this place – a not wanting to
know about it, but wanting to know about it. It became part of the
fear, another part of the unknown in terms of this whole story. The
Justice Minister stepped into those sheds.

NAOMI LONG:

> We looked at various possible locations – and I think it's important
> to say that despite speculation on social media around that time,
> Dundonald Ice Bowl and the SSE Arena were never even considered
> as options. The Northern Ireland Temporary Resting Place (NITRP) at
> Kinnegar came about after we made a request for military assistance
> following a discussion with Executive colleagues. In terms of preserving
> dignity for the dead, it was ideal in that it was self-contained, well
> screened from public view and had its own controlled entry and
> exit point. We fully recognised that for some in our community the
> involvement of a military location would be a sensitive issue, which
> is why from the outset the site was unbranded and civilly managed.
> We worked with churches and other faith groups, with the Humanist
> Society, with funeral directors, with the Coroner's Office and other
> partners to ensure if the facility had to be called upon, that at every
> stage there would be privacy and dignity for the deceased.

I have spoken with someone else who has been inside that 'temporary
resting place'. He described it as 'very clinical, very bright, very well
made' – adding that it is 'massively impressive in how it was built,
but then you remember what it is for'. My source spoke about the
aisles and the rows of metal shelving – five-high, if he remembered
correctly: 'It's like a big storeroom, built professionally by people

who hoped it would never be needed.' This is also the hope of the Justice Minister.

NAOMI LONG:

As somebody whose background is in construction, I was fascinated to see the facility and so visited the site on a warm, sunny spring day. Stepping into the storage rooms was a chilling experience in more ways than one. The sheer scale of these two immaculate spaces, held at temperatures of -4° and -20°, brought home the enormity of the potential loss of life in a way that numbers alone never could. And yet, despite the sobering nature of that realisation, I could not help also be hugely impressed at how quickly we went from what were essentially large industrial sheds to what I think is possibly the best temporary morgue facility on these islands. That's not just a boast on behalf of the Justice department, it's the view that has also been expressed to me by the police officers specially trained in body recovery in emergency situations, who agreed to manage the facility should it be called upon. A huge amount of work and thought went into it from start to finish and I have to say the officials in the department were extraordinary in the way they dealt with this difficult issue on a personal level and in how they turned it around in such a short space of time.

One member of the team lost a family member to the coronavirus during this period and it brought home to all of us just how real the issues were. When I watched the news and saw mass graves in New York and bodies piled up in storage containers or lining the floors of morgue corridors, in cities around the world, I have no regrets at the investment we made in this facility because I could not countenance people here having to see their loved ones' remains treated in that way. I believe that the facility we have provided is a dignified resting place and one that remains important, as it stands ready and can be operational within 48 hours if required. Despite being an incredible project, it is one that I hope we will never, ever need to use.

My walk changed. Not the route or the steps I took, but what I thought and what I saw. I wrote about this at the time: how the broken structures that stand up out of the water looked like soldiers standing to attention, and then, in another thought, how they became a quiet line, wake-like, waiting to pay their respects. I wrote also that too much of this will wreck our heads – this, the new fear of a different time. Health Minister Robin Swann was and is dealing with this round-the-clock; still no escape from the threat of this virus or from the pressures of the accompanying decision-making.

ROBIN SWANN:

There have been many seriously difficult periods during the Covid-19 pandemic and, even now with the passage of time, there are particular moments that caused sleepless nights then, that even now still send a chill down my spine.

I was in office for two weeks before the UK's first Civil Contingencies Committee (COBRA) meeting on the coronavirus was called. A fortnight earlier, the little I knew about such meetings was that they were convened during times of national emergency or major disaster. I would never have contemplated ever having to attend, let alone participate, in one. In the days and weeks that followed, many such meetings were called and, unfortunately, the international picture was increasingly bleak and frightening.

As part of a generation that grew up during the latter half of the Troubles, sometimes I think many of us in Northern Ireland became partly desensitised to what would understandably terrify many other societies. Yet it was clear early on that this virus was coming and no one knew how or when it would end, or how deadly it had the potential of being. Given the health and social consequences of an impending epidemic, all attention turned to planning and preparing for the reasonable worst-case scenario of a global influenza pandemic, with no vaccine.

This was a war with different frontlines and uniforms. The hospitals became the battlefields, with the constant fear that they could be overwhelmed. Once a week, we were encouraged to go to our doorsteps to applaud the doctors and nurses and other staff, to rattle pots and pans and to make noise to show our appreciation. It seemed inadequate. Not enough. Many of us could shelter from the threat. Avoid the news. Switch off. Others could not.

ROBIN SWANN:

It was at a very early UK-wide brief at which we were advised of the very real prospect of an 80 per cent infection rate across the population, during which 1 per cent of those would sadly lose their lives. I have always had a habit of hearing numbers and doing calculations in my head, and at that I came to a figure of 15,000 deaths for Northern Ireland alone. That figure and that calculation was what really brought the enormity of what we could face, if we didn't react to this as a community; [there was] the potential of losing over four times the number of people that we lost during three decades of Troubles. The single most terrifying moment for me however was a day or two later whenever I was informed of the prospect of us not having enough body bags to place the victims of Covid-19 in.

Thankfully, through the heroic actions of our citizens and health workers we were able to minimise the number of deaths, but the fear I felt when informed of not having something as basic as enough body bags and coffins is one I never want to experience again. But never did I contemplate that being Health Minister and informing people of my concerns, and giving guidance on how we should act to help protect ourselves and our loved ones, would result in death threats and threats of violence towards my family and myself.

I wrote earlier that the Ulster Unionist decision to join the executive was at the last minute on 11 January 2020. When party leader Steve Aiken nominated Robin Swann, neither could have known the scale of the next challenge: those associated pressures; the threat to the population and then those other threats made against the minister and his family. The other parties could have had the health portfolio, but they left it to be picked up further down the order of choices. It had been identified as a priority in the New Decade, New

Approach document. The pandemic took that priority and urgency to a completely different place.

The crisis focused minds. It looked like the making of our politics. For the first time in a long time, I began to believe in Stormont. I could see its purpose, its potential, the beginnings of a working relationship in that lead office of the executive. Arlene Foster and Michelle O'Neill finding the same page in public, even if there were differences and battles in the background on those issues of response, equipment, timing and testing. I began to think it could work. Of course, there were other big issues in waiting – Brexit and legacy among them – and the centenary and the 'New Ireland' conversations; but if you can build a relationship, then at least there is a chance. Stormont was better than the alternative of Boris Johnson and Dominic Cummings (who has since left Downing Street). Then, in the summer of 2020, our politics was tested again.

Bobby Storey's importance in the IRA's war and the making of its peace has already been referred to. He was part of a headline jail escape in 1983, but he was quickly recaptured and was eventually released before the first of the ceasefires in 1994. He then became one of those contradictions in the peace – part of what Sir Hugh Orde described earlier as a messy endgame. Storey's name was attached to the planning of the Thiepval Barracks bomb of October 1996 (the first IRA attack in Northern Ireland after the collapse of its ceasefire months earlier). Then, in 2002, assessments linked him to the planning of a break-in and the theft of Special Branch documents from the Castlereagh base in Belfast, and, in that same year, to a republican intelligence-gathering episode known as 'Stormontgate'.

The intelligence war that continued after the ceasefires happened in a two-way street; it was not just Special Branch and MI5 trying to get inside the republican head and thinking but also vice versa. Police also believe that Storey was the mastermind behind the £26.5 million Northern Bank robbery in central Belfast in 2004, their jigsaw pieces in relation to everything dating back to the Thiepval Barracks bombs falling into place after the events and not before. If the assessments are correct, then Storey had this quite remarkable ability to walk around and away from all of that sophisticated surveillance gadgetry of watching and listening.

He was arrested again in 2015 after members of the IRA were linked to the murder of Kevin McGuigan in Belfast; it was a reprisal shooting months after a senior republican – Jock Davison – was shot dead in the city (at the time of the McGuigan shooting, I was told police had 'no intelligence or evidence' to link him to the Davison killing). Several days after Storey was released unconditionally, he appeared at a Sunday morning news conference with Martin McGuinness, Mary Lou McDonald, Gerry Adams and the then Sinn Féin MLA Jennifer McCann. This said something about his standing in the republican leadership; his place in that top tier. Storey said the PSNI had no basis for arresting him: 'At no time during my detention did the police present a shred of evidence or intelligence, which in either my opinion or the opinion of my solicitor, warranted my arrest.'

At this news conference, Storey likened the IRA to a caterpillar that had turned into a butterfly and flown away. His line was a tease and a taunt, spoken at a time of intelligence and police assessments that detailed the remnants of an existing IRA structure, including its army council. This was 2015 – ten years after the statement that ended the armed campaign – and the McGuigan murder was the issue that Peter Robinson believed 'held the greatest likelihood of bringing the Executive down' during his period as First Minister. Stormont was on the brink, and we were being reminded again that these transitions are never a straightforward walk from war to peace. There are always obstacles, some more obvious than others.

Why is all of this relevant to the story of Covid-19 and the lockdown restrictions? Bobby Storey died in June 2020; his funeral in west Belfast on the last day of that month was attended by the Sinn Féin leadership, including Stormont deputy First Minister Michelle O'Neill and party president Mary Lou McDonald. Hundreds of men and women in white shirts and black ties lined the route and thousands of others looked in. Social distancing forgotten – guidelines ignored. At Milltown Cemetery, the most senior figures, spanning several decades of the republican leadership, carried the coffin: Sean Murray, Sean Hughes, Martin Lynch, Gerry Kelly, Martin

Ferris and Gerry Adams – a picture that spoke a thousand words; that spoke of Storey's standing inside the republican community. It was Adams who gave the oration to Storey – another oration to one of the IRA's most senior leaders. Politics was in another row. Anyone with their eyes open would have seen it coming.

I arrived in west Belfast before 8.30 a.m. and left within an hour or so, long before the funeral began. That early, I could see in the build-up what this was going to be. While I was there, pockets of those men and women in white shirts and black ties had already begun to gather, some in the carpark at the Kennedy Centre shopping complex, others elsewhere, including at the Felons Club. The police were carrying out a search at the church, where the funeral mass would happen. I had arranged to meet with BBC correspondent Julian O'Neill at around 9 a.m., and minutes later, I told him I was not staying. In these days of the virus, I did not want to be in the vicinity of a crowd of that size, something I told a veteran republican when he saw me walking in the opposite direction of the funeral. The political row was inevitable and it could have been avoided. This was a day when republicans thought of themselves. 'He [Bobby Storey] was entitled, and they [Sinn Féin] were entitled' was the scathing observation of one source.

In the immediate fallout, the decision of First Minister Arlene Foster to withdraw from joint Covid-19 news conferences with the deputy First Minister was entirely understandable. There was an obvious credibility issue. Eventually, Michelle O'Neill acknowledged the damage that had been done – that the public health message had been undermined. She expressed regret. In September 2020, in another period of concern about the virus and its deadly presence, the joint news conferences resumed. The public health message was also undermined in November 2020 when the DUP twice used its veto inside the executive to block four-party support for proposals and papers brought forward by Robin Swann on the need to extend a series of restrictions; only a week later, they were to perform gold-standard political gymnastics by supporting an even tougher lockdown. In all of this, those earlier hopes that I had for this new executive have faded. I understand and know the standing of Bobby

Storey in the republican community. I also understand the place of John Hume in the peace process. When he died in August 2020, his was an entirely different funeral. One was the right decision; the other, the wrong decision. I do not accept the argument that Bobby Storey was 'too big' for it to be any other way. There is no one so big to stand above everyone and everything else. If republicans are serious about a 'New Ireland' conversation, then they need to think beyond themselves. In the worst of the Covid-19 period, people died without their family beside them. People were buried without their family beside them. What was the message on that June day in 2020? Were others 'too small' – less entitled? Respect happens in a two-way street.

CHAPTER 11

Centenary and uncertainty – Union versus unity

The grip is no longer as tight. It's not yet at the point of desperately holding on, but the Union is slipping – not as safe as described in the Combined Loyalist Military Command (CLMC) ceasefire announcement when it responded to the IRA in 1994. As I wrote in the opening pages of this book, this is Ulster's next crossroads and nightmare. The next turn on the road – but in which direction? In this centenary year, the future is uncertain. It perhaps explains, in part, the resistance to an Irish Language Act; unionists are afraid to give something that they feel will, in some way, further diminish or undermine their Britishness. Yet the price for a restored Stormont was an Irish Language Act by another name; it was the only way of having a Northern Ireland Assembly in time for that centenary moment. There are those who can see the signposts on the road ahead, and they haven't the confidence they once had.

Brexit, like a piece of heavy machinery on fragile ground, has left cracks across the four nations of the Union. At the top of British politics, there are those who clearly prioritised exiting the EU over everything else. The consequence of this is the reality of the Irish Sea border and the anger – so evident in 2021 – in parts of the loyalist/unionist community. Once more, they sense betrayal and sell-out.

In recent months, I reread a sequence of twenty-plus statements from the Ulster Unionist Party from October 2019 expressing concern about that sea border – about Northern Ireland being walked into a no-man's land and being placed on the window ledge of the Union. The party was nowhere near the negotiations, yet it could see the shape of the agreement. Are we so foolish to believe that Johnson and Cummings could not? They knew what they were doing.

It was also in October 2019 that then Secretary of State Julian Smith began a direct engagement with loyalists, who, at the time, had been exploring the possibility of using a conduit to have their concerns heard in Downing Street. The questions raised by loyalists in their meetings and conversations with Smith have previously been referred to; they included: what are the tangible, concrete ideas for strengthening the four nations of the Union, and what exactly is meant by 'unfettered' trade?

The 2019 general election added to their fears. Unionists no longer hold the majority of Northern Ireland seats at Westminster; this was the price for their part in the Brexit play that has brought forward the conversation on a 'New Ireland' and a border poll. Centenary is not just about 100 years of Northern Ireland. On the other side of the coin, it is about 100 years of partition.

As indicated earlier, I compiled reports for the BBC in August 2019, twenty-five years on from the first of the ceasefires by the IRA that brought a response from loyalists in October 1994. I won't ever forget the hell of the years before – that surge in loyalist violence in the 1990s when the talks between Hume–Adams and Dublin became public as well as secret contacts between the British government and the republican leadership; both dialogues were deliberately manoeuvred into public attention. Loyalists feared a sell-out but were persuaded that there had been no secret deals and that the Union was safe. That was then, and there is a very different now. Lord Robin Eames – then Church of Ireland Primate – helped persuade the loyalist leadership of that time.

I was present in Fernhill House in Belfast in 1994 when Gusty Spence read the words of that loyalist ceasefire statement, and I learned recently that Winston Irvine was also there. He was 20 years old then. We did not know each other, but we do now. On his journey, he completed a Masters at Maynooth University in International Peacebuilding, Security and Development, and he has become part of the public stage as a spokesman for the loyalist community.

In October 2019, Irvine was involved in those meetings with Arlene Foster that I referenced earlier and, then, with Julian Smith. These separate meetings were about the implications of Brexit – what it would mean for the Union. They were an opportunity for loyalists to express their concerns and to ask their questions. At this uncertain moment in history, now so obvious and real in 2021, I asked Irvine to write here, to let his words breathe and to give us the pulse and the mood of the loyalist community.

WINSTON IRVINE:

As we mark the centenary of the formation of the state of Northern Ireland, the partition of Ireland and consider the Ireland of today, we are brought into direct contact with the historical moment in which diverging constitutional, political and ideological differences were encapsulated within an historic British–Irish political accord. This resulted in the establishment of two distinct jurisdictions on the island of Ireland. The consequences of this accord remain highly controversial and divisive, leaving in place a complex set of problems and grievances, and an unresolved conflict sustained to a lesser or greater degree by all sides. Like most complex and contested political arrangements, they mean different things to different people and are dependent on the particular interpretative structure one uses to convert actions and lived experiences into 'meaning', and more importantly, how its narrative is devised and nurtured, relative to its specific audience. Sound familiar? Well, it is, albeit its application has had a different political framework, set in a more recent era – namely that of the Good Friday/Belfast Agreement – the period of the 1998 peace accord.

For unionists and loyalists, the centenary of the foundation of Northern Ireland will mark a momentous moment and represent an expression of great occasion and national pride. However, there are also those who are detecting a feeling of uncertainty and perhaps even a sense of foreboding of what the future might hold for the

Union of Great Britain and Northern Ireland. This is especially so when judged against what is clearly a growing chorus of voices and perspectives ... already deemed as being predisposed to the aspiration of a United Ireland ... who are talking up the prospects of a different union, one involving the island of Ireland as a whole under one unified geographical and political entity. There is also the rise of English, Scottish, Welsh, and Irish nationalist sentiment across the United Kingdom and Ireland, not to mention the shifting trends and patterns in how people are self-designating when it comes to demographic categorisation.

Irvine wants thoughtful and thinking dialogues in 2021 – not separate and competing conversations. The task is how to discuss the centenary and partition without them becoming the two ends of one rope pulling against each other to create another of those impossible knots. A more thinking approach is how to achieve one conversation that brings together both that sense of foreboding that Irvine has described and identified and, from another part of the community, that growing sense of expectation. It is about moving those at the two ends of the rope into some middle place of managed and facilitated discussion – loosening the conversation. A vote in itself does not create a 'New Ireland'. You have to move people in their minds and in their thinking. It is there that the real borders and barriers exist – the different understandings and interpretations and arguments of the lived experiences of the past 100 years, and how you begin to decommission those mindsets. In this conversation, we walk in another minefield. It is no place for careless steps.

WINSTON IRVINE:

For many nationalists and republicans, the arrival of the centenary of the state of Northern Ireland will represent a new form of grievance and disaffection and serve as a reminder of how this issue is firmly fixed within the imagination of that community. As I see it, because of these parallel and polarised political forces, we are being guided to and along different paths, moving towards very different destinations, the outworking of which means we are locked on to a collision course – sooner or later, these two entirely legitimate political aspirations are certain to clash.

And, so, today, as the call for a border poll grows bigger and louder, and as the machinery of both governments begins to re-orientate their positions according to their respective audiences, relative to the question of Northern Ireland's constitutional future, the path to peace is constrained once again by binary choices concerning the national question. All the while unionist fervour for Northern Ireland's place within the United Kingdom becomes even more ingrained within the psyche of unionists and loyalists – therefore setting the scene for both sides to begin to unilaterally dictate the terms of their own solution. Something that is likely not to end well.

Therefore, this centenary year should serve as a wake-up call for everyone. And we should demand urgent action of ourselves and others in order to avoid any future calamity. There is, in my view, real merit in looking forwards and backwards, as a course of action in abstracting out lessons and learning for today and tomorrow. As far as unionists and loyalists are concerned, this will require a reversion in thinking and in action, in my opinion, to a time when the leaderships and movements of Ulster Unionism and Loyalism were united in common cause, with one over-arching political goal: to copper-fasten Northern Ireland's place within the United Kingdom – a subject that we will return to.

That joined-up thinking was how loyalism and unionism found its way through the negotiations and political agreements of the 1990s. A Combined Loyalist Military Command delivered the ceasefire, and loyalists remained inside the talks with UUP leader David Trimble as other unionists shouted in from the outside. The loyalist and unionist communities have fractured and frayed since then, but this next turn on the road – the 2021 conversation and what happens beyond – demands careful steering and management. Can loyalism and unionism find one voice and one position at this time; can they find the confidence of the 1990s to speak not just among themselves but also to others?

WINSTON IRVINE:

Let me say something of that period from 1994–1998, a time in which bitter conflict and communal hostilities were at fever pitch, and what is undeniably a centrepiece of the historical backdrop that has shaped modern Northern Irish political development. In a somewhat tour de force in peace-making, it is a phase of the peace and political process that is also widely recognised as being a defining era that established loyalism's political leadership credentials – given the major contribution from people such as Gusty Spence, Gary McMichael, David Ervine, Davy Adams, Billy Hutchinson, Billy Mitchell, Plum Smith, Hugh Smyth, to name but a few.

In this next big discussion, there is no one-side answer. So, what are the steps that might avoid that collision and clash that Irvine writes about? Is there a path through the minefield that I describe? There is only one place and one way to test this. It is in a dialogue that brings all the sides and arguments together. This template is the process that made the Good Friday/Belfast Agreement. A chair in the room for all who want to talk, and people from outside of us to help the conversation.

WINSTON IRVINE:

Bound by a shared sense of common purpose and cause, the leaderships and memberships of the Ulster Unionist Party and political representatives of the PUP and UDP, who represented the loyalist paramilitary groupings, helped successfully negotiate the 1998 political agreement, and its historic peace accord that marked the end of major hostilities in and about Northern Ireland. An accomplishment unrivalled in Anglo–Irish relations, by any standards. Therefore if you accept the view that unionism and loyalism can be a real force for the common good when it acts in unison, then it follows that in order to best meet the challenges and uncertainties of today, and in the near future, there is much to be gained from re-visiting and re-evaluating the formulae that helped previous successful unionist and loyalist leadership movements transcend previous historic animosities.

Although it must be borne in mind that all political solutions relate to a point in time, and as grounds shift and change, they need to be revisited. And as we acknowledge the uncertainty of the future, in which there are no guarantees, or foregone conclusions and where nothing is inevitable, unionists and loyalists must embrace and repurpose the lessons from 1994–1998, that there is nothing to fear or lose from respectful, reasoned and reciprocal dialogue. In the past and at critical stages unionists and loyalists have spoken within and across divisions, understanding that engaging with your opponent does not make you any less British, loyalist or unionist. Something that unionists and loyalists of today need to come to terms with.

Those conversations within and outside the loyalist community can be equally challenging. Change is difficult. Compromise is often reduced to a conversation about winning and losing. I was with Irvine as part of a panel discussion in Carrickfergus, County Antrim in October 2019, when there was an explosion of emotions in a packed hall. At times, it was raw – a chance to vent about restrictions on flying the Union Flag, on marching, on bonfires. There was a sense that, on the past, it was the security forces who were being pursued and not the IRA. Unionism/loyalism is unnerved. The border poll conversation is adding to those fears. In that anger, there is danger. The centenary year – 2021 – could easily become the next divisive conversation.

WINSTON IRVINE:

In reflecting back over my own experiences of those early days of the peace and political process, as a young man – who was active inside loyalism in the run up to and during that 1994–1998 period – it was hard not to have felt somewhat awestruck by the incredible events and people that were shaping and influencing political change all around us. Whilst inside various clandestine and backroom political meetings, involving senior loyalist leadership figures and Progressive Unionist Party members, as people debated and searched for a way out of the quagmire of armed conflict and the political stagnation – sometimes in a manner in which heated debate turned into people having stand-up rows with one another – there was nothing more impressive or illuminating than sitting alongside people while they teased their way through the intricacies of ceasefires. Or as they discussed in detail the major concerns over Northern Ireland's sovereignty, of prisoners and policing and justice issues, and of the need to be able to see beyond their own immediate political interests and attempt to read between the lines and behind the lines of political opponents, in order to understand what lay beneath their rhetoric and political posturing. All of which was about bending the needle in the direction of the safety and security of the United Kingdom, as we know it today.

Those meetings, the heated discussions – that trying to work out and understand the other – became the crafting of the loyalist ceasefire statement. It was about finding a way to a new place; part of this process was about the right choice of words to make and mark that moment.

WINSTON IRVINE:

Even though twenty-seven years have passed, the extraordinary scenes and impressions from inside Fernhill House – that stately home that was to play a crucial role as part of Lord Carson's campaign against Home Rule – are still current. It was here that Gusty Spence delivered the Combined Loyalist Military Command ceasefire statement of 1994. I, and others in the room, became transfixed by the words and the moral weight with which they were being spoken and heard. The words, 'abject and true remorse', spoken by Gusty, on behalf of himself and others, were the beginning for me in understanding the scale and extent of the power of reaching out across differences. Whether consciously or subconsciously, it was clear that history was literally being written and transformed in that very moment.

Looking back from the here-and-now, and paying new attention to identifying key lessons that can be extracted from the past in order to structure the future, is, in my opinion, one of the clearest answers to facing head-on the present uncertainties that have been articulated. What can unionism and loyalism learn from that 1994–1998 period? What are some of the key challenges they face? And more importantly, what can be done to address them in 2021? Given the scale and pace of the dynamic changes occurring internally and externally within the context of the United Kingdom, particularly those which concern Northern Ireland – namely a border poll, increased support for a united Ireland, demographic shifts and trends – unionism and loyalism in all their various shades need to build the context and capacity in which a serious dialogue between them and others can occur. Co-operation and coherence within and across unionism and loyalism should be seen as a prerequisite for long-term political stability. Empowering loyalists in a legitimate sense means they are less likely to look for authority from other sources. Events surrounding the period from 1994–98 would certainly lend itself to that assertion.

Irvine is challenging his community to open its eyes; to see beyond itself; to think of the next arguments; to be part of these arguments. Not just his community but all communities. This cannot be about talking to yourself in the mirror; not if we want to avoid that collision course described earlier in his writing. Change is inevitable. In 1998, the Good Friday/Belfast Agreement was part of it. What is the next agreement?

WINSTON IRVINE:

Perhaps one of the most important challenges for those of a pro-union persuasion is the question: what kind of future Northern Ireland do you want to see for unionists, nationalists and the non-aligned?

People need to see a vision of the future that they are being asked to move toward. They also need to feel and believe and become part of a collaboratively designed vision and narrative that is going to capture and serve the interests that are important to them and that of their family. They need to build a dream that is uplifting, forward-orientated, inclusive and relevant to the people that they are trying to convince. The question then becomes, how do you do that?

There is something profoundly powerful in reaching out beyond differences, beyond your own tribe. In practical terms, it means engaging in conversation, in processes of dialogue, in peaceful co-operation, in the broadest of terms, thereby localising engagement across differences at multiple levels. Otherwise, it is impossible to see how you could bridge the moral, tribal, political, constitutional differences that are encapsulated in the differing aspirations that define the deep-rooted divisions between the main traditions on the island.

If Unionism and loyalism are to chart a new course, they need to stop looking for scapegoats, bogeymen and traitors, and start nurturing thinkers, allies and next-generation leaders. So, as we contemplate this centenary year, and for the Union to be truly inclusive, proponents of the United Kingdom would do well to draw upon and harness the very best of the British, Welsh, Scottish and Irish traditions, as a tribute to its 100th anniversary.

There are challenges in Irvine's words – both within his community and across the communities: the challenge to talk and, perhaps, as in 1998, make the impossible compromise and agreement. Loyalism had credibility then. Those he named helped David Trimble carry the weight of the Good Friday Agreement, but, more than that, they also helped Gerry Adams and Sinn Féin understand what was possible – including republicans adjusting their demands on a timeframe for prisoner releases so as not to break Trimble and the possibility of the unionist community accepting that agreement. The loyalists of 1998 understood republicans in a way that the unionist leadership did not, all of which contributed to possibilities.

So, there is also the challenge of going back in time to learn in the present. A dialogue that does not involve all the relevant voices will not work. Sinn Féin cannot lead the conversation on a 'New Ireland' – should not lead that conversation, nor can the SDLP or the Irish government. This needs a much broader initiative – perhaps, the two governments appointing an international chair as they did with

Senator George Mitchell in the shaping of the Belfast Agreement. Then, inviting all opinions into the room with a blank canvas to begin with. What is this 'New Ireland'? What is Britishness and unionism within it? What is the political construct in the North? How does it work financially? How does it work, also, in terms of education and health?

Forty years after he gave that 'H' Block oration for the hunger striker Bobby Sands, the republican Jake Mac Siacais believes '2021 offers us an opportunity to close the book on this final chapter of Stormont and to imagine ways in which all of us who share these islands can do so in ways which accommodate peaceful co-existence, mutual respect and real social justice.' He was speaking with me as we walked and talked on that political hill in the grounds of the Stormont estate in late November 2020. He spoke of repeated attempts 'at breathing life into the cadaver that is Stormont' and argued that this runs against logic. He quoted the late Charles Haughey, that the North was a failed political entity, and added his own thought that 'The North is, was and will continue to be a failed political entity.'

The veteran republican spoke of the need for 'a blank sheet conversation where we honestly engage with the malaise at the heart of this society'. 'British policy in Ireland was an utter failure, which ill-served everyone. It's time for real dialogue and real politic.' It is a conversation of sides and opinions that will pull at the two ends of the one rope, but it is a dialogue that cannot be avoided.

Mac Siacais knows the Hume–Adams process in its finest detail and knows that John Hume spoke of an 'agreed Ireland'. If you do not have an agreement, then it is not agreed. The Belfast republican also knows that you cannot leave the loyalist/unionist community behind: 'If you bring an alienated, demoralised, broken unionist minority into all-Ireland arrangements, then you're simply creating a stick for your own back.' This is what I meant when I wrote earlier that a 'New Ireland' is about so much more than a vote. Are we going to build the future on top of an unresolved past, repeat the mistakes of recent decades? This conversation needs creative thinkers, imaginative pens; new ideas inside a new script. It needs outside help. It needs an organised beginning and then the drawing of that 'New Ireland' on that blank page. It also needs patience, and it needs time – the working out of the journey and the best roads to take. The 'New Ireland' cannot, should not, be the 'Old Ireland'.

What became more clear as we turned into 2021 was the need to step carefully on that political eggshell that is Northern Ireland. The Union is already different as a result of Brexit and the sea border, and there are many questions. Who is best placed to sell the benefits of the Union? Surely not those who were loudest in the Brexit debate and who have done so much damage to that cause. We hear them now trying to distance themselves from that, but it is too late. Who, in this debate, will lead for unionism? As I write, there are again questions about Arlene Foster's leadership. And, for those in other communities, making the argument for a New Ireland, there is learning from the Brexit project and experience. Don't ask the question until you have the answers. And, in this conversation about the future, it is important to remember this, that Northern Ireland or the North is no longer a place of just two tribes. Everything is changing.

Afterword

Hume – 'his long war for peace'

I don't know how many times I read or heard John Hume's name in the course of reporting that transition from conflict to peace, and its many twists and turns. I read it in the vitriol of political and media commentary that chastised and challenged him for the 'sin' of daring to talk with Adams. For too many, the more comfortable option was condemnation. So, words were spat at Hume like piercing shrapnel and then spread out in headlines written to admonish. The conflict continued. Hume, with others, was trying to end it.

His talks with Adams had been encouraged by Fr Alec Reid and Taoiseach Charles Haughey, and it is in 1988 that Hume's 'real involvement begins'. In a reference to the continuing violence, one source described it as a 'completely mad year' – 'bonkers'. Who believed in peace then? SDLP–Sinn Féin talks began as party delegation meetings and developed into that critical one-to-one dialogue involving Hume and Adams.

As we move into the 1990s, I also read Hume's name in the chilling statements of loyalist organisations; many of them were dictated to me with accompanying codewords used to authenticate their source and content. Often, the purpose was to admit killings, to threaten more, and there is a pattern in this period of using the Hume–Adams dialogue as the excuse. Hume put his health and his life on the line for peace. There is no bigger contribution – no more that can be asked of any individual. He put people before party politics, had the vision to see what others could not and made the ceasefires and political agreements possible. He believed Adams could deliver; he believed it because he was bold enough to step into a dialogue with the republican leader and find out for himself. In 1998, Hume was jointly awarded the Nobel Peace Prize with the unionist leader David Trimble.

Before then, I had read his name in the explanations of that dialogue with Adams and in the arguments that were made for another way – for an alternative to arms and for an 'Agreed Ireland'. In August 1994, when the IRA announced 'a complete cessation of military operations', it was Hume, along with Adams and others, who made that possible. Right up to that announcement, senior SDLP colleagues had questioned Hume and doubted Adams and the IRA. For a fleeting moment, the IRA thought about briefing the party's deputy leader Seamus Mallon on that impending statement, but they chose not to; they decided that it was not their business – that it was up to Hume. When that ceasefire collapsed in February 1996, it was Hume, along with Adams, who went to meet the IRA leadership. They met them to try again. Peace-building is not about one moment. It is about many.

On Monday, 3 August 2020, I read Hume's name again in two statements that arrived in my email box within minutes of each other. The first from his family with the news that he had died in the early hours of the morning after a short illness. Then, just minutes later, a statement from the SDLP leader Colum Eastwood, including this line: 'It is no exaggeration to say that each and every one of us now lives in the Ireland Hume imagined – an island at peace and free to decide its own destiny.' Hume's death was just weeks before his party would celebrate its fiftieth anniversary.

In a tweet, the political journalist Aoife Moore captured the love and respect for him in his home city: 'When John Hume first got dementia, he would still go on long walks. You'd always see him along the Foyle. As it progressed, people would walk with him to make sure he was alright. A few people I know walked him home. John Hume looked after us, so Derry looked after him. RIP John.'

On 5 August 2020, in a couple of BBC radio interviews, I recalled a meeting with Hume in February 1995 – months after the ceasefires, but, as we know now, a long way from peace. He drank black coffee, smoked continuously and talked almost in a whisper. He was restless, fidgeting with his lighter, and he struck me as a man under immense pressure. Who else could have carried the weight of that effort? On the news of Hume's death, President Clinton spoke of 'his long war for peace'. It is the perfect phrase to summarise Hume's mission and that wider challenge of building politics on top of conflict. As in Derry, at the McGuinness funeral those several years earlier, Clinton again found the right words.

Throughout his dialogue with Adams, Hume persevered. At different moments, he needed Clinton. Needed the late Charles Haughey, the late Albert Reynolds. Needed the late Fr Alec Reid. Needed the late Martin McGuinness. Needed the late Mo Mowlam. Needed the late Seamus Mallon. At times, needed the encouragement of the late Brendan Duddy, the key link and intermediary in that backchannel that ran between the British government and the republican leadership. Those who helped make the peace are leaving us. Add David Ervine, Gusty Spence, William 'Plum' Smith and the Presbyterian minister Roy Magee to that list.

They have left the work still to be done to those in leadership roles today. Perhaps the biggest challenge is to get beyond blame. How does that leadership of Adams and others free today's republican generation of the questions about the IRA? When will unionists/loyalists see beyond *what* happened and look into the *why* – how a shameful politics became the fire? It is not good enough to say the conflict should never have happened. It did happen, and it cannot be undone.

When will two governments accept and understand that a legacy process cannot be shaped from within the political systems in Britain and Ireland, that this needs to be designed and written by others, by people with the skills and the words to bring together the different narratives and perspectives of those conflict years, including what is often called the 'dirty war' and the collusion that was part of it.

In 2020, the coronavirus emerged as a different threat; but it also brought back those fears and memories of the conflict years and created that image of a 'mass grave' in the mind of the senior police officer Tim Mairs as he stood inside that emergency mortuary at Kinnegar in Holywood. It made him think of the threats of yesteryear and today and the different responses. There is no line thick enough to draw over or under or through our past.

So, what is the learning in all of this? That you can never hide from what was there before. There is no such thing as rubbing it out. Somehow, no matter how difficult, the questions that are being avoided must be answered to be included in an assessment that is best written from outside of us – the lines that explain and help us understand what happened and why. Written in ink and not in blood. Written to learn from and not to repeat. A 'New Ireland' – North and South – built on our past will never be a new house. It will crumble and fall into that 'mass grave'.

As I put my pen down, I have many thoughts and questions. Have we really achieved the Ireland that Hume imagined – that place at peace with itself? That is not how it feels. Not now. There is more a sense of fear, anger – uncertainty. The coronavirus has, of course, contributed to this. Every day has been a story of deaths, cases and the numbers of people in intensive care. Brexit has left its imprint – its mark has disturbed relationships. Once more, politics feels broken. That Smith–Coveney moment and initiative in January 2020 now seems a lifetime ago – forgotten in these latest days of fury. Community tensions are obvious. Policing became part of the mess. This is the context of 2021. The mood in which that next big conversation of Union versus Unity is happening. In what is meant to be a year of celebration, Northern Ireland – the North – has been unsettled; unsure of its next steps. We could, in the words of one of the contributors to this book, be 'plunged headlong into another political maelstrom'. Winston Irvine writes: 'As we search for a solution to this chaos, we might do well to remember – as history shows – that simply merging two nations and two opposing political cultures into one sovereign, democratic framework, did not produce the elixir to cure our political ills beyond a short term flicker of hope.' Our new conversation is happening inside an old frame; politics destabilised – a tug-of-war between hope and fear, and, once again, the knot is tightening.

Chronology

From ceasefires to peace

1988: Quiet conversations about peace

This was the year when the Social Democratic and Labour Party (SDLP) and Sinn Féin met in party delegation meetings, which by the 1990s had developed into the Hume–Adams dialogue, with Dublin informed. These talks, as well as secret contacts between the British government and the republican leadership, became public knowledge in 1993, deliberately manoeuvred out into the open. Violence continued, but within a year, the Irish Republican Army (IRA) and the major loyalist organisations had declared ceasefires – the first steps on a long road to peace.

1994: The year of the ceasefires

March 1994: A Combined Loyalist Military Command (CLMC) statement sent in private to Archbishop Robin Eames to share with the UK government stated, 'Being mindful of what is called the "peace process", the CLMC wishes to offer to their Government terms for consideration which would enable hostilities from this source to cease.'

31 August 1994: A CLMC statement before the IRA ceasefire announcement stated, 'The CLMC wish to make it quite clear that we will not be dancing to the pan-nationalist tune.' The statement calls on unionist leaders Ian Paisley and James Molyneaux to go to Downing Street to seek answers to questions: 'Is our Constitution being tampered with or is it not? What deals have been done?'

31 August 1994: The IRA announces 'a complete cessation of military operations' from midnight.

13 October 1994: The CLMC says it 'will universally cease all operational hostilities' from midnight.

December 1994: The government begins exploratory dialogue with Sinn Féin and loyalist parties – the Progressive Unionist Party (PUP) and Ulster Democratic Party (UDP).

1995: 'There shall be no first strike'

Throughout the year, arguments continue over the decommissioning of weapons.

February 1995: The Frameworks for the Future document is published, setting out proposals for government in Northern Ireland, and relationships within the island of Ireland and between the two governments.

25 August 1995: A CLMC statement reads, 'The CLMC wish to reassure the people of NI that provided their rights are upheld, the CLMC will not initiate a return to war. There shall be no first strike.'

8 September 1995: David Trimble becomes the new Ulster Unionist Party leader.

29 September 1995: An IRA statement reads, 'The entire decommissioning issue is a deliberate distraction and stalling tactic by a British Government acting in bad faith.'

12 October 1995: On the eve of the first anniversary of the loyalist ceasefire, Gusty Spence says the time is now ripe for political dialogue: 'The guns are silent. Let them remain silent. I say now is the time to move.'

1996: Breakdown

9 February 1996: The IRA ends its ceasefire from 6 p.m. Their statement reads, 'The cessation presented an historic challenge for everyone and Óglaigh na hÉireann commends the leadership of nationalist Ireland at home and abroad. They rose to the challenge. The British Prime Minister did not.' An hour later, a bomb explodes in London Docklands.

28 February 1996: John Hume and Gerry Adams meet the IRA leadership.

12 March 1996: A CLMC statement warns that IRA attacks 'cannot be permitted to continue without a telling response from this source … We will give blow for blow.'

7 October 1996: There is an IRA bomb attack inside the Army Headquarters at Thiepval Barracks, Lisburn.

November 1996: The IRA holds a General Army Convention.

1997: Split

May 1997: The British general election takes place; Tony Blair and Labour achieve a landslide victory.

19 July 1997: There is an IRA statement announcing 'a complete cessation of military operations from 12 o'clock midday on Sunday, 20 July 1997. We have ordered the unequivocal restoration of the ceasefire of August 1994. All IRA units have been instructed accordingly.'

September 1997: Sinn Féin joins talks leading to the Good Friday Agreement. Trimble and the Ulster Unionist Party enter this phase of talks with the loyalist parties, the PUP and UDP.

October 1997: The IRA holds a General Army Convention. Resignations follow, including a number at a senior level. These are the roots of the dissident IRA. The intention had been to dislodge the Adams/ McGuinness leadership. An assessment from a senior Northern Ireland Office (NIO) security official includes, 'The situation is that Adams and McGuinness still have the Movement … There are no bodies on the border. The net effect is a crack of the whip over the two governments to get on with it [the talks].'

1998: History and horror

As talks continue, the emerging dissident IRA carries out a number of bomb attacks.

10 April 1998: The Good Friday Agreement is made; it includes a 108-seat assembly and a 12-member executive. It addresses north–south and east–west relations and sets out processes for prisoner releases, decommissioning and police reform.

29 April 1998: An IRA statement describes the agreement as 'a significant development'. On decommissioning, the statement reads, 'Let us make it clear that there will be no decommissioning by the IRA. This issue as with any other matter effecting the IRA, its functions and objectives, is a matter only for the IRA, to be decided upon and pronounced upon by us.'

May 1998: Another IRA convention changes its constitution to allow members to take seats in the new assembly.

May 1998: Majority support for Good Friday Agreement in referendum.

June 1998: The assembly election yields the following results: Ulster Unionist Party (UUP), 28 seats; SDLP, 24 seats; Democratic Unionist Party (DUP), 20 seats; Sinn Féin, 18 seats; Alliance, 6 seats; UK Unionist Party (UKUP), 5 seats; PUP, 2 seats; NI Women's Coalition, 2 seats; independent anti-agreement unionists, 3 seats.

15 August 1998: The dissident IRA bomb Omagh.

7 September 1998: The dissident IRA announce complete ceasefire.

11 September 1998: This date marks the beginning of the phased release of republican and loyalist prisoners.

18 December 1998: The first act of decommissioning by the Loyalist Volunteer Force (LVF).

After the Belfast Agreement, arguments continue over IRA decommissioning, summarised in the phrase 'no guns – no government'. This is the tug-of-war and the battle for the implementation of the 1998 accord.

1999: 'We've jumped, you follow'

29 March 1999: An IRA statement on 'the disappeared' includes, 'We believe we have established the whereabouts of the graves of nine people, some of whom were members of Óglaigh na hÉireann who were executed for activities which put other Óglaigh na hÉireann personnel at risk or jeopardised the struggle.' An accompanying IRA briefing includes, 'As part of this investigation we also endeavoured to locate the burial site of British SAS operative Robert Nairac. We were unable to do so.'

9 September 1999: The Patten Report, or *A New Beginning: Policing in Northern Ireland*, is produced. This is a major reform package, including the end of the Royal Ulster Constabulary (RUC) title and the process leading to the Police Service of Northern Ireland (PSNI). Chris Patten states, 'We believe that it is possible to find a policing solution to the policing problem, but only if you take the politics out of policing. That is a key part of this report – the depoliticisation of policing.'

16 November 1999: The Mitchell Review of the implementation of the Good Friday Agreement ends, leading to a sequence of statements. The IRA does not commit to actual decommissioning but, in a statement, confirms it will appoint a representative 'to enter into discussions' with General John de Chastelain and the Independent International Commission on Decommissioning (IICD).

27 November 1999: The Ulster Unionist Party votes to establish the executive. This happens on 29 November. The Ulster Unionist

Council is to reconvene in February 2000, meaning decommissioning should occur before then. Party leader David Trimble says, 'We've done our bit, Mr Adams, it's over to you. We've jumped, you follow.'

27 November 1999: A statement from Gerry Adams includes, 'I welcome the decision today to establish the institutions but I am disappointed that Mr Trimble has stepped outside the Mitchell Review and the Good Friday Agreement by unilaterally introducing a new element, a new deadline, which seeks to dictate and totally undermines and contradicts the agreed role of the IICD.'

2 December 1999: The first meeting of the executive.

2000: Phased process of prisoner releases is completed

The continuing battle is this argument about the decommissioning of IRA arms linked to the stability or instability of the political institutions.

January 2000: Gerry Adams states, 'We want to see all of these matters resolved. I think that they can be resolved, but I think the way they're being tackled at the moment is the road to disaster.'

31 January 2000: A report from IICD states, 'Our sole task is decommissioning and to date we have received no information from the IRA as to when decommissioning will start.' (The report was not made public until 11 February.)

11 February 2000: Devolution is suspended.

6 May 2000: An IRA statement announces a confidence-building measure of arms inspections by third parties who will report to IICD. Inspections are to happen 'within weeks'.

27 May 2000: The Ulster Unionist Council votes to return to government.

25 June 2000: There is confirmation of the first arms inspections.

28 July 2000: The phased process of prisoner releases is completed.

2001: First act of IRA decommissioning

In August and September 2001, in continuing arguments over decommissioning, there are two technical suspensions of devolution, then – weeks later – the IRA completes its first act of putting arms beyond use.

22 October 2001: In a speech by Gerry Adams at Conway Mill, west Belfast, he states, 'Martin McGuinness and I have also held discussions with the IRA and we have put to the IRA leadership the view that if it could make a groundbreaking move on the arms issue that this could save the peace process from collapse and transform the situation.'

23 October 2001: An IRA statement on the first act of decommissioning states, 'This unprecedented move is to save the peace process and to persuade others of our genuine intentions.'

23 October 2001: A statement from the IICD reads, 'We have now witnessed an event – which we regard as significant – in which the IRA has put a quantity of arms completely beyond use.'

4 November 2001: The PSNI is founded, succeeding the RUC.

2002: Politics collapses

8 April 2002: The IRA announces the second act of decommissioning.

October 2002: A culmination of alleged IRA activities, including training and intelligence-gathering leads to the suspension of devolution.

2003–04: Adams and the IRA jump, Trimble decides not to follow

21 October 2003: A choreographed sequence of events designed to restore devolution collapses. There was a speech by Gerry Adams, statements from the IRA and the third, and largest, act of putting arms beyond use – before David Trimble paused the sequence and steps towards restoring devolution over a lack of detail on the extent of decommissioning. In the election that follows, the DUP becomes the largest unionist party. Protracted, arms-length negotiations in 2004, exploring the possibility of an agreement between the DUP and Sinn Féin, fail on the demand for photographic proof of IRA decommissioning. An expected fourth act of putting arms beyond use is postponed. At the end of 2004, the IRA is linked to a major bank robbery in Belfast. Devolution does not return until 2007.

2005: An end to the armed campaign

6 April 2005: An Adams speech, addressing the IRA, includes, 'In the past, I have defended the right of the IRA to engage in armed struggle. I did so because there was no alternative for those who would not bend the knee, or turn a blind eye to oppression, or for those who wanted a national republic. Now, there is an alternative … Can you take courageous initiatives which will achieve your aims by purely political and democratic activity?'

7 May 2005: David Trimble resigns as Ulster Unionist Party leader.

28 July 2005: An IRA statement reads, 'The leadership of Óglaigh na hÉireann has formally ordered an end to the armed campaign. This will take effect from 4 p.m. this afternoon. All IRA units have been ordered to dump arms.' Prime Minister Tony Blair gives a statement: 'This is a step of unparalleled magnitude in the recent history of Northern Ireland … the statement is of a different order to anything before.' Taoiseach Bertie Ahern also gives a statement: 'The end of the IRA as a paramilitary organisation is the outcome the governments have been working towards since the cessation of military activities in 1994. If the IRA's words are borne out by verified actions, it will be a momentous and historic development.'

1 August 2005: There is news that the Northern Ireland-based battalions of the Royal Irish Regiment are to be disbanded as part of the military response to the IRA statement. The Army will end its support role to the police – Operation Banner – on 1 August 2007.

19 August 2005: Mo Mowlan, the NI Secretary of State at the time of the Good Friday Agreement, dies.

26 September 2005: An IRA statement, signed P. O'Neill, reads, 'The leadership of Óglaigh na hÉireann announced on July 28th that we had authorised our representative to engage with the IICD to complete the process to verifiably put arms beyond use. The IRA leadership can now confirm that the process of putting our arms beyond use has been completed.'

30 October 2005: A statement from the Loyalist Volunteer Force declares, 'The leadership of the LVF have today ordered all their military units to stand down. This decision is taken as a direct response to recent IRA actions and statements.'

2006: 'not all PIRA's [the Provisional IRA's] weapons and ammunition were handed over for decommissioning'

1 February 2006: Included in a report by the Independent Monitoring Commission is an assessment of the extent of IRA decommissioning the previous September; it reads, 'We have since received reports that not all PIRA's weapons and ammunition were handed over for decommissioning.'

13 June 2006: Former Taoiseach Charles Haughey dies.

8 July 2006: In a meeting in Belfast, I noted the last statement dictated to me in the name of the IRA's P. O'Neill. It read, 'Following a public request from the family of Jean McConville, the IRA carried out a thorough investigation of all the circumstances surrounding her death. That investigation has confirmed that Jean McConville was working as an informer for the British Army. The conclusion of this investigation was reported to Michael McConville. The IRA accepts that he rejects this conclusion. The IRA regrets the suffering of all of the families whose loved ones were killed and buried by the IRA.' Twenty-four hours earlier, on 7 July 2006, there had been a statement from the Police Ombudsman, which included, 'There is no evidence that Mrs McConville gave information to the police, the military or the Security Service. She was not an informant.'

10 October 2006: On the eve of the St Andrews talks, Adams makes a speech to a republican audience in the Europa Hotel, including, 'So let it be clear Sinn Féin's focus on policing is about depoliticising the police force and changing it from an armed wing of the state to a service for the people.' He also said, 'Our support for policing and law and order is not a response to unionist demands. Neither is it a tradeable commodity to be retained or given away as part of a deal.'

October 2006: The St Andrews talks and agreement pave the way for the restoration of devolution months later. Among the steps to be taken before then is the requirement that Sinn Féin support the new policing arrangements. That endorsement follows an IRA convention and a Sinn Féin special Ard Fheis in January 2007.

2007: New Government – New Days

8 January 2007: Loyalist politician and former UVF prisoner David Ervine dies. Four days later, on 12 January, Gerry Adams attends his funeral, as do former Taoiseach Albert Reynolds, PSNI Chief Constable Sir Hugh Orde and Secretary of State Peter Hain.

28 January 2007: At the special Sinn Féin Ard Fheis, a motion endorsing new policing arrangements passes with overwhelming majority. That same weekend, the IRA meets in an Army Convention.

26 March 2007: A statement from DUP leader Ian Paisley declares, 'On Saturday the DUP Executive overwhelmingly endorsed a motion committing the party to support and participate fully in government in May this year. This is a binding resolution … Today, we have agreed with Sinn Féin that this date will be Tuesday 8 May 2007.'

26 March 2007: A statement by Sinn Féin President Gerry Adams reads, 'While it is disappointing that the institutions of the Good Friday Agreement have not been restored today, I believe the agreement reached between Sinn Féin and the DUP, including the unequivocal commitment made by their party Executive and reiterated today, to the restoration of the political institutions on 8 May, marks the beginning of a new era of politics on this island.'

3 May 2007: Statements by the Ulster Volunteer Force (UVF) and Red Hand Commando Command Staff declare, 'as of twelve midnight, Thursday 3rd May 2007, the Ulster Volunteer Force and Red Hand Commando will assume a non-military, civilianised, role.'

8 May 2007: A new day of devolution. Ian Paisley and Martin McGuinness become First Minister and deputy First Minister. The executive is nominated.

11 November 2007: A statement from Ulster Defence Association (UDA) reads, 'all active service units of the Ulster Freedom Fighters will as from 12 p.m. tonight stand down with all military intelligence destroyed and as a consequence of this all weaponry will be put beyond use'.

2008: Paisley steps down – Robinson steps up

March 2008: Ian Paisley announces decision to stand down as First Minister and DUP leader.

24 May 2008: Gerry Adams gives an oration for Brian Keenan, saying, 'It will only be when the history of this period is properly written that the real extent of the key role Brian played can be told. For now, let me say that he was central to securing the support of the IRA leadership and rank and file for a whole series of historic initiatives which made the peace process possible.'

5 June 2008: New DUP leader Peter Robinson becomes First Minister.

2009: The Past in the Present

28 January 2009: The Consultative Group on the Past (Eames/ Bradley) Report is published in an explosion of emotions inside the Europa Hotel, Belfast. The report recommends an Independent

Legacy Commission, a Reconciliation Forum and investigation and information-recovery strands. Its most controversial proposal was for a recognition payment to all families who had lost loved ones in the conflict period. The report is not implemented. A variation of these proposals, minus the recognition payment, would emerge in all subsequent legacy negotiations.

March 2009: Two soldiers and a police officer are murdered in dissident IRA attacks. Martin McGuinness describes those behind the shootings as 'traitors to the island of Ireland'.

April 2009: Senior republican Bobby Storey describes the actions of the dissident groups as 'futile, purposeless, pointless, a waste of life and a waste of freedom'.

27 June 2009: There is a loyalist news conference at which the UVF and Red Hand Commando confirm the decommissioning of weapons and explosives. The statement read by Harry Stockman includes, 'The leadership of the Ulster Volunteer Force and Red Hand Commando today confirms it has completed the process of rendering ordnance totally, and irreversibly, beyond use.' The PUP leader Dawn Purvis comments, 'This is a truly momentous day ... Peaceful, stable democracy is the way forward.' On this date, the IICD also reports on a beginning to decommissioning by the Ulster Defence Association (UDA)/Ulster Freedom Fighters (UFF).

29 June 2009: The IICD confirms a 'major decommissioning event involving arms, ammunition, explosives and explosive devices' by the UVF and associated Red Hand Commando.

28 August 2009: It is Sir Hugh Orde's last day as PSNI Chief Constable. He leaves to become President of the Association of Chief Police Officers (ACPO); Matt Baggott becomes the new Chief Constable.

11 October 2009: An Irish National Liberation Army (INLA) statement declares, 'the armed struggle is over and the objective of a 32-county Socialist Republic will be best achieved through exclusively peaceful political struggle'.

29 November 2009: Sinn Féin Chair Declan Kearney, speaking at a republican commemoration in Dunloy on the delayed devolution of policing and justice powers and the DUP, states, 'Their continued intransigence is a serious political mistake. It is a train wreck political strategy and political consequences will be inevitable.' DUP MP Jeffrey Donaldson responds, 'It's yet more threatening noises from Sinn Féin with the clear implications that they are prepared to walk away from the political institutions.' On dissidents, Declan Kearney said the IRA 'war' had been fought 'to a conclusion'. 'There is no other IRA today. Nor is there an armed struggle to be finished. Those who choose to masquerade otherwise should disarm and disband.'

2010: 'Its business was war and, in the madness that is war, the IRA did many things which deeply hurt people'

6 January 2010: A UDA statement reads, 'Today the leadership of the Ulster Defence Association can confirm that all weaponry under its control has been put verifiably beyond use.' The decommissioning happened at the Ballykinlar Army base on Tuesday, 5 January. Lord Robin Eames was present as a witness: 'I pray that this historic moment can lead to a more peaceful future for the next generation.'

8 February 2010: A statement from the leadership of the Irish National Liberation Army (INLA) confirms, 'that the INLA has disarmed through a joint facilitation group consisting of a local, a national and an international organisation. This was done in a process in accordance with international standards.' A statement from the IICD reads, 'The IICD can confirm that it has conducted events in which quantities of firearms, ammunition, explosives and explosive devices belonging to the INLA have been decommissioned. The events were attended by witnesses chosen by the INLA. The INLA representatives have informed us that the arms decommissioned constitute all those under the control of the INLA leadership.'

31 March 2010: Gerry Adams' blog includes, 'It was not a perfect organisation and it made many mistakes. Its business was war and, in the madness that is war, the IRA did many things which deeply hurt people. I regret that very much and I have worked with others to ameliorate this.'

4 April 2010: Gerry Adams, speaking at the Easter Commemoration, Milltown Cemetery, west Belfast, states, 'I am glad the war is over. Any post conflict phase – any transition – is bound to be difficult. For all survivors, victims, former combatants. The war should never be glamorised or repeated.'

11 April 2010: At midnight, policing and justice powers devolved to Stormont. Minutes later, a dissident IRA bomb explodes at Palace Barracks, Holywood, which houses the NI Headquarters of MI5. David Ford becomes Justice Minister in the executive.

2011: Decommissioning – lessons learned

2 April 2011: Police officer Ronan Kerr is killed by the dissident IRA in an under-car bomb explosion.

4 July 2011: The final report of the IICD, given to the governments on 28 March 2011, is published. On lessons learned, it reads, 'when it became clear that decommissioning would not be rushed, and that it would indeed be tied to progress being made in the political arena, patience became a necessity'. **Author's note**: The decommissioning debate began with republicans declaring 'not a bullet-not an ounce' and significant loyalist figures suggesting that 'rust' would be the way of addressing the issue of arms. In this context, the IICD achieved remarkable progress. Other key learning is that demands do not work – such as the DUP asserting the need for photographic proof of the process in 2004. The IRA and the main loyalist organisations did things their way in consultation with the IICD. We know, of course, that not all weapons were decommissioned. Beyond the statements announcing ceasefires, ending the armed campaign and the civilianisation of organisations, trust is a slow process – part of that 'long war for peace'.

25 September 2011: Loyalist leader Gusty Spence dies. He read the 1994 CLMC ceasefire statement, including its words of 'abject and true remorse'. Commenting, William Smith, who chaired the ceasefire news conference, says, 'He was a self-taught, articulate man – very shrewd. We were the students of Gusty.' Smith describes debates in jail in the 1970s in which he said Spence was exploring 'a way out of the darkness'.

27 October 2011: The date of the Irish presidential election. Michael D. Higgins becomes President. First count: Higgins, 701,101; Sean Gallagher, 504,964; Martin McGuinness, 243,030. Higgins is elected on the fourth count. McGuinness had temporarily stepped aside as deputy First Minister to contest the election. John O'Dowd had deputised for him.

2012: 'Sorry' – the hardest word

February 2012: Ahead of talks with Secretary of State Owen Paterson on the question of the past, Peter Robinson rules out a truth commission and amnesty: 'What would be the purpose of having a Truth Commission when we know without a doubt that the terrorists will not be coming forward to tell the truth? All you would get, once again, would be the police and Army in the dock and history being distorted.'

March 2012: Sinn Féin Chair Declan Kearney states, 'Regardless of the stance of others, we should recognise the healing influence of being able to say sorry for the human effects of all actions during the armed struggle. All sensible people would wish it had been otherwise; that these events had never happened, that other conditions had prevailed. The political reality is those actions cannot be undone, or disowned.' Former Methodist President Harold Good responds, 'It reads as a genuine offering from one part of a hurting community to another.'

31 March 2012: Mike Nesbitt becomes the Ulster Unionist leader, succeeding Tom Elliott.

27 June 2012: At a Cooperation Ireland event in the Lyric Theatre, the Queen and Martin McGuinness shake hands. **Author's note**:

I wrote at the time that this meeting was about the challenges after conflict: healing, reconciliation, ending enemy relationships, thinking beyond the bombs and bullets but not forgetting Lord Mountbatten and those shot on 'Bloody Sunday'. In the period that followed, we listened as senior republicans spoke on the anniversaries of IRA attacks in which there were multiple civilian fatalities – a description of 'Bloody Friday' as 'unjustifiable' and the bombing of Claudy as 'indefensible'. It was part of a wider dialogue under the heading 'Uncomfortable Conversations', which gave us an indication of the type of 'corporate' rather than 'individual' answering and accountability that might be possible as part of some wider truth-recovery or informational-retrieval process.

25 October 2012: The senior republicans Sean Murray and Danny Morrison take part in a Memorial debate organised by loyalists for the UDA leader John McMichael, killed in an IRA under-car bomb attack in 1987.

1 November 2012: The dissident IRA murder prison officer David Black as he is driving to work.

December 2012: A decision by Belfast City Council to fly the Union Flag only on designated days sparks what came to be called the flag protest.

2013: Drawing a line – the legacy debate continues

7 June 2013: Chief Constable Matt Baggott and other senior officers, as well as Protestant clergy, attend a Sinn Féin-organised event – 'a city of equals in an island of equals' – at the Europa Hotel in Belfast. The keynote speaker is Martin McGuinness. Ulster Unionist leader Mike Nesbitt withdrew from the conference. The audience included Gerry Adams and Ted Howell, former PUP leader Dawn Purvis, Kate Turner of the Healing Through Remembering project and Alan McBride of the WAVE Trauma Centre. **Author's note**: I chaired the event. I was told beforehand that Martin McGuinness would make a significant statement on legacy, including that nobody should go to prison as a result of inquiries and investigations. These lines were removed from the speech. I was told they were vetoed by Adams and other senior republicans.

June 2013: The G8 summit is hosted in County Fermanagh.

20 November 2013: Attorney General John Larkin states, 'It strikes me that the time has come to think about putting a line set at Good Friday 1998, with respect to prosecutions, inquests and other inquiries.'

22 November 2013: Father Alec Reid dies.

31 December 2013: The Haass–O'Sullivan talks end without five-party consensus. A final paper – detailing the negotiations and proposals – is forwarded to First Minister Peter Robinson and deputy First Minister Martin McGuinness. Legacy proposals include a Historical Investigations Unit (HIU) and Independent Commission on Information Retrieval (ICIR). Haass and O'Sullivan ask for it be published. This legacy structure is repeated in the Stormont House Agreement the following year.

2014: Stormont House Agreement – then, disagreement

30 June 2014: Sir George Hamilton becomes PSNI Chief Constable; he will serve in this post for five years.

21 August 2014: Former Taoiseach Albert Reynolds dies.

September 2014: Hamilton, speaking to British-Irish Association, states, 'To continue to ignore, hesitate, or procrastinate, on the past will have unpredictable and far-reaching consequences. It requires all of us to be selfless, to go beyond our comfort zones and have challenging conversations, such as the one initiated by the Attorney General almost a year ago.'

12 September 2014: Former First Minister and DUP leader Ian Paisley dies.

23 December 2014: The date of the Stormont House Agreement, including proposed legacy structures. This includes a new HIU and ICIR.

2015: The picture darkens – murder and the IRA army council

Throughout much of this year, there are fears that Stormont could fall. There are increasingly dire warnings linked to welfare reform, and then later, the crisis shifts to the murder of Kevin McGuigan and police and intelligence assessments on a remaining IRA structure, including the army council.

9 March 2015: Former Ulster Unionist leader Jim Molyneaux dies.

5 May 2015: Former senior IRA figure Gerard 'Jock' Davison is murdered in Belfast.

6 August 2015: Chief Constable Sir George Hamilton and deputy First Minister Martin McGuinness take part in Féile debate in west Belfast: 'Will the questions of the past ever be answered?'

12 August 2015: Kevin McGuigan murder.

22 August 2015: In a statement on the McGuigan murder, Sir George Hamilton speaks of a line of enquiry 'that has shown connections and cooperation between Action Against Drugs as a group and a number of individuals who are members of the Provisional IRA … we are currently not in possession of information that indicates that Provisional IRA involvement was sanctioned or directed at a senior or organisational level within the Provisional IRA or the broader republican movement'. Hamilton also gives an assessment on the IRA structure: 'We assess that in the organisational sense the Provisional IRA does not exist for paramilitary purposes. Nevertheless, we assess that in common with the majority of Northern Ireland paramilitary groups from the period of the conflict, some of the PIRA structure from the 1990s remains broadly in place, although its purpose has radically changed since this period. Our assessment indicates that a primary focus of the Provisional IRA is now promoting a peaceful, political republican agenda.'

18 September 2015: A statement from Secretary of State Theresa Villiers indicates that UK security agencies and the PSNI will carry out a factual assessment on the 'structure, role and purpose of paramilitary organisations in Northern Ireland'. The assessment is to be independently reviewed.

19 October 2015: The assessment confirms that the remaining IRA structure includes a 'Provisional Army Council' – the assessment describes a strategy that has 'a wholly political focus'.

14 November 2015: Colum Eastwood elected leader of the SDLP.

2016: Build-up to breakdown

11 January 2016: Arlene Foster becomes First Minister, succeeding Peter Robinson as he retired from frontline politics.

5 May 2016: The polling day for the assembly election. The final seats are tallied by 7 May: DUP, 38; Sinn Féin, 28; UUP, 16; SDLP, 12; Alliance, 8; Greens, 2; People Before Profit, 2; Traditional Unionist Voice (TUV), 1; Independent, 1.

25 May 2016: New Stormont Executive nominated: First Minister, Arlene Foster; deputy First Minister, Martin McGuinness; Justice, Claire Sugden; Economy, Simon Hamilton; Finance, Máirtín Ó Muilleoir; Education, Peter Weir; Infrastructure, Chris Hazzard; Agriculture, Environment and Rural Affairs, Michelle McIlveen; Communities, Paul Givan; Health, Michelle O'Neill; junior ministers, Alistair Ross and Megan Fearon. The Ulster Unionists and SDLP form a Stormont opposition rather than taking seats in the executive.

8 June 2016: William 'Plum' Smith, who chaired the news conference for the 1994 CLMC ceasefire announcement, dies.

23 June 2016: The date of the Brexit referendum. UK result: Leave, 51.9 per cent; Remain, 48.1 per cent. Northern Ireland result:

Remain, 55.8 per cent; Leave, 44.2 per cent. The following day, David Cameron announces decision to resign as Prime Minister.

11 July 2016: Theresa May becomes new Conservative Party leader.

13 July 2016: May becomes Prime Minister. Boris Johnson is announced as Foreign Secretary.

14 July 2016: James Brokenshire becomes the new Northern Ireland Secretary of State.

7 October 2016: Martin McGuinness writes to the Prime Minister. A statement from McGuinness on legacy negotiations includes, 'Unfortunately we are rapidly coming to the conclusion that the British Government isn't serious – and never was serious – about resolving the outstanding legacy issues which were not concluded in the "Fresh Start Agreement" [November 2015].'

8 November 2016: The unveiling of Irish artist Colin Davidson's portrait of Queen Elizabeth at a London event. Northern Ireland political leaders are present, including Arlene Foster and Martin McGuinness.

9 November 2016: Donald Trump is elected US President.

16 December 2016: A statement by Martin McGuinness includes, 'I spoke by phone this afternoon with the First Minister Arlene Foster. I outlined my serious concern that the credibility of the political institutions is being undermined by the serious and ongoing allegations surrounding the design, operation, abuse and ending of the Renewable Heating Incentive Scheme ... I also said that in the public interest, she should stand aside from the role as First Minister while the investigation is underway.'

16 December 2016: A DUP statement reads, 'The First Minister will not be stepping aside, but instead is focused on ensuring the full facts about this issue emerge and proposals are brought forward which can make a significant reduction in the future financial burden the Executive would face. The First Minister does not take her instructions from Sinn Féin, but from the electorate.'

2017: Ructions and resignation

7 January 2017: A Gerry Adams speech to a republican audience at the Felons Club in west Belfast is read as a final demand for Arlene Foster to step aside: 'If the First Minister does not take the actions that society desires and deserves and which a sustainable process of change requires, then Sinn Féin will bring this ongoing and totally unacceptable state of affairs to an end.'

9 January 2017: Martin McGuinness resigns as deputy First Minister 'in protest at the DUP's failure to accept the principles of power-sharing and parity of esteem and their handling of the RHI crisis'. The McGuinness statement says, 'There will be no return to the status quo.' Arlene Foster responds, saying, 'Sinn Féin's actions are not principled – they are political.'

16 January 2017: Secretary of State James Brokenshire announces assembly elections, to take place on 2 March.

19 January 2017: In a series of interviews, Martin McGuinness says he won't run in the March elections.

23 January 2017: Michelle O'Neill becomes the Sinn Féin leader in the North.

2 March 2017: The polling day for the assembly elections. Final results: DUP, 28 seats; Sinn Féin, 27 seats; SDLP, 12 seats; UUP, 10 seats; Alliance, 8 seats; Green Party, 2 seats; TUV, 1 seat; People Before Profit, 1 seat. Independent Unionist Claire Sugden is also elected. Unionism loses its overall majority in the Stormont chamber.

4 March 2017: Gerry Adams comments, 'Clearly the unionist majority in the Assembly has been ended, and the notion of a permanent or a perpetual unionist majority has been demolished.'

21 March 2017: Martin McGuinness dies.

12 May 2017: Brendan Duddy, the key link in a secret backchannel connecting the British government and republican leadership, dies.

8 June 2017: The date of the UK general election. The DUP wins ten of the Northern Ireland seats and makes a confidence and supply deal with the Conservative Party, propping up a minority government. Sinn Féin wins seven seats and the Independent Unionist Lady Sylvia Hermon holds her seat in North Down. The SDLP loses all three of its Westminster seats.

14 June 2017: Simon Coveney is appointed Minister for Foreign Affairs.

18 November 2017: Gerry Adams announces that he will not stand in the next Dáil elections and that this is his last Ard Fheis as Sinn Féin President.

2018: Adams steps down – changes at the top

8 January 2018: Karen Bradley becomes NI Secretary of State.

20 January 2018: Mary Lou McDonald is confirmed as Sinn Féin President-elect.

10 February 2018: Mary Lou McDonald becomes Sinn Féin President. Michelle O'Neill is made Vice President.

May 2018: The publication of the Northern Ireland Office (NIO) consultation paper, *Addressing the Legacy on Northern Ireland's Past*. This paper is concerned with the structure agreed in the Stormont House Agreement of December 2014, including an HIU and ICIR.

21 November 2018: Clare Bailey becomes Green Party NI leader.

2019: Election – a day of reckoning

18 April 2019: Journalist Lyra McKee shot dead by dissident IRA while observing rioting in Derry.

2 May 2019: The date of the council elections. Results NI: DUP, 122 seats (24.1 per cent of vote); Sinn Féin, 105 seats (23.2 per cent of vote); Ulster Unionists, 75 seats (14.1 per cent of vote), SDLP, 59 seats (12 per cent of vote); Alliance, 53 seats (11.5 per cent of vote).

7 May 2019: The beginning of a new phase of all-party negotiations at Stormont.

23 May 2019: The date of the European elections. In Northern Ireland, unionists lose their second seat to Alliance leader Naomi Long. Diane Dodds (DUP) and Martina Anderson (Sinn Féin) are also elected.

24 May 2019: Simon Byrne is appointed as the new PSNI Chief Constable.

24 July 2019: Boris Johnson becomes Prime Minister. Julian Smith is appointed Northern Ireland Secretary of State.

12 December 2019: The date of the UK general election. Results NI: DUP, 8 seats; Sinn Féin, 7 seats; SDLP, 2 seats; Alliance, 1 seat. The DUP Westminster leader, Nigel Dodds, loses North Belfast to John Finucane, Sinn Féin. Emma Little-Pengelly, DUP, loses South Belfast to Claire Hanna, SDLP. Elisha McCallion, Sinn Féin, loses Foyle to Colum Eastwood, SDLP. Stephen Farry, Alliance, wins North Down.

2020: Stormont deal – its maker sacked

9 January 2020: The Secretary of State Julian Smith and Tánaiste Simon Coveney publish their New Decade, New Approach deal.

11 January 2020: A new Northern Ireland executive is formed, ending the three-year-long standoff at Stormont. Arlene Foster is First Minister. Michelle O'Neill is deputy First Minister.

24 January 2020: Former MP, SDLP deputy leader and deputy First Minister Seamus Mallon dies.

8 February 2020: The date of the Irish general election. Percentage share of first preference votes: Sinn Féin, 24.5 per cent (37 seats); Fianna Fáil, 22.2 per cent (38 seats); Fine Gael, 20.9 per cent (35 seats).

13 February 2020: There is a Cabinet reshuffle. Julian Smith is sacked as NI Secretary. He is replaced by Brandon Lewis.

21 June 2020: Former senior IRA leader Bobby Storey dies.

3 August 2020: Former SDLP leader and Nobel Peace Prize winner John Hume dies.

24 December 2020: UK and EU agree post-Brexit trade deal.

2021: Trump Out

20 January 2021: Inauguration of Joe Biden as 46th US President. Kamala Harris Vice President.

Appendices

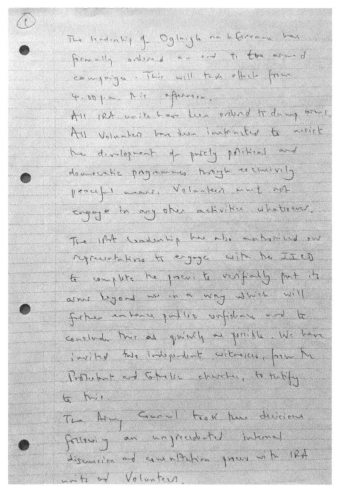

Handwritten history: Many of the big moments of the peace process were choreographed – one move, then the next. In July 2005, the day before the IRA announced the end of its armed campaign, Gerry Adams gave the Northern Ireland Office a preview of the planned statement. It was a typed text, which he would not allow to be photocopied. So, over four pages, then NIO Political Director Sir Jonathan Phillips made a handwritten note to fax to Downing Street. Sir Jonathan has given us permission to reproduce that note.

We appreciate the honest and forthright
way in which the consultation process was
carried out and the depth and content of
the submissions. We are proud of the ~~completely~~
comradely way in which this truly historic
discussion was conducted.

The outcome of our consultations show
very strong support among IRA Volunteers for
the Sinn Féin peace strategy. There is also
widespread concern about the failure of the
two governments and the unionists to fully
engage in the peace process. This has
created real difficulties. The overwhelming
majority of people in Ireland fully support
the peace. They and friends of Irish unity
throughout the world want to see the
full implementation of the Good Friday
Agreement.

Notwithstanding these difficulties our decisions
have been taken to advance our republican
and democratic objectives, including our
goal of a united Ireland. We believe
there is now an alternative way to

achieve this and to end British Rule in
our country.

It is the responsibility of all Volunteers
to show leadership, determination and courage.
We are very mindful of the sacrifices of
our patriot dead, those who went to jail,
Volunteers, their families and the wider republican
base. We reiterate our view that the armed
struggle was entirely legitimate.

We are conscious that many people suffered
in the conflict. There is a compelling imperative
on all sides to build a just and lasting
peace.

The issue of the defence of nationalist and
republican communities has been raised with
us. There is a responsibility on society to
ensure that there is no re-occurrence of
the pogroms of 1969 and the early 1970s.
There is also a universal responsibility to
tackle sectarianism in all its forms.

The IRA is fully committed to the goals of
Irish unity and independence and to building

the Republic outlined in the 1916 Proclamation.

We call for maximum unity and effort by Irish republicans everywhere. We are confident that by working together Irish republicans can achieve our objectives. Every Volunteer is aware of the import of the decisions we have taken and all Oglaigh are compelled to fully comply with these orders.

There is now an unprecedented opportunity to utilise the considerable energy and goodwill which there is for the peace process. This comprehensive series of unparalleled initiatives is our contribution to this and to the continued endeavours to bring about independence and unity for the people of Ireland.

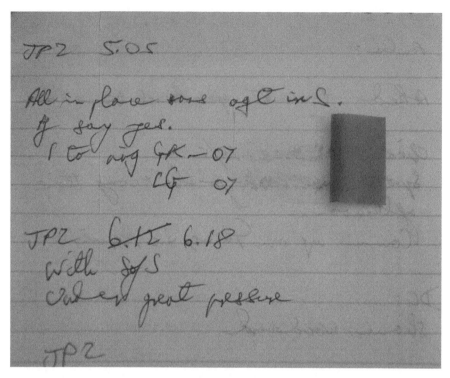

Links in the chain: The next move was the release of the IRA prisoner Sean Kelly. Robin Masefield was then Director General of the Northern Ireland Prison Service. On a page of his notebook from July 2005, you read the initials JP – Jonathan Phillips. Also the initials GK and LG – the republicans Gerry Kelly and Leo Green. We have removed their telephone numbers. When the order was given for Sean Kelly to be released, Masefield called Gerry Kelly with the news.

Read all about it: A copy of *An Phoblacht* from July 2005 with the IRA statement placed on top. The news now public. The armed campaign over.

Headline words: A signed copy of the November 2017 speech by Gerry Adams signalling his decision to step down as Sinn Féin President some months later. For decades, he has been the most-influential republican leader.

OFFICIAL SENSITIVE NON PAPER

SECTION ONE

IDENTITY RIGHTS AND FREED OF CULTURAL EXPRESSION

Previous agreements and cor ments

The Importance ntity in the context of Northern Ireland has long been recognised

In the Belfast / wer of Government in Northern Ire

"shall
dive
of f
fre
a
c

In the
civil
bac
of

ss of

themselves
hoose, and
citizenship is
y any future

lated to identity
recognised in

Official Sensitive: One of numerous documents leaked to the author during the never-ending Stormont negotiations. Rowan's notebook covers the source of the leak.

Index

Action Against Drugs 227

Action for Community Transformation (ACT) 162

Adair, Johnny 121

Adams, Davy 77, 199

Adams, Gerry 15, 66, 92, 103–26, 203; Ard Fheis address (2017) 110, 115, 123; Assembly election (2017), comment on 230; blogs 47, 119, 132; Dáil elections and 231; Easter Commemoration 223; Ervine, David and xvii, 85; 'Facing the Questions of the Past' 79, 81, 82; Felons Club, speech at 16, 17, 20, 230; Foster and 16, 61; General Election (2017) (UK) 99; Hain, meetings with 104–6; *Hope and History: Making Peace in Ireland* 121–2; Hume and 28, 75, 115; IRA and 45, 103, 104, 105, 106, 111, 119; IRA decommissioning and 104–8, 215, 216; IRA leadership, meeting with 212; IRA membership, denial of 112; IRA, views on 119, 222–3; Irish Language Act and 100–1; Keenan's funeral oration 113–15, 121, 220; Kelly's book, foreword to 120; McGuinness and 1–2, 93–6, 105, 226; McKenna's funeral oration 120–1; Milltown Cemetery address 118–19; *Negotiator's Cook Book, The* 33; *Never Give Up* 123, 124; orations delivered by 113–15,

120–1; peace process xiii, 33, 73, 117–18; perception of 95–6, 112–13, 115–16; policing, Sinn Féin and 219; Presbyterians and 111; questions about 110, 115; Sinn Féin and 103, 110, 115, 123, 124, 125; Sinn Féin press conference 178; Sinn Féin-DUP agreement 219–20; steps down as Sinn Féin President 231; Storey and 191, 192; Stormont crisis and 3, 8; Stormont negotiations 129, 132; Whitelaw, talks with 69, 94–5, 103, 123, 124; *see also* Hume–Adams talks

Ahern, Bertie 106, 107, 217

Aiken, Steve 125, 180, 189

Alderdice, John Alderdice, Baron 40–2, 43

Alliance Party 40, 49, 62, 66, 148–53; Assembly elections 213, 228, 230; council elections 231; General Election (2019) 164, 165, 232; Stormont negotiations 168, 171

Anderson, Revd Brian 159

Anderson, Martina 149, 150, 232

Archibald, Caoimhe 178

Association of Chief Police Officers (ACPO) 221

Baggott, Matt, PSNI Chief Constable 34, 221, 225

Bailey, Clare 149–50, 162, 163–4, 231

Baker, Sam 24, 33

Barton, Rosemary 65

BBC 62, 65, 66, 142; broadcasting restrictions 71–2; General Election (2019) (UK) 165, 166; Hume, meeting with 207–8; 'Long War, The' (documentary) 79–80; reports on NI 195; Storey funeral 192

Belfast Agreement *see* Good Friday Agreement

Belfast City Council 148–9, 163, 181, 225

Belfast City Hall 5

Belfast Telegraph 69, 76, 113, 128

Biden, Joe 232

Black, David 225

Blair government 43, 104

Blair, Tony 105, 106, 107, 180, 212

Blevins, David 135

Bloody Friday 119, 225

Bloody Sunday 69, 74–5, 94, 119, 225

border poll 99, 142, 150, 152, 195, 198, 200

Bradley, Denis 29, 34, 69–70, 72, 86–7, 145; Eames/Bradley Report 29, 51, 220–1

Bradley, Karen, Secretary of State 125, 128, 134, 157, 173, 231

Breen, Suzanne 128

Brexit, impact of 155, 158

Brexit xviii, 47, 92, 99; implications for Northern Ireland 196; Irish Sea border xviii, 158, 194, 205; Northern Ireland and 142, 149–50, 151, 155, 158, 161, 163; referendum (2016) 50, 228; referendum results 228–9; rejection in Northern Ireland 138, 228–9; Smith, Julian and 180; Union and 205; Westminster and 100

British Army: Bloody Sunday 94; Royal Irish Regiment 54, 217; SAS 70, 214; veterans 53–4

British Government 53–4; IRA, talks and 72, 94–5; secret back-channel 69, 72, 88, 120, 208, 230

British–Irish Association 226

British–Irish Secretariat 134

Brokenshire, James, Secretary of State 21, 54, 99, 157, 229, 230; perception of 157

Byrne, Simon, PSNI Chief Constable 232

Cahill, Joe 113

Cameron, David 86, 229

Campbell, Colonel Mark 54–6

Campbell, John 139

Carroll, Gerry 50

Carthy, Matt 15, 178

Catney, Pat 65

centenary year, Northern Ireland xviii, 174, 190, 194, 195, 196–8, 200

Charles, Prince 18, 19, 115, 118

Civil Contingencies Committee (COBRA) 188

Clinton, Bill: Foster, courage of 93; Hume, tribute to 208; McGuinness's funeral 68, 69, 70, 90, 92, 93

Co-operation Ireland 96, 136, 224–5

COBRA 188

Combined Loyalist Military Command (CLMC): ceasefire 73, 194, 198, 210, 211; ceasefire statement 201, 223–4, 228; warning to IRA 212

Community Foundation for Northern Ireland 76

Conmy, Kevin 134

Conservative government: Cabinet reshuffle 180, 232; Confidence and Supply deal with DUP 101, 139, 140, 158, 231; DUP and 100, 170; majority 162; minority government 100, 231

Consultative Group on the Past 51–2, 220–1

council elections (NI) (2019) 231

Coveney, Simon xi, xii, 125, 182; Co-operation Ireland conference 136; Foreign Affairs ministry 231; funeral of Lyra McKee 146; 'New Decade, New Approach' 168–9, 172, 232; news conference at Stormont Castle 156–7; press conference 178; Smith, Julian and 139, 174, 209; Stormont negotiations xv, xvi, 156, 162, 166–7, 173–5

covert human intelligence sources (CHIS) 118

Covid-19 pandemic xii, 175, 183–9, 208–9; emergency mortuary xii, 183, 184–7, 209; funeral, Sinn Féin leadership and xv, 191–2; 'Project Dignity' 184

Crawley, William 165, 166

Cummings, Dominic 180, 190, 195

Dallat, John 65

Davidson, Colin (artist) 22, 59, 229

Davison, Gerard (Jock) 191, 227

de Chastelain, General John 214

Deeny, Eamon 125, 129, 134

Democratic Unionist Party (DUP) 43; Assembly elections 213, 228, 230; British government and 99; Confidence and Supply deal 101, 134–5, 137, 139, 140, 158, 231; Conservatives and 100; council elections 231; criticism of 222; devolution of policing and justice powers 46; General Election (2017) 98, 100, 231; General Election (2019) 162, 164–5, 173, 174, 232; Good Friday Agreement and 47; Johnson, Boris and 158–9; language acts 131;

local elections 149; McGuinness's resignation 20; Paisley stands down as leader 220; peace centre and xiv, 8; power-sharing 49, 63–4; Sinn Féin, agreement with 219–20; Sinn Féin and 1, 9, 10–11, 22, 46, 47, 48, 49, 63–4, 217; Stormont, collapse of 20; Stormont draft agreement 135–6; Stormont majority, loss of 62; Stormont negotiations 125, 128, 129, 130–4, 137, 153, 167, 170, 174; veto used by 192

devolution xiv–xv, 220; justice powers 5, 12, 29, 46, 223; policing 5, 12, 29, 46, 223; Sinn Féin and 12; suspension of 215, 216

direct rule 20, 23, 157–8

'disappeared, the' 109, 120, 214

dissident IRA 23, 39, 81, 83, 95, 222; bomb attacks 145, 213, 223; ceasefire announced 213; criticism of 221; killings 144, 145, 156, 221, 223, 225, 231; roots of 212

Dodds, Diane 149, 150, 232

Dodds, Nigel 16, 98, 100, 128; Brexit and 165; General Election (2019) 162, 165–6, 232; Stormont negotiations 128, 134, 135

Doherty, Dominic 7

Doherty, Pearse 66, 178

Donaldson, Sir Jeffrey 100, 135, 222

Downing Street Declaration (1993) 28

Drumcree parade 116

Duddy, Brendan 208, 230

Dunlop, Revd Dr John 11, 110, 111–12

Eames, Robin, Baron 29, 34, 69, 195, 210

Eames/Bradley Report 29, 51, 220–1

Easter Commemoration 223

Easton, Ross 138, 167, 169, 170, 176–9

Eastwood, Colum 150; General Election (2019) 165, 166, 232; Hume, tribute to 207; leadership of SDLP 228; Smith, Julian and 154–5, 156; Stormont negotiations 125

Edwards, Rodney 2–3, 18–20

Elizabeth II, Queen: McGuinness and 88, 224–5; McGuinness family, message to 68; portrait, unveiling event 22, 59–60, 229; visit to Irish Republic 60

Elliott, Tom 165, 224

Empey, Reginald, Baron 158

Ervine, David 48, 77, 156, 199, 208; death 47, 219; funeral xvii, 85, 219; UVF and 49

Ervine, Jeanette xvii

European elections 149–50, 158, 163, 232

Farry, Stephen 125, 149, 150–3, 164, 171, 232

Fearon, Megan 17, 228

Féile an Phobail 36, 73, 80, 227

Ferris, Martin 114, 191–2

Fianna Fáil 33, 181, 182, 232

Fine Gael 33, 181, 182, 232

Finucane, John 165, 166, 178, 232

Finucane, Katherine 82

Finucane, Pat 30, 82

flag protest 225

flags 5, 6, 8, 144, 200, 225

Ford, David 171, 223

Forde, Stephen, Dean 146, 148

Foster, Arlene 125; Adams and 16, 61; collapse of Stormont xvii–xviii, 132; Covid-19 pandemic 190; 'Draft Agreement Text' 136; DUP leadership 66, 98, 205; as First Minister xvii–xviii, 15, 49, 180, 228, 232; funeral of McGuinness 90–1, 93; IRA attack on policeman father 90, 93; Irish Language Act and 133, 136; loyalists and 158–9; McGuinness and 1, 19–20, 60, 90, 229; newspaper interview 2–3, 18–20; Queen's portrait event 60, 229; refusal to stand aside 4, 15, 16, 17, 19–20, 99, 229, 230; Renewable Heat Incentive (RHI) scheme xiii–xiv, 4, 229; Sinn Féin, views on 48, 61, 65; Storey funeral fallout 192; Stormont negotiations 125, 128, 131, 133, 134, 135, 167

Frameworks for the Future 211

G8 Summit (2013) 86–7, 226

General Election (2017) (UK) 98–100, 231

General Election (2019) (UK) 139–40, 162–166, 171, 173, 174, 232; DUP and 154–65, 162, 173, 174, 232; Sinn Féin and 165, 166, 232; unionists and 195

General Election (2020) (Irish) 33, 181, 232

Gibney, Jim 35, 166

Gildernew, Michelle 165

Givan, Paul 48, 228

Glencree Peace Centre 118

Glenholmes, Eibhlin 16–17, 82

Good Friday Agreement (1998) 2, 25, 30, 78, 106, 116–17, 145–6; DUP and 47; implementation 39, 214; Independent Monitoring Commission and 43; international chair 203–4; IRA and 45, 213, 214; Irish government and 157, 158; loyalists and 198, 199, 202, 203; Mitchell Review 214, 215; prisoner release provisions 53; Sinn Féin and 203, 212; support for 213; twentieth anniversary 124; UUP and 198, 199, 212

Good, Revd Dr Harold 76, 92, 146, 147, 224

Gordon, Gareth 139

Green, Leo 51–4

Green Party (NI): Assembly elections 228, 230; General Election (2016) 62, 149; General Election (2019) 162–5

Guardian 99–100

Haass, Richard 6, 8, 29, 35, 143–4, 226

Hain, Peter, Baron 103–8, 110, 219; Adams, meetings with 104–7

Hamilton, Sir George, PSNI Chief Constable 2, 13, 22, 36, 73, 226; 'Facing the Questions of the Past' 79, 80–3; Féile an Phobail debate 36, 73, 80, 227; funeral of McGuinness 83–5, 90; IRA structure, assessment of 227–8; McGuigan murder, statement on 227; McGuinness and 79, 80–3

Hamilton, Simon 125, 228

Hanna, Claire 162–3, 164, 232

Harris, Kamala 233

Haughey, Charles J. 124, 204, 206, 208, 218

Hazzard, Chris 17, 228

Healing Through Remembering (HTR) 34–5, 36, 37, 225

Henderson, Deric 86, 87, 88, 89–90, 93, 144; *Reporting the Troubles* (Henderson and Little) 86

Hermon, Lady Sylvia 231

Higgins, Michael D. 68, 90, 146, 148, 224

Hill, Judith 159

Historical Enquiries Team (HET) 78

Historical Investigations Unit (HIU) 35, 54, 131, 226, 227, 231

Holywood, County Down 183, 185, 209

Howell, Eileen 35

Howell, Ted 22, 25, 34–6, 46, 51, 225; internment 35; *Negotiators Cook Book, The* 33; perception of 34, 36, 38

Howson-Smith, Lilah 138, 140–1, 154, 156, 162, 168, 170

Hughes, Brendan 118–19

Hughes, Sean 24, 191

Hume, John 112, 145–6, 165; Adams and 28, 75, 115; an 'agreed Ireland' 204; criticism of 206; death 207, 233; dialogue and persuasion 2, 24, 40, 41, 42; funeral 193; 'his long war for peace' 208; IRA leadership, meeting with 212; Nobel Peace Prize 207; peace-building and 206–7; tributes to 207

Hume–Adams talks 79, 88, 104, 124, 195, 204, 206–7, 208, 210

Hume–Adams–Reynolds initiative 124

hunger strikes 5, 7, 35, 51, 63, 73, 204

Hutchinson, Billy 156, 199

Imelda May 184

Impartial Reporter, Foster interview 2–3, 18–20

Implementation and Reconciliation Group (IRG) 35

Independent Commission on Information Retrieval (ICIR) 35, 54, 131, 226, 227, 231

Independent International Commission on Decommissioning (IICD) 106, 214, 215, 216, 218, 221, 222; final report 223

Independent Monitoring Commission (IMC) 40, 43, 218

Independent Reporting Commission (IRC) 148

Interaction 116

Irish Language Act 179, 194; DUP and 99, 179; Foster and 61, 133, 136; lack of 29, 48; Sinn Féin and 99, 101–2, 132, 143; Stormont negotiations and 130, 131, 132, 133, 135, 136, 137, 143; unionists and 194

Irish Language Commissioner 179

Irish National Liberation Army (INLA) 221, 222

Irish News 69

Irish Republican Army (IRA) xiv, 2, 11; Adams and 45, 103, 104, 105, 106, 111, 119; agents, killing of 79–80; armed campaign cessation 54, 61, 95, 104, 106–9, 122–3, 207, 211, 217–18; Army Convention 219; army council 29–30, 110, 114, 121; bank robbery 217; Belfast republicans and 21–2; bomb attacks 72–3, 121–2, 225; British Government, talks and 72, 94–5; ceasefire, breakdown of 211–12; ceasefire restoration 212; ceasefire statement 68–9, 142; ceasefires 11, 18, 39, 45, 74, 77, 116, 210; decommissioning 13, 18, 76, 104, 105, 106, 213, 214, 215, 216, 223; 'disappeared, the' 109, 120, 214; endgame strategy 73; General Army Convention 212; Gibraltar killings 70; leadership in 1970s 27; London Docklands bomb 212; McGuinness and 45, 49, 70–1, 79–80, 91, 96–7, 123; peace process and 26–9, 40, 43, 45; peace strategy 61; Provisional Army Council 228; Shankill road bomb 121–2; Sinn Féin's views on 11–12; statements signed P. O'Neill 109, 218; structure, assessment of 227–8; structures 29–30, 44, 109, 110, 191; Thiepval Barracks, bomb attack 190, 212; TUAS strategy 28; unionist/loyalist community and 54; *see also* dissident IRA; Provisional IRA (PIRA)

Irish sea border xviii, 158, 194–5, 205

Irish Times 25, 33, 145; McGuinness obituary 69; Sinn Féin meeting 21–3; Smith interview 77

Irvine, Winston xv, xvi, xvii, 36, 162, 195–203; Brexit, implications of 196; the future 202–3; International Peacebuilding, Security and Development (thesis) 195–6; loyalism and unionism 198–200, 202; Northern Ireland centenary year 196–8; peace process 200–1; solution, search for 209

Jennings, Una xiii, 56–9

Johnson, Boris 139, 153, 158, 160, 190; Cabinet reshuffle 180; Conservative majority 162; DUP and 158–9; as Foreign Secretary 229; Irish sea border and 195; perception of 159; as Prime Minister 232; visit to Stormont 180, 181

Johnston, Tim 13, 129, 153, 167

justice powers, devolution of 5, 12, 29, 46, 47, 223

Kearney, Declan 15, 46, 66, 178, 222, 224

Keenan, Brian xiv, 23, 24, 122; funeral oration by Adams 113–15, 121, 220

Kelly, Gerry 8, 24, 66, 115, 191; *Playing My Part* 120

Kelly, Sean, release from prison 104, 105, 107, 108–9

Kenny, Enda 90

Kerr, Ronan 223

Labour Party (British) 212

Larkin, John, Attorney General 226

Larmour, Mark 128, 169

legacy debate 225–6

legacy issues 50–6, 208–9; Bradley's views on 145; Campbell's views on 54–6; Green's views on 51–4; Jennings' views on 56–9; proposals 226

Legacy of Violence Project 118

Lewis, Brandon, Secretary of State 232

Little, Ivan, *Reporting the Troubles* (Henderson and Little) 86

Little-Pengelly, Emma 100, 162, 163, 164, 232

local elections 148–9

London Docklands bomb 212

Long Kesh xiv, 5, 7, 35, 60, 61

Long, Naomi xii, 125, 148–9, 150, 163; European elections (2019) 232; Stormont negotiations 168, 171; temporary mortuary, provision of 184–7

Lost Lives (Thornton et al.) 30, 110

Lowry, Shane 153

loyalism, unionism and 198–200, 202, 203

Loyalist Volunteer Force (LVF) 214, 218

loyalists: ceasefire 73, 76, 77, 143, 195, 198, 201, 210; decommissioning 214, 221; Foster and 158–9; Good Friday Agreement and 198, 199, 202, 203; McGuinness and 73, 74–6; reconciliation 74–6; Smith, Julian and 156, 161–2, 195; Stormont and 156; Union, concerns about 195, 196–7

Lynch, Martin 22, 24, 33, 79, 82; IRA army council 25; Sinn Féin, political director of 39; Storey funeral 191

McAleese, Mary 74

McAuley, Richard 110, 124

McBride, Alan 225

McBride, Sam 61–2, 66, 139; *Burned* xv

McCallion, Elisha 123, 166, 232

McCann, Eamon 49

McCann, Jennifer 191

McCartney, Rab 162

McCartney, Raymond 7, 49

McConville, Jean 109, 118, 218, 219

McConville, Michael 218

McDermott, Mandy 76–7, 78

McDonald, Jackie 34, 73, 74–5, 161

McDonald, Jim 77

McDonald, Mary Lou 39, 66, 123, 125, 156; General Election (2020) (Irish) 181; press conference 176, 178; Sinn Féin President 231; Storey funeral 191; Stormont draft agreement 135

McDowell, Michael 106

McGinley, Paul 153

McGlone, Roisin 116, 117, 118

McGuigan, Kevin xiv, xv, 2, 13–14, 62, 82–3, 191, 227

McGuinness, Martin: Adams and 93–6, 105, 113, 226; Assembly election (2016) 49; BBC interview 71–2; death 68, 89, 230; as deputy First Minister 83, 85, 86, 88, 220, 226, 228; dissident IRA, views on 83, 221; 'Facing the Questions of the Past' 79, 80–3; Féile an Phobail debate 73, 80, 227; Foster and 1, 4, 60; funeral 67, 68–9, 83–6, 88–92, 113, 147; G8 Summit (2013) 86–7, 89; Hamilton and 79, 80–3; ill health 16, 20; IRA and 45, 49, 70–1, 79–80, 91, 96–7, 123; IRA statement 107; Irish presidential election 224; legacy issues, views on 50; letter to Theresa May 50, 54, 229; loyalists and 73, 74–6; obituaries 69–70; Paisley and 1, 42, 88, 104; 'part of the rage of his time' 69, 92; peace centre plan and 6, 8; peace process xiii, 33, 69, 73, 90, 96; perception of 22, 49, 59–60, 70, 73, 87; personality 88, 89, 112; power-sharing and 6, 9; Queen Elizabeth and 88, 224–5; Queen's portrait event 22, 59–60, 229; reconciliation and 59–60; Renewable Heating Incentive scheme, views on 4; resignation xi, xiii, xv, xvii, 1–2, 15, 18, 20, 101, 230; Robinson and 6, 9; speech, lines removed from 225–6

McIlroy, Rory 153

McIlveen, Michelle 228

McKee, Lyra: funeral 146–7, 148, 173; murder of 144–6, 156, 173, 231

McKenna, Kevin 24, 113, 120–1

McKittrick, David 110

McLaughlin, Maeve 49

McLaughlin, Mitchel 34

McMichael, Gary 77, 199

McMichael, John 225

Mac Siacais, Jake 26–9, 73; 'H' Block oration for Sands xiv, 204; IRA, perception of 27–9

Magee, Revd Roy 208

Maghaberry Prison 107, 108–9

Magill, Revd Martin 146–7, 148, 173

Maidstone prison ship 35

Mairs, Tim xii–xiii, 56, 209

Mallie, Eamonn 5, 8–9, 68, 86, 110; article on peace centre 6; McGuinness's funeral 91; Stormont draft agreement 135, 136

Mallinder, Louise 36

Mallon, Nichola 125

Mallon, Seamus 207, 208, 232

Martin, Micheál 156, 182

Masefield, Robin 108–9, 110

Maskey, Alex 181

May, Theresa 50, 54, 160; DUP and 98–9; elected Conservative Party leader 229; funeral of Lyra McKee 146; General Election (2017) 98–100; McGuinness's letter to 50, 54, 229; Stormont negotiations 132

Maze/Long Kesh peace centre xiv, 60, 61; EU funding 7; McGuinness and 6; newspaper article on 6; plan put on hold 6; Robinson and 5, 6, 7; unionists' views on 5

Merkel, Angela 86

MI5 25, 44, 145, 190, 223

Milltown Cemetery, Belfast 191, 223; address by Adams 118–19; Easter Commemoration 223; Storey funeral 191–2

Mitchell, George 39, 204

Mitchell Review 214, 215

Mitchell, William 162

Molyneaux, James (Jim) 11, 41, 210, 227

Moore, Aoife 207

Morrison, Danny 8, 225

Mountbatten of Burma, Louis Mountbatten, 1st Earl 225

Mowlam, Mo 208, 218

Murphy, Conor 66, 125, 156, 178

Murphy, Thomas 24

Murray, Sean 22, 24, 25, 33, 116; Memorial debate 225; peace process and 36, 38; Sinn Féin and 36; Storey funeral 191

Mythen, Fergal 125

Nairac, Robert 214

Negotiators Cook Book, The (Adams, Howell, Wilson) 33

Neill, Rosemary 129, 139, 167

Nesbitt, Mike 62–6, 224, 225

'New Decade, New Approach' 137, 156, 168–9, 232; health portfolio 189–90; Irish Language Commissioner 179; publication of 171–2, 179, 232

'New Ireland' 48, 66, 190, 193, 197; Brexit and 142, 195; broader initiative, need for 203–5; building trust and reconciliation 60; international chair suggestion 203–4; loyalist/unionist community and 204; solution, search for 209

News Letter 61–2, 69, 139

Ní Chuilín, Carál 178

Nobel Peace Prize 207

Nolan Show 131

Northern Bank robbery 190

Northern Ireland Assembly 8–9, 40, 45–6, 92; election (1998) 213; election (2016) 49–50, 228; election (2017) 62, 64–6, 230

Northern Ireland Executive 12, 13, 14, 15, 46; absence of 22–3; DUP and 21; new executive (2020) 180; nominated (2016) 228; UUP and 63, 214–15

Northern Ireland Office (NIO) 155–6, 157, 158; *Addressing the Legacy in Northern Ireland's Past* 231; communications officer 139; IRA leadership 212–13; language acts 131; Stormont negotiations 125, 126, 127, 128, 129, 130

Northern Ireland Policing Board 109, 118

Northern Ireland Prison Service 108

Northern Ireland Protocol 152

Northern Ireland Women's Coalition 213

Obama, Barack 86

O'Dowd, John 160, 178, 224

Óglaigh na hÉireann 212, 214, 217, 218; *see also* Irish Republican Army (IRA)

Omagh bomb 145, 213

Ó Muilleoir, Máirtín 17, 63, 228

O'Neill, Julian 192

O'Neill, Michelle 15, 16, 17, 39, 66, 123, 178; challenge to position as Vice President 160; Covid-19 pandemic 190; as deputy First Minister 180, 232; 'Draft Agreement Text' 136; Health ministry 228; Sinn Féin party leadership 21, 22, 24, 230; Sinn Féin Vice President 231; Storey funeral and 191, 192; Stormont negotiations 125, 130, 132, 134, 160

Oral History Archive 35

Orde, Sir Hugh, PSNI Chief Constable xiv, 30–2, 34, 104, 109, 219, 221

O'Sullivan, Meghan 6, 8, 29, 35, 144, 226

Paisley, Ian 5, 9, 18, 41, 210; death 226; as First Minister 114, 220; government, statement on 219; McGuinness and 1, 42, 88, 104; retirement 46; stands down as First Minister 220

Paisley, Ian, Jnr 100, 132, 136

Panorama documentary, 'Long War, The' 79–80

parades 6, 8, 36, 117, 144

paramilitaries 55–6, 76, 77, 148, 199; deaths attributed to 55

partition, centenary year 195, 197

Paterson, Owen, Secretary of State 224

Patten, Chris 214

Patten Report 30, 31, 117, 214; *New Beginning, A: Policing in Northern Ireland* 214

peace centre *see* Maze/Long Kesh peace centre
peace process xiii, xiv, xv, 24, 25, 26–7, 92, 200–1; Adams and xiii, 33, 73, 117–18; Downing Street Declaration and 28; IRA and 26–9, 40; McGuinness and xiii, 33, 69, 73, 90, 96; shadowy figures and 31–2, 39–40, 44; violent organisations and 40–2
People Before Profit 49, 50, 62, 228, 230
Phillips, Sir Jonathan 104, 106, 107, 108
Phoblacht, An: Kearney's blog 15; obituary, Eileen Howell 35
Police Service of Northern Ireland (PSNI) xii, xiv, 56, 214, 216, 228
policing 32, 47, 56, 61, 223; devolution, DUP and 46; Patten Report 30, 31, 117, 214; Sinn Féin and 219
Poots, Edwin 125
Powell, Jonathan 104, 105, 106
Presbyterians, Adams and 111
Press Association 3, 86
Prison to Peace 76
prisoner releases 11, 53, 77, 92, 119; phased process 213, 215; *see also* Kelly, Sean
Progressive Unionist Party (PUP) 47, 199, 201; Assembly election (1998) 213; government, exploratory dialogue 211
'Project Dignity' 184, 186
Provisional IRA (PIRA) xv, 13–14, 40, 62, 218–19, 227–8; *see also* dissident IRA; Irish Republican Army (IRA)
Purvis, Dawn 34, 47–9, 61, 156, 221
Putin, Vladimir 86

Rea, Winston 76
reconciliation 59, 74–5; funerals, attendance at 83–6; loyalists and 74–6; McGuinness and 59–60, 61, 74–5; republicans and 59–60
Red Hand Commando 77, 220, 221
Reid, Revd Alec 206, 208, 226
Reid, Ken xv, 100–1, 165
Renewable Heat Incentive (RHI) scheme xiii–xiv, xv, 15, 60; *Burned* (McBride) xv; 'cash for ash' 3–4; fallout 16, 17, 132; Inquiry 99; McGuinness's views on 229; report 182
republicans: outreach/reconciliation and 59–60; Stormont and 50, 60–1; unionists and 48
'Respecting Languages and Culture' 130, 131
Reynolds, Albert 124, 208, 219, 226
Robinson, Gavin 100
Robinson, Peter xiv–xv, 1, 2, 10, 11–14; DUP leadership 220; as First Minister 5, 9, 11–14, 110, 191, 220, 226; funeral of McGuinness 90; G8 Summit (2013) 86; IRA and 110; 'letter from America' 6, 7, 8; McGuinness and 6; peace centre plan and 5, 6, 7, 8; perception of 88; retirement 228; Sinn Féin and 6, 11; Truth Commission, views on 224
Ross, Alistair 228
Royal Portrush Golf Club 153
Royal Ulster Constabulary (RUC) xii, 214; Special Branch 34

St Andrews Agreement 47, 64, 219
Sands, Bobby 63, 66, 73; 'H' Block oration for xiv, 204; hunger strike 204; mural 73
'shadowy figures' 23, 24–44, 30; peace process and 31–2, 39–40, 44; Stormont negotiations and 128
Shankill Road bomb 121–2

Sheridan, Peter 76, 96, 97

Shevlin, Myles 94

Sinn Féin xiii 160; Adams and 103, 110, 115, 123, 124, 125; Ard Fheis (2007) 219; Ard Fheis (2017) 110, 115, 123, 124; Assembly elections 49–50, 228, 230; attitude towards in Republic of Ireland 181–2; council elections (NI) (2019) 231; criticism of 222; devolution and 12; DUP, agreement with 219–20; DUP and 1, 9, 10–11, 22, 46, 47, 48, 49, 63–4, 99, 217; fall of Stormont (2017) 15, 20; Foster's views on 48, 61, 65; funeral of Bobby Storey xv; General Election (2017) (UK) 99; General Election (2019) (UK) 165, 166, 232; General Election (2020) (Irish) 181, 232; Good Friday Agreement and 203, 212; government, exploratory dialogue 211; IRA army council, views on 11–12; Irish Language Act and 101–2, 132, 143; leadership 123; local elections 149; McGuinness and 95; McGuinness's resignation 1–2; meeting at Felons Club 21–3; National Officer Board 2; O'Neill, Michelle as party leader 21, 22, 24, 230; peace process 43; perception of 112; policing and 219; Policing Board and 109; power-sharing 8, 49, 63–4; press conference 176, 178; RHI scheme, Foster and 4; Robinson and 6; SDLP-Sinn Féin talks 206; Storey funeral 191–2; Stormont draft agreement 135–6; Stormont House Agreement and 54; Stormont negotiations 125, 128, 129, 130–1, 132, 134, 135, 153, 170; welfare reform and 13

Sky News 16, 66, 135

Smallwoods, Ray 74

Smith, Julian, Secretary of State vii–ix, xi, xii, 100, 232; Brexit and 155, 180; Coveney and 139, 174, 209; DUP and 139–40; loyalist community and 156, 161–2, 195; 'New Decade, New Approach' 168–9, 171, 172, 232; perception of 142, 154–5, 174, 176, 181; press conference 178; sacking as Secretary of State 180, 232; Stormont, final deadline 160, 167, 170–1; Stormont negotiations 141–4, 153–4, 161, 162, 166–75; Stormont, restoration of xv–xvi 232; tweets 153–4, 181; WhatsApp 154

Smith, Owen 129

Smith, William (Plum) 73, 76–7, 116, 199, 208; death 228; funeral 77–8; *Inside Man* 76; peace process, the past and 78; Spence, perception of 224

Smyth, Hugh 199

Social Democratic and Labour Party (SDLP) 2, 40, 49, 65, 112, 150; Assembly elections 213, 228, 230; council elections 231; Eastwood as leader of 228; General Election (2017) 231; General Election (2019) 162–3, 166, 232; opposition stance 228; SDLP-Sinn Féin talks 206, 210; Stormont negotiations 171

Special Branch and Security Service 25, 44

Spence, Gusty 77, 195, 199, 208, 211; CLMC ceasefire statement 201, 223–4; death 223; perception of 224

'Stakeknife' 120

Stephens, Sir Jonathan 125, 128, 130, 169, 176, 178–9

Stockman, Harry 161, 162, 221

Stockman, Revd Steve 147

Storey, Bobby 22, 24, 33, 79, 82, 190–3; death 33, 191, 233; funeral xv, 113, 183, 191–3; IRA and 25, 118, 122, 191; news conference 191; Northern Bank robbery and 190; oration given by Adams 192; release from prison 19; 'Stormontgate' and 190; Thiepval Barracks bomb and 190

Stormont: Adams and 125; all-party negotiations 231; collapse (2017) xiii, xvii–xviii, 15, 20–1, 132; deadlines/red lines 101; draft agreement 135–6; IRA guns and xiv; legislation, Westminster and 159; loyalist representation, absence of 156; negotiations 125–37, 140–1, 142–3, 153–4, 159, 166–75; negotiations, final deadline 160, 167, 170–1, 174–6, 177; 'New Decade, New Approach' 137, 156, 168–9, 171–2, 179, 189–90; people's protest rally 158; Petition of Concern 131; political institutions, sustainability of 180; power-sharing difficulties xiv–xv, 8, 14, 16, 17; republicans and 50, 60–1; restoration (2020) xi, xv–xvi, 15, 178; talks, round-table meeting 125; three-year standoff, ending of 178; welfare reform issue xiv, 13

Stormont House Agreement (SHA) 29, 50, 53, 131, 226–7; delay in implementation 51; legacy structures 226, 227, 231; Sinn Féin and 54

'Stormontgate' 190

'Stuck in the Past' event 36

Sugden, Claire 49, 228, 230

Swann, Robin 125, 158, 159, 180, 183; Covid-19 pandemic 185, 188, 189, 192

Taylor, Peter 88; 'Long War, The' 79–80

Thiepval Barracks, Lisburn 190, 212

Thompson, Harry 74, 75, 76

Thompson, Judith (Victims' Commissioner) 36

Tonge, John 19

Traditional Unionist Voice (TUV) 228, 230

Trimble, David 11, 46, 47, 198; decommissioning issue 216–17; devolution and 217; executive, establishment of 212, 215; Good Friday Agreement 203, 212; Nobel Peace Prize 207; resignation as DUP leader 217; Sinn Féin and 112, 203; UUP leadership 211

Troubles, the xiii, 32, 55–6, 70, 73, 78, 93

Trump, Donald 229, 233

Turner, Edgar, Canon 36–7, 38

Turner, Kate 34, 36–8, 225

Twitter 25, 58, 63, 133, 181

UK Unionist Party (UKUP) 213

Ulster Defence Association (UDA) 74, 77, 121, 220, 221, 222

Ulster Democratic Party (UDP) 199, 211, 212

Ulster Freedom Fighters 220, 221

Ulster Scots language 130, 131

Ulster Television 62, 65, 66, 100–1, 159

Ulster Unionist Council 214, 215

Ulster Unionist Party (UUP) 10, 11, 47, 49, 62, 65, 112, 150, 224; Assembly elections 213, 228, 230; council elections 231; executive, establishment of 214–15; Good Friday Agreement and 198, 199, 212, 214–15; Irish sea border 194–5; Northern Ireland Executive, withdrawal from 63; opposition

stance 228; Stormont negotiations
  171, 180, 189; Trimble and 211, 217
Ulster Volunteer Force (UVF) 77, 220,
  221
Union, Northern Ireland and 161–2
Union Flag 5, 200, 225
unionism: Brexit and 205; loss of
  Stormont majority 61–2, 64;
  loyalism and 198–200, 202, 203
unionists: independent anti-agreement
  unionists 213; Irish Language Act
  and 194; republicans and 48

Varadkar, Leo 132, 146, 148, 156, 182
Villiers, Theresa, Secretary of State 228
Voices from the Grave (Moloney) 118

WAVE Trauma Centre 225
Weir, Peter 228
West Belfast Festival 73, 83
WhatsApp 154, 158, 167
White, Raymond 34
Whitelaw, William 69, 94–5, 103, 123,
  124
Wilsey, Sir John 72
Wilson, Padraic 25, 33, 36, 118

Young, David 3–4